W.J. KEITH was born and brought up in England. He is a member of the Department of English at University College in the University of Toronto and the author of *The Rural Tradition: a study of the non-fiction prose writers of the English countryside* and *Richard Jefferies: a critical study.*

This book examines some of the ways in which 'nature poets' have expressed their experience of and response to the natural environment. W.J. Keith studies the techniques of nine poets of the nineteenth and twentieth centuries: William Wordsworth, John Clare, William Barnes, Thomas Hardy, Robert Frost, Edward Thomas, Edmund Blunden, Andrew Young, and R.S. Thomas. This is not a theoretical study of any unified philosophy of nature, but rather a comparative study of the poets which discovers several experimental attitudes in their work. A major emphasis is Wordsworth's influence on his successors, which Professor Keith finds to be far more subtle than is generally recognized.

The volume will be a welcome companion to Professor Keith's previous book, *The Rural Tradition*, a study of non-fiction rural writers. This work places greater emphasis on viewpoint and angles of narration, but both map out a loose but definable literary tradition out of which each writer has developed his particular strengths.

W.J. KEITH

The Poetry of Nature

RURAL PERSPECTIVES IN POETRY FROM WORDSWORTH
TO THE PRESENT

UNIVERSITY OF TORONTO PRESS
Toronto Buffalo London

© University of Toronto Press 1980
Toronto Buffalo London
Printed in Canada
Reprinted 1981

Canadian Cataloguing in Publication Data

Keith, William J., 1934–
    The poetry of nature
    Includes index.
    ISBN 0-8020-5494-3
    1. English poetry – History and criticism.
    2. American poetry – History and criticism.
    3. Nature in literature. I. Title.
    PR508.N3K44   821'.009'36   C79-094903-2

O many are the poets that are sown
By Nature.
WILLIAM WORDSWORTH

A poet does not stand in the presence of natural facts alone, he stands also in the presence of other poets of nature and their poems.
REUBEN A. BROWER

CONTENTS

PREFACE

Great things are done when Men & Mountains meet;
This is not done by Jostling in the Street.

WILLIAM BLAKE

The Poetry of Nature might be described as a book about what happens when men and mountains (and other natural objects) meet, and the encounter is recorded in verse. I have isolated and discussed the particular kind of 'nature poem' that is my main concern in the introductory chapter. I see Wordsworth as the first English poet to develop the artistic possibilities of this 'human nature poetry,' and the second chapter concentrates on his experiments with perspective and angles of narration. Subsequent chapters are devoted to the practice of individual poets, and in each case I begin by discussing the forms (often indirect and sometimes ambiguous) that Wordsworth's influence and example take. Although I have tried to make each chapter as self-sufficient as possible, my approach depends upon my considering each poet in relation to the others, and the book clearly gains in coherence and (I think) in effectiveness if it is read as a whole. Like my earlier study, *The Rural Tradition*, which concerned itself with the non-fiction prose writers of the English countryside, this book sees the poets and poetry treated here as forming a loose but palpable 'line' that benefits from being examined in sequence and on its own.

Much of the book consists of close readings of individual poems. I have tried in each case to quote all the essential lines, but most of the poems are too long to reproduce in full; the reader is therefore recommended, whenever possible, to consult a complete text. The poems in question are for the most part accessible in numerous editions and anthologies. Only in cases where poems are less easy to locate have I given formal references to specific editions.

As usual, I am grateful to a number of colleagues and friends who gave me useful advice during the writing of this book. R.P. Bilan and Michael Kirkham both read an earlier draft and made various suggestions that have improved the final version. Others read individual chapters and gave me the benefit of their specialized knowledge; these include Johanne Clare (for Clare), Michael Millgate (for Hardy), John F. Lynen (for Frost), and John Studley (for Blunden). None of the above is in any way responsible for my readings of the poets as a whole, but all have contributed to whatever merit the book may possess.

I acknowledge with gratitude the fact that this book has been published with the help of a grant from the Canadian Federation for the Humanities, using funds provided by the Social Sciences and Humanities Research Council of Canada, and a grant from the Publications Fund of University of Toronto Press. Much of the research and writing took place during a sabbatical leave, and for this period of leisure I am indebted to my university, my department, and my college, and to the Canada Council (as it was then) for awarding me a Leave Fellowship. I also owe a debt of gratitude to Miss Jean C. Jamieson and Miss Judith Williams, both of the University of Toronto Press, for advice and encouragement at crucial stages in the preparation of the typescript. Last but certainly not least, I would like to thank my wife Hiroko for cheerfully accepting the mass (mess?) of books and papers strewn haphazardly about our living-room floor during the years in which the book was being written.

W.J.K.
English Department, University College, University of Toronto,
September 1979

ACKNOWLEDGMENTS

Acknowledgments are due to the following for permission to quote from copyright material: To Curtis Brown, Ltd., for quotations from John Wain's 'Reason for Not Writing Orthodox Nature Poetry' (in *A Word Carved on a Sill*). To Granada Publishing, Ltd., for quotations from the following works by R.S. Thomas: *Poetry for Supper, Song at the Year's Turning, Tares*. To Holt, Rinehart and Winston, Publishers, for quotations from *The Poetry of Robert Frost* edited by Edward Connery Lathem. Copyright 1923, 1928, 1930, 1939, © 1969 by Holt, Rinehart and Winston. Copyright 1942, 1951, © 1956, 1958, 1962 by Robert Frost. Copyright © 1967, 1970 by Lesley Frost Ballantine. Reprinted by permission of Holt, Rinehart and Winston, Publishers. To Jonathan Cape Ltd., publishers of Robert Frost for the British Commonwealth and Empire excluding Canada, for quotations from *The Poetry of Robert Frost* edited by Edward Connery Lathem. To Macmillan (London and Basingstoke) for quotations from the following works by R.S. Thomas: *Frequencies, Laboratories of the Spirit*. To Macmillan Publishing Co., Inc. (New York), for quotations from *The Complete Poems of Thomas Hardy* (ed. James Gibson) originally published in *Human Shows* (copyright 1925 by Macmillan Publishing Co., Inc., renewed 1953 by Lloyds Bank, Ltd.) and *Winter Words* (copyright 1928 by Florence E. Hardy and Sydney E. Cockerell, renewed 1956 by Lloyds Bank, Ltd.). To Martin Secker and Warburg, Ltd., for quotations from Andrew Young's *Complete Poems* (ed. Leonard Clark).

THE POETRY OF NATURE

ONE

Introduction

'Nature poetry' is a term so broad and all-embracing that it can no longer be said to hold any important place in the vocabulary of literary criticism. It can include anything from Thomson's *Seasons* to a W.H. Davies lyric or even Ted Hughes's 'Crow' poems; it can be narrowed to an isolated image ('the swan's down-feather' in *Antony and Cleopatra*, for example) or expanded to contain a philosophy of life. In his poem 'Lucretius versus the Lake Poets,' Robert Frost has caught the awkward ambiguity of the term in a facetious but witty rhyme: 'Nature' can mean either 'pretty scenery' (Wordsworth, etc.) or 'the Whole Goddam Machinery' (*De Rerum Natura*). Even if we set aside the whole question of 'natural philosophy,' the subject remains enormous. In the last two hundred and fifty years poems descriptive of 'pretty scenery' have been innumerable and for the most part third-rate. Predictably, the Romantic cult of natural objects and the natural life produced a counter-reaction. In an industrial age, moreover, such poetry is regarded, at best, as a minor genre that can exist only on the peripheries of the modern world. Small wonder, then, that 'mere nature poetry' is a phrase that recurs with deadening regularity in twentieth-century critical writing.

I feel no strong commitment to the term, though I shall continue to use it in the absence of a better phrase; I am convinced, however, that within the intractable mass that we call 'nature poetry' there is a smaller, better-defined type of verse that not only proves worthy of attention on its own merits, but benefits from being studied as a generic unit. In a little-known article contributed to the American magazine *Forum* in 1897, the Canadian poet Charles G.D. Roberts made a distinction which, though simple enough when articulated, is by no means self-evident, and can prove helpful at this point. 'The poetry of nature,' he wrote, 'may be roughly divided into two main classes: that which deals with pure description, and that which treats of nature in some one of its many relations with humanity.' Purely descriptive verse, he contends, is 'little more than a presentation of some of the raw materials of poetry,' and he concludes that nature poetry at its best 'is not mere description of landscape in metrical form, but the expression of one or another of many vital relationships between external nature and "the deep heart of Man."' [1] Admittedly the subject remains large, but, however rough and ready this distinction may prove when rigorously scrutinized, it at least suggests divisions and boundaries, and can even help us to separate the grain from the chaff. Above all, if we confine ourselves to nature poems that are at one and the same time 'human nature poems,' the subject cannot be dismissed as minor or irrelevant. Indeed, the relation of the human mind to all that exists outside it, the connection between interior and exterior landscapes, the inseparable links between man and his environment, all these are matters of central importance to the modern consciousness. While the poets I shall be discussing here are seldom concerned directly with such weighty issues, their personal encounters with the natural world may be seen as individual examples of the overriding human urge to understand the universe in which we find ourselves.

In the following chapters I shall examine some of the ways in which so-called nature poets (and for convenience I limit my attention to those for whom the subject comprises a major part of their poetic material) have communicated their experience of, and response to, the natural environment. The emphasis will fall as much on the observer as on his subject-matter; I argue, indeed, that the two cannot properly be separated. A major concern will be Wordsworth's influence upon his successors, which I believe to be far subtler than is generally recognized; but this is by no means a constraining influence. On the contrary, I am impressed by the varied possibilities within this kind of poem that Wordsworth's exploratory genius made possible, and I am especially interested in the technical considerations that such poetry involves. In particular I wish to stress the literary-critical advantage of treating the chosen poets in relation to each other. This relation may be one of contrast or comparison, but in either case the result, I believe, is an enriched appreciation of the subtlety of the poems and the artistry of the poets.

One could argue, of course, that there is in fact no possibility of separating Man and Nature. Can there be such a thing as a purely descriptive poetry? Is it practically possible to write a poem in which the reader is unconscious of a particular human speaker or unaware of any human content in the landscape described? Perhaps not, but the poet can certainly regulate our consciousness of his presence within the poem and can control the extent to which the emphasis falls upon the external scene or upon a human response towards it. Wordsworth's 'Written in March' – not, incidentally, the kind of nature poem that I am concerned with in the rest of this book – is a useful test case, since it presents natural objects in what would seem to be the simplest and most direct way possible. It begins as follows:

> The Cock is crowing,
> The stream is flowing,
> The small birds twitter,
> The lake doth glitter,
> The green field sleeps in the sun.

The simplicity of diction and syntax seems determined by a desire to communicate baldly, without any intrusive comment, the external scene as it presents itself before him. Indeed, its relative lack of interest (compared with Wordsworth's major poems) derives from this deliberate suppression of his own response. None the less, the human element cannot be excluded for long. In the immediately succeeding lines,

> The oldest and youngest
> Are at work with the strongest,

we see countrymen at work, and at the opening of the second stanza the snow retreats 'like an army defeated' and human reference enters (as it does so often) through illustrative simile. But if 'Written in March' begins as an attempt at a 'pure' nature poem, the experiment clearly fails in the closing lines:

> The Ploughboy is whooping – anon – anon:
>   There 's joy in the mountains;
>   There 's life in the fountains;
>   Small clouds are sailing,
>   Blue sky prevailing;
>   The rain is over and gone!

I refer not to the presence of the ploughboy but to words like 'joy' and 'life' which imply a human consciousness responding to the landscape, and particularly to the undeniably human emotion expressed through the movement and rhythm of the verse. I can think of no poem by Wordsworth that is closer to purely descriptive poetry than this, and its insistence on becoming a 'human nature poem' (whatever our reservations about its artistic success) is surely significant.

For a more complex instance we may turn to Hardy's 'Last Week in October,' which is short enough to quote in full:

> The trees are undressing, and fling in many places –
> On the gray road, the roof, the window-sill –

Their radiant robes and ribbons and yellow laces;
A leaf each second so is flung at will,
Here, there, another and another, still and still.

A spider's web has caught one while downcoming,
That stays there dangling when the rest pass on;
Like a suspended criminal hangs he, mumming
In golden garb, while one yet green, high yon,
Trembles, as fearing such a fate for himself anon.

Here Hardy seems to have taken special pains to be as objective as possible, and has deliberately excluded an 'I' from his poem; but as soon as we observe (as we surely do) that the poem is unmistakably Hardyesque, we have implicitly denied its 'objective' status since it betrays the hallmarks of a human maker. In fact, Hardy has controlled the reader's response with remarkable dexterity. The human references are, until the last line, confined to imagistic association – not only, as in the Wordsworthian example, through simile ('Like a suspended criminal'), but through metaphor: the trees are 'undressing' and their leaves are transformed into 'robes and ribbons and yellow laces.' But the human connection upon which the whole poem depends becomes clear in the final line where the green leaf 'trembles'; this could be merely metaphorical, but then Hardy moves unequivocally into what we call, inadequately, pathetic fallacy – 'as fearing such a fate for himself anon.' Not 'itself,' we notice, but 'himself.' To say that he employs personification or pathetic fallacy is true but (within the context) unhelpful. The effectiveness of 'Last Week in October' derives from the subtlety with which Hardy presents his material, his deliberate stance in communicating an individual response without recourse to the first person. His technique lies not in the mere employment of rhetorical devices and figures of speech but in the totality of response (control of viewpoint, diction, rhythm, allusion, etc.) that the poem communicates.

The relation between nature and human nature, then, is central to the verse I shall be considering. This explains why I begin with Wordsworth rather than with the poetry of the eighteenth century. Nature poetry was a prominent feature of Augustan verse, as numerous scholarly accounts have testified, but there is little evidence of that kind of personal encounter and reaction with which I am exclusively concerned. Although the Augustans knew that the proper study of mankind was man, their nature poetry emphasized the descriptive. As John More pointed out as early as 1777, while writing of Thomson's *Seasons*, 'by *descriptive poetry*, we chiefly mean what refers to external nature, and what has no direct connection either with the human character, or any department of social life.'[2] In such poetry the observer, if noticeable at all, is present primarily as spectator, a faithful recorder who communicates what he sees; often, indeed, he is not far removed from the field-naturalist. If he draws conclusions from his observations, they are (so far as is possible) general conclusions, objective, usually didactic, and sometimes even 'scientific.' His experience in the landscape brings about no discernible change in the speaker.

There can be little that is distinctive, let alone unique, about a first-person singular in such conditions. The poet-speaker aligns himself with one of a series of prescribed conventions. Thomson's stance in *The Seasons* represents one of the commoner attitudes:

> I solitary court
> The inspiring breeze, and meditate the book
> Of Nature, ever open, aiming thence
> Warm from the heart to learn the moral song.
>
> ('Autumn,' ll. 669–72)

Solitary, meditate, moral song: the development is familiar. Numerous other examples could be cited without difficulty. The sensitive, feminine sympathy of Anne Finch, Countess of Winchilsea, provides an alternative approach, as does Cowper's surprisingly individual melancholy – surprising, that is, when compared with the numbing sameness of so much 'retirement poetry.' But in all these instances, we feel that the mood is fixed from the start and is overlaid upon the natural world. Thomson, convinced already that the manifold works of nature make up 'an harmonious whole' ('Hymn,' l. 26), can assign any seasonal phenomenon to its place within the total scheme. Anne Finch's 'Nocturnal Reverie' exists because the night-scene proved coincident with her state of mind. Cowper's gentle, sheltered landscape is deliberately chosen by the poet because it reflects the terms of his own personality. The natural world offers no dramatic challenge; the poet is not presented with a shock that might affect his attitude – any shocks that do occur, like Thomson's 'cogenial horrors' in 'Winter' (l. 6), are themselves conventional. There are few equivalents to Wordsworth's encounter with the daffodils or with the leech-gatherer on the lonely moor, Clare's discovery of the mouse's nest, the possible challenge to Hardy's pessimism in 'The Darkling Thrush,' the enigma represented by the giant buck in Frost's 'The Most of It,' or the violence and terror that emanate from Edmund Blunden's 'Pike.' It was not until the development of an interest in subjective response, fostered by the Romantic movement, that the nature poet offered his unique on-the-spot reactions as well as his observations and the generalized meditation they were expected to provoke. Wordsworth was being more original than perhaps we realize when he wrote in his Preface to *Lyrical Ballads* (1802): 'What then does the Poet? He considers man and the objects that surround him as acting and re-acting upon each other, so as to produce an infinite complexity of pain and pleasure.'[3] The critical commonplace that the

'Ode to a Nightingale' tells us more about Keats than about the nightingale takes on new interest in this context. The subject seeing proves at least as significant as the object seen.

But it is not so much the 'I' as the artistically deliberate manipulation of the 'I' that becomes all-important. What we find for the first time in Wordsworth (though this is still obscured by those determined to trace a rigidly consistent philosophical attitude throughout his poetry) is the creation of an appropriate 'I' for the particular natural confrontation. In order to communicate the experience of the poem, the poet must be firmly in control of his point of view. Hitherto, when an effect depended upon an appropriate angle of narration, this occurred too often merely as the result of happy accident. In Stephen Duck's *The Thresher's Labour* (1730), for instance, the freshness of the poem derives to a considerable extent from the fact that we see the labouring life from the inside, through the thresher's eyes rather than through those of a detached observer. But the reason for this is only too clear: Duck's circumstances at the time of writing – he had not yet been taken in tow by the literati – meant that this was the only possible viewpoint he could adopt. It was, literally, the only one he knew; the effect, though dramatic, was unplanned. We shall meet a similar situation from time to time in the poetry of John Clare. Wordsworth, however, constructs his best poems in such a way that the speaker is seen in a suitable setting and/or a suitable mood, and is viewed from an artistically appropriate angle.

I am inevitably concerned, then, with matters of structure, and particularly with perspective. But here again some initial distinctions need to be made. Eighteenth-century nature poetry was itself preoccupied with perspective, but this was mainly visual, analogous to the perspective in landscape painting; I focus my attention here on an essentially poetic perspective involving the relation, in both physical and emotional terms, between the poet and the natural world in which he finds himself. Does he present himself directly or create a separate persona for his purpose? Do we look through the protagonist's eyes or is he presented as himself a part of the landscape? Is the narrator an observer or a participant? A native or an outsider? A teacher or a learner? All these questions are worth asking and can throw light on the unique qualities of the poem.

To take a reasonably straightforward example, here is the opening stanza of R.S. Thomas's poem, 'The Welsh Hill Country':

> Too far for you to see
> The fluke and the foot rot and the fat maggot
> Gnawing the skin from the small bones,
> The sheep are grazing at Bwlch-y-Fedwen,
> Arranged romantically in the usual manner
> On a bleak background of bald stone.[4]

The poem continues for two more stanzas, but they are syntactically parallel, and its essential structure can be derived from the lines quoted. There is no employment of the first-person singular in this poem, but we realize immediately that we are being addressed by an individual; it is equally apparent that the point of the poem depends upon the perspective from which we are invited (or, rather, forced) to view the subject-matter. Furthermore, we do not need to be familiar with Thomas's other poems to appreciate the tone and attitudes of the speaker. The poem is, sardonically but literally, about the problem of aesthetic distance – that distance which, an earlier poet has told us, lends enchantment to the view. The reader is cast into the role of a tourist approaching the country from afar. The narrator, on the other hand, is a native who speaks knowledgeably from within the landscape; he knows intimately the ugly and unpleasant details which are invisible until one is close. This example is particularly convenient because Thomas makes use of a visual perspective in order to contrast it with a specifically poetic one. The scene we are offered contains a formal 'background' and the sheep are 'arranged romantically in the usual manner' – that is to say, according to the traditional principles of 'the picturesque.' This is the kind of prospect that an eighteenth-century traveller might have viewed with a Claude-glass. But the poet has deliberately placed us in the position of a beauty-seeking tourist so that he can draw attention to the inadequacy of the viewpoint.

Poetic perspective is wider than its visual counterpart because it can encompass time as well as space. This can be illustrated by reference to Hardy's 'At Middle-Field Gate in February.' The opening stanzas read as follows:

> The bars are thick with drops that show
> As they gather themselves from the fog
> Like silver buttons ranged in a row,
> And as evenly spaced as if measured, although
> They fall at the feeblest jog.
>
> They load the leafless hedges hard by,
> And the blades of last year's grass.
> While the fallow ploughland turned up nigh
> In raw rolls, clammy and clogging lie –
> Too clogging for feet to pass.

So far the poem seems purely descriptive. Once again, there is no discernible 'I,' though the likening of the drops of mist to 'silver buttons ranged in a row' and the metaphorical description of the wet ploughland 'in raw rolls' suggest an idiosyncratic viewpoint on the part of the poet. (In fact, the use of conspicuous poetic imagery often converts what would otherwise be a piece of straightforward description into a 'human nature poem.') But the final stanza unequivocally reveals the thought-process of a specific narrator:

> How dry it was on a far-back day
>> When straws hung the hedge and around,
>> When amid the sheaves in amorous play
>> In curtained bonnets and light array
>> Bloomed a bevy now underground!

Only Hardy could have written that. Anyone possessing even a nodding acquaintance with his characteristic verse could not fail to identify the sentiment, the language (especially 'far-back' and 'bevy') and the tone of controlled nostalgia that shapes and individualizes the conventional structure. But the point to be emphasized here is that, in contrast to R.S. Thomas's spatial perspectives (the reader's 'too far' against the narrator's implied close-up), Hardy's viewpoints are temporal: now compared to then. The landscape recalls to the aging man a scene from the past, and this despite – or even, perhaps, because of – the radical contrasts: February instead of harvest, clammy fog instead of warm dryness, a deserted scene instead of a gay and crowded one. The poem is about time and memory, but the specific title and the identifying annotation at the close ('Bockhampton Lane') show that the process of recalling the past is dependent upon the poet's keen sense of locality. 'At Middle-Field Gate in February,' like so many of Hardy's poems, is a 'spot of time,' and he can only achieve his effect by extreme precision in evoking the spirit of place and distinguishing between time present and time past. We carry away from the poem a visual image of the aged poet leaning over the gate lost in reverie. Through Hardy's inconspicuous but deliberate control of poetic perspective, we can observe the poet in the landscape while at the same time accepting and responding to the form of the poem, which is best described perhaps as an inner monologue.

I have chosen to dwell on these two examples, of course, because they illustrate the importance of poetic perspective with an admirable clarity. Admittedly, viewpoint is seldom as integral to the effect of a poem as it is here. None the less, in a remarkable number of instances we shall find that the success of a poem involving a natural encounter is considerably enhanced by an appropriate angle of presentation. It is not too much to say that the most skilful poets are those who are prepared to learn in this regard from the technical experience of their predecessors, and who then go on to apply the expertise gained to new and original ends. For all the rural poets since his time the example of Wordsworth is supreme.

TWO

William Wordsworth

INVOLVEMENT AND INTERCHANGE

Wordsworth is, first and foremost, a poet of personal engagement. If we turn to his mature verse from the characteristic nature poetry of the eighteenth century, or even from his own *Evening Walk* and *Descriptive Sketches* written under the influence of eighteenth-century tradition, what we first notice is its vigorous energy and involvement. This is manifest not only in attitude and subject-matter but, more palpably, in the fast-flowing rhythmic movement of the verse, as the following well-known but representative examples will illustrate:

> And so I dare to hope,
> Though changed, no doubt, from what I was when first
> I came among these hills; when like a roe
> I bounded o'er the mountains, by the sides
> Of the deep rivers, and the lonely streams,
> Wherever nature led. ('Tintern Abbey,' ll. 65–70)

> I was a Traveller then upon the moor,
> I saw the hare that raced about with joy;
> I heard the woods and distant waters roar;
> Or heard them not, as happy as a boy.
> ('Resolution and Independence,' ll. 15–18)

> Oh! when I have hung
> Above the raven's nest, by knots of grass

> And half-inch fissures in the slippery rock ...
> With what strange utterance did the loud dry wind
> Blow through my ear!   (*Prelude*, I, 330–2, 337–8)[1]

We respond to a sense of personal urgency behind the poetry. The speaker is not merely a passive observer and recorder of natural phenomena but an energetic participator. He bounds like the roe, is joyous with the hare, and takes into himself the 'utterance' of the wind as it blows through him. An active inhabitant of an 'active universe' (*Prelude*, II, 254), he bears witness to a profound interchange between man and nature.

I am concerned here with the expression of this interchange, and can therefore avoid any extended description and definition of Wordsworth's 'nature,' a subject that has been debated in numerous books ranging from topographical accounts of 'Wordsworthshire' to learned commentaries on his natural philosophy. All that needs to be noted here (and the quotations in the previous paragraph help to establish the point) is that, for Wordsworth at his most characteristic, 'nature' is primarily a matter of landscape and the elements. The physical features of Somerset and the Lake District (mountains and moors, valleys, streams, stretches of water) and the meteorological conditions under which they are seen (rain, winds, mist, sun, and shadow) are paramount. Although he wrote a number of poems about flora and fauna – 'To the Daisy,' 'The Small Celandine,' 'The Green Linnet,' 'The Cuckoo,' etc. – these subjects did not engage him sufficiently to give rise to his most profound and lasting verse. For the most satisfying treatment of the wild life of the countryside we must turn to the work of John Clare. But in tracing the varied human responses to the forms of nature, and the equally varied ways in which the natural world can affect the human mind, Wordsworth is unrivalled.

Nowhere is the interrelationship more forcefully celebrated than in 'I Wandered Lonely as a Cloud,' a poem central to the Wordsworthian experience and therefore worth considering in some detail. Here, in an effect that appears spontaneous but as we shall see is exquisitely contrived, the worlds of man and nature are tightly interwoven even in the opening lines:

> I wandered lonely as a cloud
> That floats on high o'er vales and hills,
> When all at once I saw a crowd,
> A host, of golden daffodils.

The 'I' is immediately linked through simile to a natural object ('lonely as a cloud'), the daffodils are then presented in collective terms normally reserved for human beings ('a crowd, / A host'), and by the end of the first stanza they are seen not only as 'fluttering' but also, in human terms, as 'dancing.' Similarly, one set of natural objects is firmly and deliberately likened to another; the 'I' compared to a cloud at the opening of the first stanza is duly balanced at the opening of the second by the daffodils 'continuous as the stars.' There are, in fact, three natural sets in the poem corresponding to the three natural elements in the landscape – the daffodils on the land, the waves on the water, the clouds and stars in the sky – and all are eventually presented in terms of each other. First, the cloud 'floats on high o'er vales and hills,' a metaphor arising, one presumes, from the reflection of the cloud within the lake; the daffodils can then be likened (this time by way of memory) to the stars, and at the opening of the third stanza the waves dance just like the flowers.

When all the varying forms of nature are so triumphantly united in celebration, how can the lonely human being fail to be drawn into the scene?

> A poet could not but be gay,
> In such a jocund company.

The human being involved is not merely a generalized 'I' but quite explicitly and necessarily a poet, since the vision of the interconnecting forms of the natural world is clearly a poet's vision and can only be communicated through poetic means. Thus, even the use of the word 'company,' which is at one and the same time a synonym for 'crowd' and 'host' and a contrast to the speaker's original loneliness, is indicative of an essentially poetic manipulation of language. The interlinking connotations of human words complement the interlinking dance of natural things. Moreover, in the well-known last stanza the delight experienced in the passing moment is preserved both in the poet's memory and within the record of his poem. The 'inward eye / Which is the bliss of solitude' succeeds in combining the potentially creative loneliness with which the poem started and the social unity achieved by the 'jocund company' of flowers. The poem rises to its climax when the poet's heart is able to join the company and to extend it in human time as, in imagination, he 'dances with the daffodils.' The emphasis here should fall not on the obvious and rather crude rhyme but on the intellectual and poetic achievement of 'dances.' The confrontation between man and nature has become a continuing union.

'I Wandered Lonely as a Cloud' flows so smoothly and effortlessly that, until we realize its complexity, we are tempted to regard it as a straight transcription of experience. In order to measure the full extent of the 'shaping spirit of Imagination' that moulded the poem, we need to compare it with the account of the original incident in Dorothy Wordsworth's Journal (15 April 1802):

> When we were in the woods beyond Gowbarrow park we saw a few daffodils close to the water-side. We fancied that the lake had floated the seeds ashore, and that the little colony had so sprung up. But as we went along there were more and yet

more; and at last, under the boughs of the trees, we saw that there was a long belt of them along the shore, about the breadth of a country turnpike road. I never saw daffodils so beautiful. They grew among the mossy stones about and about them; some rested their heads upon these stones as on a pillow for weariness; and the rest tossed and reeled and danced, and seemed as if they verily laughed with the wind, that blew upon them over the lake; they looked so gay, ever glancing, ever changing. This wind blew directly over the lake to them. There was here and there a little knot, and a few stragglers a few yards higher up; but they were so few as not to disturb the simplicity, unity, and life of that busy highway.[2]

We realize at once that Wordsworth has been radically selective, and has not hesitated to alter biographical circumstances to create the quintessent[...] experience conveyed by the poem. 'We saw a few daffodils,' writes Doro[...] but Wordsworth suppresses this first glimpse to achieve the forceful imme[...]cy of 'all at once I saw a crowd, / A host, of golden daffodils.' Dorothy is ca[...]ul to specify the locality in which the flowers were seen, but this informatio[...] not needed in the poem. Dorothy records that they discussed the possible or[...]ns of the colony, but such ecological speculation has no place in Wordsworth'[...]etic experience. Similarly, Dorothy notices that some of the flowers 'reste[...]heir heads upon ... stones as on a pillow for weariness,' but this detail, con[...]ting with the required sense of movement and energy, is excluded, as a[...] the unsuitable references to 'a country turnpike road' and the 'busy highwa[...] But the most striking change, of course, is reflected in Wordsworth's t[...]e: 'I Wandered Lonely as a Cloud.' A solitary speaker is a poetic necessi[...]y, so Dorothy herself is ruthlessly banished from the poem.

It would be difficult to exaggerate the significance of these changes. Wordsworth first reduces the biographical experience to its basic ingredients, and then builds upon this foundation the major effects of his poem. The elements of earth, water, and air are implicit within the scene, and duly recorded by Dorothy in their specific manifestations (flowers and trees, lake, and wind), but it is Wordsworth the poet, the 'maker,' who relates these images to each other, and reinforces the sense of union between speaker and natural objects by combining form and content into a firmly structured artistic whole. If we have responded adequately to the challenge of the poem, we are aware not only of the experience in nature that so affects the poet, but of the poet's own art which has added a further universalizing dimension to the experience. 'I Wandered Lonely as a Cloud' can be described as nature poetry in a very exact sense, since 'nature' and 'poetry' are here fused.

'There Was a Boy' is another poem that embodies this characteristically Wordsworthian sense of involvement and interrelation; indeed, it presents and celebrates the perfect if momentary coalescence of man and nature. From the first description of the stars as they 'move along the edges of the hills,' the interchange is stressed, but it culminates, of course, in the commerce between the boy and the owls. He can lure them into sound by his 'mimic hootings' while they in turn 'shout ... / Responsive to his call' (my italics). And even when, for an unspecified reason, the duet is broken up, the resultant stillness is equally productive:

> Then, sometimes, in that silence, while he hung
> Listening, a gentle shock of mild surprise
> Has carried far into his heart the voice
> Of mountain-torrents; or the visible scene
> Would enter unawares into his mind
> With all its solemn imagery, its rocks,
> Its woods, and that uncertain heaven received
> Into the bosom of the steady lake.

By making every word count, Wordsworth succeeds here in communicating what we might otherwise be tempted to describe as the inexpressible. The 'gentle shock of mild surprise,' doubly paradoxical, prepares us for the communication beyond words which is so important a part of Wordsworth's natural supernaturalism. (It recalls in 'Tintern Abbey' the 'sensations sweet, / Felt in the blood, and felt along the heart' [ll. 27–8] and the voice of nature speaking through the River Derwent as it 'flowed along [his] dreams' in The Prelude [1, 274].) Moreover, we should note that the scene enters 'unawares' into the boy's mind, that for all its obvious substantiality it is also 'imagery,' and that the interchange between nature and man occurs as quietly and naturally as the reflection of the paradoxical 'uncertain' heaven into the bosom of the equally paradoxical 'steady' lake.

The most obvious difference between 'There Was a Boy' and 'I Wandered Lonely as a Cloud' may be located in the separation of narrator from protagonist. Scholars tell us that the boy in question can be shown to be Wordsworth himself, because manuscript lines exist in which the incident is told in the first person (see Prelude, pp. 639–40). This, though likely enough, seems to me to fall short of proof since, if Wordsworth can change from first to third person, he is equally capable of moving in the opposite direction. Besides, Wordsworth himself mentions a William Raincock of Rayrigg in his notes on the poem preserved by Isabella Fenwick (Prelude, p. 547), and T.W. Thompson has identified the grave in the last verse-paragraph as that of John Tyson, who died in August 1782 at the age of twelve.[3] One suspects that the boy combines some of the external characteristics of Raincock and Tyson with Wordsworth's own imaginative sensibility, but the important questions to ask at this point are:

why is the poem constructed as it is? why does Wordsworth dissociate himself from the boy both in the poem as a separate entity and also as it fits into Book v of *The Prelude*?

Any answers to these questions must necessarily remain hypothetical, but the following explanation seems to me both likely and convincing. The anonymous boy could be any boy. Wordsworth did not want the experience to be offered as individual and unique; still less, I suspect, did he want it categorized as part of a portrait of the artist as a young man, which would carry even more limiting connotations. For this reason, I believe, he not only presents the incident from an omniscient perspective but underlines the separation by appearing, deliberately and somewhat ostentatiously, in his own person at the graveside in the concluding lines which most critics have judged unconvincing. I have no wish to quarrel with this consensus – indeed, I agree with it – but it is important to understand why the lines are there. They are an attempt, albeit a clumsy one, to provide a commentator for the story since the boy, even if kept alive, could hardly have articulated the experience for himself. This experience, though available to anyone, could only have been expressed by a poet. 'There Was a Boy' is an example of Wordsworth's frequent practice of introducing a poetic interpreter between his subject and the reader.[4]

The preceding discussion should have demonstrated that a consideration of Wordsworth's nature poetry cannot ignore the technical resources that he brought to the writing of verse. Throughout the 'great decade' of his productive poetic life, as the prefaces to succeeding editions of *Lyrical Ballads* make clear, he was a tireless experimenter, and I shall be arguing that it is for his original experiments with viewpoint and perspective rather than for any abstract 'philosophy of nature' that Wordsworth proved a decisive influence on his poetic successors. In the ensuing sections of this chapter I shall discuss a number of alternative ways of presenting the confrontation of man and the external world in Wordsworth's verse before offering some general conclusions about his central importance in the tradition of nature poetry in English.

EARLY EXPERIMENTS

Two early poems, 'Lines Left upon a Seat in a Yew-Tree' and 'A Night Piece,' will repay critical examination at this point. Both are concerned with the man-nature relation, but they approach the subject indirectly. In each case, the relation is imperfect and it is described and analysed by a detached observer. Although neither poem can be judged wholly successful, they are both of particular importance because in them we can see Wordsworth evolving, fitfully and often clumsily, the structural techniques that were to prove so central to his poetic achievement.

'Lines Left upon a Seat in a Yew-Tree' is an address by a local resident to an imagined traveller, explaining to him the circumstances under which the seat was constructed and drawing a suitable moral from the anecdote. The traditional elements loom large, and Geoffrey Hartman has shown the extent to which Wordsworth was indebted here to the classical and eighteenth-century genre of the poetic inscription.[5] At the same time we can recognize within it the seeds of a later poetic form, the dramatic monologue. 'Nay, Traveller! rest,' the poem begins, and while this inevitably suggests to the literary historian 'the traditional *Siste Viator* of the epitaph,'[6] it also catches the sound of an actual speaking voice. Despite the title, which represents part of the traditional element in the poem, the reader cannot help visualizing a literal encounter between speaker and traveller. The traveller learns something from this meeting at a particular spot in much the same way as the narrator is presented as learning from the Wanderer at the site of Margaret's home in 'The Ruined Cottage,' or the rather different narrator from the leech-gatherer on the lonely moor in 'Resolution and Independence.'

Like so many of Wordsworth's poems, 'Lines Left upon a Seat in a Yew-Tree' is indebted to local history but is in no way confined to it. In *Wordsworth's Hawkshead*, T.W. Thompson has assembled all the available information about the Rev. William Braithwaite of Satterhow upon whom Wordsworth based his central character, the recluse who built the seat; but, since Braithwaite lived until 1800 and so was still alive when the poem was first published in the 1798 edition of *Lyrical Ballads*, the situation presented here is clearly a poetic construct. Wordsworth doubtless took his inspiration from what he knew of Braithwaite, as he acknowledges indirectly in the Isabella Fenwick notes (*PW* i. 329), but he had no hesitation in altering the circumstances to fit his broader creative purpose. He chose to emphasize the contrast between the youth who 'to the world went forth / A favoured Being' and the older misanthrope who retired in proud disdain from a world which had decided that it 'owed him no service.' The recluse, then, combines within himself the qualities of both resident and traveller, and Wordsworth has subtly constructed his poem so that both narrator and listener bear separate relations to the main subject; the resident speaker or writer of the lines represents what the recluse might have been if he had never left to work in the larger world, while the traveller to whom the lines are addressed embodies what he might have become if he had not returned to his native place.

Many of the characteristic concerns of the mature Wordsworth can be recognized here. It is, for instance, an early example of a poem arising from an *object*, and although the yew-tree seat lacks the haunting quality of Michael's unfinished sheepfold, its suggestiveness as the recluse's 'only monument' – in the double sense of achievement and memorial – is still impressive. Again, this is no simple poem about the 'influence of natural objects'; rather, it concerns the failure of the recluse to derive comfort from the external scene:

> he many an hour
> A morbid pleasure nourished, tracing here
> An emblem of his own unfruitful life.

He casts his own misanthropy and self-pity on to the landscape. Moreover, as Hartman has noted, the poem differs from Wordsworth's earlier poems like *An Evening Walk* and *Descriptive Sketches* in that 'the natural setting is drawn into the poetry not so much as a thing of beauty that should startle the traveller but because it mingled with human life and still mingles presently in the poet's imagination.'[7] The yew-tree in question stands 'far from all human dwelling' yet has strong human associations. Its immediate surroundings of 'barren rocks' contrast with the loveliness of the 'distant scene' – balanced in eighteenth-century fashion in the subtitle ('a desolate part of the shore' against the 'beautiful prospect') – while an additional contrast is set up within the poem between the actual landscape and the 'far lovelier' scene that the recluse imagines. We find, too, a potentially fruitful contrast between the man's influence on the natural scene (he piled the stones, spread the mossy sod, and even 'taught this aged Tree / With its dark arms to form a circling bower') and the way in which the world of nature ultimately (though perhaps only partially) 'subdue[s] him to herself.'[8]

For my immediate purpose, the technical qualities of the poem, which will become characteristic of Wordsworth's later work, stand out in conveniently clear relief. While the prime subject is the relation between the unnamed recluse and a desolate part of the shore near Esthwaite Water, the story and moral are conveyed by the writer/speaker, mouthpiece of the poet, to the traveller who stands as surrogate for the reader. In this way, the interrelation between man and the world of nature has been interestingly expanded and complicated. The meaning behind the poem is filtered through a second consciousness, and this device, to be repeated by Wordsworth on numerous occasions, enables him to create several layers of implication that form a complete and many-faceted experience.

None the less, though touching and curiously memorable, the poem fails to live up to its promise. Wordsworth is experimenting with an attitude and approach that he will later use to considerable effect, but he has not yet succeeded in fully controlling the complex situation that he has built up. Most obviously, the moralizing is excessively direct. The speaker, who is not simply 'the poet' but a created persona just as the recluse is not Braithwaite but a created character, has not earned the right to his hectoring rhetorical gestures ('Nay,

Traveller! rest,' 'and so, lost Man!,' If Thou be one,' 'O be wiser, Thou!'). His connection with the recluse seems slender; all we are told is that he 'well remember[s] him.' The more the poem develops from the tradition of the verse-inscription towards the suggestion of a speaking voice, the less effective such exhortation becomes. This is but one aspect of the larger stylistic problem that the poem presents. It is customary to draw attention to the curious juxtaposition within the poem of conventional eighteenth-century diction ('what if here / No sparkling rivulet spread the verdant herb?') and what we have come to recognize as characteristically Wordsworthian cadences ('His only visitants a straggling sheep, / The stone-chat, or the glancing sand-piper'); more to the point, however, if we respond to the dramatic dimension within the poem, Wordsworth has failed to provide a convincing and consistent diction for his speaker; consequently we are uncertain about his status, and he cannot speak with the authority of, say, the Wanderer in 'The Ruined Cottage.' None the less, even at this early stage in his career, Wordsworth has begun to explore not merely his own confrontations with nature but those of other men, real or invented. Imperfect and tentative as 'Lines Left upon a Seat in a Yew-Tree' may be, it has already extended the boundaries of nature poetry and laid the foundation for future developments.

'A Night Piece' is particularly interesting as the earliest of Wordsworth's poems to have its originating experience independently recorded in Dorothy's Journal, and it can therefore tell us a great deal about his experimentation with angle and viewpoint. Her entry (Alfoxden Journal, 25 January 1798) is concise enough to quote in full:

> Went to Poole's after tea. The sky spread over with one continuous cloud, whitened by the light of the moon, which, though her dim shape was seen, did not throw forth so strong a light as to chequer the earth with shadows. At once the clouds seemed to cleave asunder, and left her in the centre of a black-blue vault: She sailed along, followed by multitudes of stars, small, and bright, and sharp. Their brightness seemed concentrated (half-moon).

From this straightforward, uncomplicated description Wordsworth incorporates many phrases ('whitened ... by the moon,' 'a black-blue vault,' 'followed by multitudes of stars') without change into his poem, but his significant contribution lies in the unusual, off-centre stance that he takes up. A version of this poem could easily be imagined in which the atmospheric effects were described by a first-person narrator who went on to present his individual response to the experience. Such an account would fit smoothly enough into one of the early books of *The Prelude*, but Wordsworth deliberately avoids this obvious procedure. Instead, the central figure becomes a 'pensive traveller' (inevitably recalling the traveller in the 'Yew-Tree' poem), who is described from side-stage by a consciousness that is never individualized into a first-person pronoun. Since the traveller has an 'unobserving eye,' the descriptive detail borrowed from Dorothy's journal is clearly offered as a contrasting response on the part of the narrator, though from some of the adjectives ('overcast,' 'heavy and wan,' 'dull') we suspect that the traveller's mood is not totally unaffected by his environment. The apparent climax comes when the appearance of the unclouded moon coincides with the awakening of the traveller's awareness of his surroundings:

> he looks up – the clouds are split
> Asunder, – and above his head he sees
> The clear Moon, and the glory of the heavens.

I say '*apparent* climax' because the description continues from the viewpoint of the unindividualized narrator. The only clue to the possible response of the traveller comes in the last four lines:

> At length the Vision closes; and the mind,
> Not undisturbed by the delight it feels,
> Which slowly settles into peaceful calm,
> Is left to muse upon the solemn scene.

'Not undisturbed' specifically implies the minimum possible reaction.[9] We are forced to conclude that the mind in question is that of the traveller, since no such assurance is required from the observant and sensitive narrator.

There is a strangely muted quality about this ending. The Vision has closed, yet its effect is never clearly indicated. But this is obviously not a straightforward nature poem about the moon breaking through a cloud; rather, it considers the possibility of such an event passing unrecorded, or only partly appreciated. Remembering Wordsworth's famous observation that poetry 'takes its origin from emotion recollected in tranquillity,'[10] one is tempted to see the subject-matter of 'A Night Piece' as the raw material for a poem existing at a time prior to the necessary recollection. Significantly, however, there is no reference to Wordsworth as poet, and the traveller may well be deliberately presented as a non-poet who can do no more than 'muse upon the solemn scene.' While Wordsworth may not quite succeed in clarifying what I believe to have been his intention, the poem remains a bold experiment, and we do it less than justice if we import into it Wordsworthian meanings and responses from other poems. It shares a common concern with human reactions to natural objects, but presents an instance in which the reaction is imperfect.

The note on this poem recorded by Isabella Fenwick when Wordsworth was an old man is teasingly ambiguous: 'Composed on the road between Nether Stowey and Alfoxden, extempore. I distinctly remember the very moment when I was struck as described "He looks up at the clouds, etc."' (PW ii. 503). He acknowledges that the poem arose from a personal experience, but offers no explanation why he should present himself in the third person with some notably un-Wordsworthian attributes. It seems clear, however, that, after undergoing an analogous experience, he chose to write the poem from a detached perspective – possibly, indeed, from Dorothy's. In converting himself into a 'pensive traveller ... with unobserving eye,' who is seen from the viewpoint of one who has the practical knowledge of a resident, he is once more adapting personal experience to the larger and more complex dimensions of his poetic subject. As a result, the 'thought' of the poem is inextricable from its form and structure.

EXERCISE IN VENTRILOQUISM

I have demonstrated, I hope, that for Wordsworth the writing of what we have come to call nature poetry is an elaborate undertaking that enlists all the resources of a mature literary technique. As soon as the importance of creating a suitable narrator to fulfil the needs of the individual poem is established, a number of complicating factors arise, one of the most important being the extent to which the central figure is able to express and comprehend his own experience. When the poet is presenting incidents from his own life (in much of The Prelude, for example), the procedure can be straightforward: Wordsworth relates the experience and then goes on to analyse it and calculate its effect upon his later development. Even here, however, the matter is generally not as simple as it first appears, and quite radical alterations and adaptations may have to be made to achieve a desired poetic effect. The difficulties are compounded when a poem demands a central figure who shares little or nothing in common with the poet himself. Wordsworth's insistence upon presenting 'low and rustic life' (Prose i. 124) leads inevitably to problems of expression and interpretation.

Many of the protagonists in his narrative poems, for example, are either inarticulate or unable to draw a more generalized meaning from their experiences. In such cases Wordsworth must invent more subtle ways to convey his meaning. Peter Bell is perhaps the most extreme instance. The famous lines about his failure to respond to the primrose by the river's brim are an index to his insensitivity, and seemingly show him at the farthest possible remove from Wordsworth. Yet his eventual conversion is a classic instance of 'the influence of natural objects,' though transposed into a grotesque and often macabre key. Margaret and Michael pose related problems; indeed, their stories require an interpretative commentary that the protagonists themselves are unable to provide, and I shall have more to say about Wordsworth's presentation of them later in this chapter. But it is 'The Thorn,' the story of Martha Ray, that presents the greatest challenge to his technical virtuosity.

Towards the end of his life Wordsworth gave the following account of the origin of 'The Thorn' to Isabella Fenwick: 'Arose out of my observing on the ridge of Quantock Hill, on a stormy day, a thorn which I had often passed in calm and bright weather without noticing it. I said to myself, "cannot I by some invention do as much to make this Thorn [prominently] an impressive object as the storm has made it to my eyes at this moment?"' (PW ii. 511). On a first reading (especially since most editions print 'permanently' for Wordsworth's 'prominently')[11] this note might, in its concern for catching the transient experience, seem more appropriate to 'I Wandered Lonely as a Cloud,' but one soon realizes that, in its own very different way, 'The Thorn' is making a comparable point. Whereas Wordsworth's response to the daffodils of Ulls-water was clear and unambiguous, his reaction to the thorn was shifting and elusive. The 'invention' he knew that he needed involved not only the creation of a story that would associate the thorn with a human life but the parallel creation of an independent narrator – independent, that is, both from Martha Ray as central protagonist and from the poet himself.

In this poem we can see Wordsworth developing a much more radical technique to accommodate the numerous and varied insights that, by this time, his poetry was beginning to reveal. His own response to the thorn-tree, as recorded in the Fenwick note, takes second place to that of Martha Ray. What the poet sees in a 'spot of time' as an uninvolved passer-by is preserved and transformed in Martha Ray's story that establishes a continuous human association with the thorn and its immediate vicinity. If it were merely a simple story about a woman and a tree there would be no need for an elaborate tissue of story-telling, but Wordsworth is concerned with a number of possible attitudes towards Martha Ray and the thorn. Indeed, one might even claim that the poem is about the difficulty and complexity of presenting the interrelations between man and nature.

That Wordsworth was conscious of the significance of the experiment may be demonstrated from the amount of space that he devotes to the poem in his critical prefaces. Granted that it proved controversial and was obviously misunderstood, he would hardly have devoted so much time to its defence had he not felt that a crucial aspect of his work was at stake. The references are reasonably well known but must be repeated here. In the 1798 advertisement to *Lyrical Ballads*, Wordsworth wrote: 'The poem of the Thorn, as the reader will soon discover, is not supposed to be spoken in the author's own person: the character of the loquacious narrator will suffcently shew itself in the course of the story' (*Prose* i. 117). But readers obviously didn't take the hint, and in 1800 he added a two-page note to the poem that begins as follows:

This Poem ought to have been preceded by an introductory Poem, which I have been prevented from writing by never having felt myself in a mood when it was probable that I should write it well. The character which I have here introduced speaking is sufficiently common. The Reader will perhaps have a general notion of it, if he has ever known a man, a Captain of a small trading vessel, for example, who being past the middle age of life, had retired upon an annuity or small independent income to some village or country town of which he was not a native, or in which he had not been accustomed to live. Such men, having little to do, become credulous and talkative from indolence; and from the same cause, and other predisposing causes by which it is probable that such men may have been affected, they are prone to superstition. On which account it appeared to me proper to select a character like this to exhibit some of the general laws by which superstition acts upon the mind.   (PW ii. 512)

In other words, as Stephen Parrish was the first to emphasize, 'The Thorn' is an early example of the dramatic monologue. [12]

Wordsworth's insistence on the specific details of his narrator's life is by no means fortuitous. A traveller who has seen much of the world, he has settled down in a community 'of which he was not a native'; he proves an idiosyncratic but appropriately neutral vehicle through which the tale can be filtered. Martha Ray's story contains the stuff out of which superstition grows; the separation of hard facts from vague rumour proves difficult, and the interpretation is even more problematic than the evidence. Like the puzzled interlocutor in the poem, we continually find ourselves asking 'But what's the Thorn? and what the pond?' (st. xix). What is the connection between woman, hill of moss, pond, and thorn? Wordsworth offers several possibilities but no firm answer. The narrator is sufficiently separated from the community to cast doubt on its rumour-ridden gossip yet sufficiently close to reject the clinical objectivity of the outsider. What he can do is to associate the human beings and natural objects, obliquely and teasingly, by the vague loquaciousness of his language. The tree is 'a wretched thing' (st. i) and 'this poor Thorn' (st. ii); Martha Ray is 'This wretched Woman' (st. vii) and 'this poor Woman' (st. viii). The heap of moss, at first 'like an infant's grave in size' (st. v, my italics), is later presented as an actual grave; it contains tints of 'scarlet bright' (st. v) while Martha wears 'a scarlet cloak' (st. vi) and the moss is subsequently described as 'spotted red / With drops of that poor infant's blood' (st. xx). Whatever the link between man and nature may be, it is so strong as to be indissoluble.

Martha Ray's association with her natural environment is complex. She is relatively young compared with the 'aged' thorn, yet a link is established through their mutual wretchedness. By contrast, the hill of moss is continually described as 'lovely' or 'beauteous' or 'fair,' and such epithets distinguish it alike from woman and tree. Here, in heightened form, is a series of comparisons and contrasts not all that far removed from the situation in 'I Wandered Lonely as a Cloud' where Wordsworth explores the relation between the solitary speaker and the 'jocund company' of daffodils. Does Martha Ray receive any soothing comfort from the natural objects with which she communes, or is the external scene a reinforcement of her miserable desolation? One thinks of the recluse in the 'Yew-Tree' poem 'on a desolate part of the shore, commanding a beautiful prospect' who can only see 'An emblem of his own unfruitful life.' We should not allow the street-ballad rhythms and the simple, inarticulate protagonist to obscure the fact that Wordsworth is creating here another aspect of the theme he treats in so many of his nature poems. On the contrary, the elaborate technical machinery with which he frames his tale is indicative of his increasing awareness of the intellectual complexity of his material.

'The Thorn' was a radical experiment for 1798, and Wordsworth had no available models to guide him. It is easy for us, used to the dramatic monologues of Tennyson, Browning, and T.S. Eliot, not to mention the impact of controlled point-of-view on the art of the novel, to judge that, technically, Wordsworth did not go far enough. We need not regret the unwritten introductory poem; that sounds like a doomed afterthought which would almost certainly have raised more difficulties than it solved, though its ghostly presence is of interest as indicating an early form of the awareness that eventually led to the Wanderer's biography in 'The Ruined Cottage.' But we cannot help lamenting the fact that we have to go outside the poem to the appended note for a sketch of the captain-narrator. This Wordsworthian ancient mariner (the basic structure complete with obsessed speaker and uncharacterized but argumentative interlocutor is virtually identical with that in Coleridge's poem) cannot be said to exist convincingly within the text. Wordsworth's contemporary readers may be forgiven for being puzzled, since the speaker's attitude, however superstitious, seems preferable to that of the even more superstitious villagers. On the other hand, the difficulty of applying firm moral judgments is at the root of the poem. The desperate questions followed by the repeated 'I cannot tell' (st. ix, xix) ultimately come closer to Wordsworth's intention. The thorn, like so many other natural objects, can be viewed from numerous angles and can contain many meanings. Wordsworth would not have been surprised at Wallace Stevens' discovery that there are thirteen ways of looking at a blackbird.

RESIDENTS AND TRAVELLERS

Wordsworth is the most original and influential writer of 'the poetry of encounter' (to borrow Lawrence Garber's useful phrase) because he was the first to envisage the variety of possibility inherent in this kind of poem. Above all (and this became the very subject-matter of 'Tintern Abbey'), he realized the extent to which the observer's own attitudes could change in the course of time. An individual will respond to the same scene in different ways, according to his mood, age, and experience. The Wye valley of 1798 produced a different poem from any that the poet could conceivably have written five years earlier, Yarrow can always be revisited, and the possibilities of nature poetry are therefore illimitable. I believe, moreover, that a number of personal circumstances in Wordsworth's life impressed this poetically stimulating recognition upon him, and that we can more readily appreciate the technical originality of his contribution to nature poetry by investigating in greater detail his relation with his native countryside.

In the third book of *The Prelude*, Wordsworth describes his move from the Lake District to Cambridge in 1787 as 'Migration strange for a stripling of the hills, / A northern villager'' (III, 34–5). Although his poetry is preoccupied with the natural world and human responses towards it, although he specifically concerns himself with 'low and rustic life,' 'villager' seems an oddly inaccurate designation. The self-portrait that Wordsworth offers in the first two books implies a child who has grown up in the country, but decidedly not a village child. The image of the northern villager, then, is not Wordsworth's own but the impression that he believes his fellow-undergraduates had of him. When we find him later in the same book referring to 'Those shepherd-swains whom I had lately left' (III, 548), and even using the phrase 'An artless rustic' (III, 586) as applicable to himself at Cambridge, we realize that in this part of his autobiographical poem he is presenting himself from a new perspective: that of the society he has just entered. This may be the same Wordsworth whom we have watched in the process of being educated by nature in the earlier books, but we are now invited to examine him from a different viewpoint.

When, in the following year and the following book, he returned home for the summer vacation, he discovered that, although little had changed at Hawkshead, a major transformation had occurred within himself. Inevitably he looked at the countryside and its inhabitants through eyes that had experience of a totally different world with which it could now be compared:

> I read, without design, the opinions, thoughts
> Of those plain-living people now observed
> With clearer knowledge; with another eye
> I saw the quiet woodman in the woods,
> The shepherd roam the hills. (IV, 212–16)

Once again, perspective is all-important, but now it is not Wordsworth himself but the people and objects around him, the subject-matter of his later poetry, which are being viewed 'with another eye.'

I have stressed the move from Hawkshead to Cambridge because it contains within itself a basic pattern of Wordsworth's experience, one which was to be repeated again and again and upon which numerous variations could be played. It is present in embryo in the 'Extract from the conclusion of a poem, composed in anticipation of leaving school' that opens most full editions of his poetry to this day. The lines begin:

> Dear native regions, I foretell,
> From what I feel at this farewell,
> That, wheresoe'er my steps may tend,
> And whensoe'er my course shall end,
> If in that hour a single tie
> Survive of local sympathy,
> My soul will cast the backward view,
> The longing look alone on you.

By Wordworthian standards, this is indifferent poetry, but the terms of his future development are clearly forecast. Hitherto he had known 'the hour / Of thoughtless youth,' as he calls it in 'Tintern Abbey'; he had explored his 'native regions' and acquired a vague sense of 'local sympathy,' but these were to be tested in later life against the world that lay for Wordsworth, as for the recluse in the 'Yew-Tree' poem, beyond the confines of the valley. The resident would develop into a traveller.

It was in the newly acquired role of traveller that Wordsworth returned to Hawkshead for the long vacation of 1788, and at this period he made the discovery, crucial to his subsequent development as poet, that the traveller views the landscape with a different eye from that of the resident. This pattern was repeated again after his visit to France, when a second reorientation had to take place; imagination and taste, to borrow the title from Book xii of *The Prelude*, were temporarily impaired and had to be restored. As we have seen, a similar experience while revisiting the banks of the Wye, the recognition that the natural world remained unaltered but that Wordsworth himself had changed, provided the stimulus for the composition of the all-important 'Tintern Abbey.'

Throughout his life Wordsworth was a keen traveller; 'Memorials of a Tour in ——' becomes a familiar title for groupings of poems. But he is also preoccupied with the idea of coming home, of responding to the claims of 'local sympathy.' The return to Hawkshead in 1788 is only one of many examples of this basic impulse; the motif of the returning traveller is repeated at various prominent points in his autobiographical work. We find it, for instance, at the opening of *The Prelude* –

> A pleasant loitering journey, through three days
> Continued, brought me to my hermitage   (I, 106–7) –

and also in 'Home at Grasmere,' where the Boy desires the liberty

> To flit from field to rock, from rock to field,
> From shore to island, and from isle to shore,

yet wishes at the same time to settle permanently:

> Here
> Must be his Home, this Valley be his World.   (PW v. 314)

Other examples readily come to mind. One of the most memorable is the contrast set up in the Lucy poems between the native who dwells 'among the untrodden ways' and the speaker whose voyages abroad impress upon him the extent of his native loyalty:

> I travelled among unknown men
> In lands beyond the sea;
> Nor, England! did I know till then
> What love I bore to thee.

The same distinction between resident and traveller is used, deliberately and creatively, in many of his non-autobiographical poems. We have already seen its structural employment in the 'Yew-Tree' poem and 'A Night Piece.' In 'Peter Bell' the roving nature of the protagonist is emphasized ('He travelled here, he travelled there' [l. 238]), and his story is told, by effective contrast, within the domestic confines of the poet's garden to a group of village residents including the vicar with his wife and the squire with his daughter. In 'The Brothers' a similar structural framework embodies the contrast. The resident priest of Ennerdale meets in the churchyard a man whom he supposes to be an idle tourist, and is led on to tell the tale of two brothers: one who remained and died in the valley, the other who, although 'His soul was knit to his own native soil' (l. 298), had been forced by circumstances to try his fortune at sea; what he fails to recognize is that the sailor-brother and the 'tourist' are one and the same. Again, in *The Excursion* Wordsworth creates four separate but (for the most part) unindividualized figures whose discussions form the basis of the poem, and sets up a deliberate polarity between the Wanderer and the resident Pastor. The former brings to the debate the experience of a lifelong traveller; the latter embodies the wisdom of one who has withdrawn from the world and become, in

Yeats's phrase, 'Rooted in one dear perpetual place.' Each presents opinions and viewpoints appropriate to his character and situation. These are the most conspicuous examples of a formal practice that became habitual to Wordsworth. Even in many of the familiar shorter poems, which we are not accustomed to regard as in any significant sense dramatic or contrived, he plays all sorts of structural permutations on the experiences and attitudes of residents and travellers.

Perspective, then, is central to Wordsworth. Indeed, I would argue that his pre-eminence lies not in the construction of a fixed and consistent intellectual system nor in the presentation of natural objects based on expert and specialized knowledge, but on an essentially poetic, creative approach to the relation between human beings and the non-human universe. In his best and most characteristic poems he is less concerned with grand generalities such as Perception, Vision, Nature, Humanity, than with the numerous and varied ways in which men come into contact with the natural world. Too much, I believe, has been written about Wordsworth's 'philosophy of nature.' It is more revealing, and infinitely more satisfying, to approach his writing with the working hypothesis that he had, not an attitude, but attitudes to the natural world, and that these attitudes were explored, juxtaposed, and tested within individual poems. Despite his later attempts, encouraged by Coleridge, to create a unified philosophical position that would contain, as it were, the whole of his poetry, what we recognize as essentially Wordsworthian are the 'spots of time,' the separate and individual poems of natural encounter. Again and again we locate the unique essence of a poem in the experience of a particular human being in a particular locality. The meaning of a poem cannot be abstracted from the circumstances out of which it springs; these include the eye that sees the natural object, the angle from which it is seen, and ultimately, of course, the character of the observer (the 'I' behind the 'eye') who responds to it. This observer may be Wordsworth himself, but more often than we yet realize he creates and moulds an individual persona who need not be completely identified with the poet himself nor with the 'I' of other poems.

VARIETIES OF 'I'

A high percentage of Wordsworth's poems are written in the first person, and it is customary to assume that in such cases 'I' and William Wordsworth are equatable. But how valid is this assumption? Can we assert with any confidence that the speakers in 'We are Seven,' the Lucy poems, 'Nutting,' 'Tintern Abbey,' 'Resolution and Independence' and 'I Wandered Lonely as a Cloud' are interchangeable? Obviously not. I have already shown how Wordsworth remoulds experience in the interests of poetic complexity in 'I Wandered Lonely as a Cloud,' and similar arguments could be offered in other cases. Wordsworth may insist that 'the little girl who is the heroine [of 'We are Seven'] I met within the area of Goodrich Castle in the year 1793' (PW i. 260), but the pedantic, arithmetically obsessed questioner, though eminently suitable here, is hardly the Wordsworth we know from biographical sources or the evidence of other, more typical poems. The speaker of the Lucy poems is similarly a construct; the sequence has attracted much (misplaced) biographical speculation, yet Wordsworth must have taken considerable pains to pare down his speaker to the basic essentials for this type of poem. He becomes, quite simply, any lover, and the poems achieve a universality because the reader can in the very act of reading subsume himself into the first person.

'Nutting' is of particular importance to any study of the Wordsworthian narrator. In the Fenwick note to the poem Wordsworth makes no attempt to disguise the fact that it 'arose out of the remembrance of feelings I had often had when a boy'; he acknowledges that it was 'intended as part of a poem on my own life [i.e. The Prelude], but struck out as not being wanted there' (PW ii. 504). Because the poem explores the relationship between man and nature in terms that are explicitly and almost obsessively sexual, 'Nutting' has commanded a good deal of attention in our post-Freudian age, and attempts have been made to offer it as a central psychological document for the study of Wordsworth and his work. However, such an approach ignores the all-important creative and poetic considerations. From the unambiguous nature of the imagery, it is clear that Wordsworth knew precisely what he was doing, and he certainly made no effort to suppress the poem (it appeared in 1800, while the poem from which it was struck out remained unpublished until after Wordsworth's death in 1850). Its omission from The Prelude is explained, not by any theory about the suppression of potentially embarrassing material, but by Wordsworth's realization that it was not specifically relevant to the growth of a poet's mind. 'Nutting' is an important part of the Wordsworthian canon because it presents an alternative example of the confrontation between man and nature. When the boy attacks the nutgrove with 'merciless ravage,' he is bearing witness to a relation startlingly different from that presented in, for example, 'I Wandered Lonely as a Cloud' or 'There Was a Boy.' Far from trying to integrate it into a neat theory of Wordsworth's 'attitude to nature,' we should see it rather as evidence that no lowest common denominator of this kind should be postulated. While 'Nutting' gains from being read in juxtaposition with other Wordsworthian poems, it recounts a separate experience and is poetically self-sufficient. It constitutes, in fact, a remarkable monument to the versatility of Wordsworth's genius.

'Tintern Abbey' is, of course, unquestionably autobiographical, yet even here we shall go astray if we fail to take account of the selectivity involved in Wordsworth's self-presentation. Although we instantly recognize in the poem some of the most characteristic features of the writer, many aspects of his personality are missing. Wordsworth the self-conscious poet, Wordsworth the didactic preacher, Wordsworth the political thinker, Wordsworth the whimsical sentimentalist who wrote many of the lesser nature poems: all these have been suppressed. Instead, we are offered a concentrated view of a developing 'worshipper of Nature' (l. 152). The biographical circumstances that led to the writing of 'Tintern Abbey' were, however, unusual. All the necessary poetic tensions and responses happily converged within the personal experience, and Wordsworth was therefore able to compose the poem orally with unusual ease and write it down (so he tells us) without the alteration of a line. Here he is not only traveller but tourist; in visiting the Wye valley he is following the example of William Gilpin and his 'picturesque' tours. The pattern of recollection is set in motion by a landscape visited before but not known intimately. The specific details are being differentiated and defined within the very process of observation ('These hedge-rows, hardly hedge-rows, little lines / Of sportive wood run wild' [ll. 15–16]). Above all, the presence of Dorothy in this case becomes integral to the poem since, by the simple expedient of making her a few years younger than she actually was, he can see in her a visible equivalent of himself as he had been five years previously. Moreover, 'Tintern Abbey' is an interior monologue, and its language fits the meditative recollection and needs to be distinguished from other examples of Wordsworthian blank verse; the voice here is less stiff and formal than that of the 'Yew-Tree' poem, more personal and colloquial than that of 'A Night Piece,' closer perhaps to 'The Old Cumberland Beggar' though less intrusively didactic than much of that poem.

If the blank verse of 'Michael' seems similar, the Wordsworthian traits revealed by the speaker in the introductory section are very different. Once again, Wordsworth has been careful to emphasize precisely those aspects of himself that suit the required tone and mood of the poem as a whole. While he is speaking out as poet,

> for the sake
> Of youthful Poets, who among these hills
> Will be my second self when I am gone,   (ll. 37–9)

even more important is his role as resident of Grasmere. This is essentially a local poem. References to 'our ancient uncouth country style' (l. 111) may sound a little patronizing (Wordsworth, as we know, was temperamentally incapable of losing himself completely in a first-person plural), but a sense of local community is none the less conveyed. Two of the rare occasions on which he uses dialect or local words occur in this poem (ll. 89–90, 168–9) and strengthen the regional emphasis. The opening invitation to turn our steps up Greenhead Ghyll is not a vague topographical gesture, but a recommendation for a rural walk. Richard (actually Robert) Bateman (l. 258) was a genuine local figure, and the 'village near the lake' (l. 135) is Grasmere. I insist on these local associations because there have been too many universalizing treatments of 'Michael' which do harm to the poem by minimizing its local matrix.

Michael's own story, probably handed down to Wordsworth by Ann Tyson, preserves a record of the regional past and rings yet another change on the theme of residents and travellers. To protect his 'patrimonial fields' (l. 224) on which he has lived all his life, Michael sends his son Luke off to London, but, instead of returning like Leonard in 'The Brothers,' Luke goes to the bad and is forced 'To seek a hiding-place beyond the seas' (l. 447). The sheepfold, a far more subtle image than the recluse's seat in the yew-tree, is made symbolic by Michael and Luke within the narrative; both natural object ('a straggling heap of unhewn stones' [l. 17]) and a human artefact, it is formally dedicated to the bond between them, and in the event, of course, the fact that it remains unfinished creates a further symbolic dimension. And again we note the formal suitability in the character of the story-teller; the introduction, with its emphasis on his earlier life, implies a middle-aged narrator equidistant, we might say, from the youthful Luke and the octogenarian Michael.

He certainly seems an older speaker than the 'I' of 'Resolution and Independence,' a poem that was actually written two years later. Indeed, a great deal can be learned about Wordsworth's poetic methods by a comparison between the narrators of these two poems. Both are poets (cf. 'We Poets,' l. 48 here) and share Wordsworth's sensitivity to natural objects; otherwise the differences are more conspicuous. We find in the later poem none of the confident authority that is so palpable a quality in 'Michael'; the radical shifts of mood suggest, on the contrary, a basic lack of stability. It would certainly be unwise to equate the 'I' here with Wordsworth himself, at least not with the Wordsworth of 1802 when the poem was written. In a letter of 14 June 1802, admittedly, Wordsworth writes of this poem: 'I describe myself as having been exalted to the highest pitch of delight by the joyousness and beauty of Nature and then as depressed';[13] but this makes no mention of the age at which he imagines himself in the situation and implies, indeed, a careful adaptation of his character to suit the dictates of the poem. When the speaker introduces himself as 'a Traveller ... upon the moor' (l. 15), we find that he has caught a feeling of joy from the hare supposedly 'running races in her mirth' (l. 11). Here we are intended, surely, to recognize the influence of natural objects on a decidedly naive level, and are consequently not surprised at the sudden change to dejection, which documents not only the narrator's instability but his obsessive selfishness. The first person rings excessively through these opening stanzas, and the whole rhetoric of the poem builds up to an encounter which will expose such gestures as at once immature and hubristic.

The meeting with the leech-gatherer is based, as we know from Dorothy's

Journal (3 October 1800), on an actual experience, but as usual the circumstances are drastically altered. The presence of Dorothy is once again suppressed, the place of meeting is transformed from what was presumably a valley path to a desolate moor, and the time of day altered from twilight to early morning. Above all, the leech-gatherer himself, who in Dorothy's version has Jewish features and 'lived by begging,' is radically metamorphosed into a pivotal figure in which natural and preternatural attributes are subtly blended. The latter tend to be overlooked because they are not recognized as pervasive Wordsworthian features (not, at least, in the poetry of the 'great decade'). But there is a unique rhetoric in this poem that should force us to acknowledge that when the narrator describes the pool by which the leech-gatherer stands as 'bare to the eye of heaven' (l. 54) he means to be taken literally. We have already had reference to 'peculiar grace, / A leading from above' (ll. 50–1) and are soon to be told that the weight cast upon the old man's frame was 'more than human' (l. 70). He is later to describe himself as 'Housing, with God's good help, by choice or chance' (l. 104) and since we have already been alerted to his 'choice word and measured phrase' (l. 95) we are obviously intended to take the reference seriously. All this leads up to the narrator's taking over such reference explicitly: ' "God," said I, "be my help and stay secure" ' (l. 139). The narrator is humbled, his selfishness recognized, the immaturity of his earlier mood exposed. The leech-gatherer, introduced in the well-known stanzas that liken him to natural objects (a huge stone, a sea-beast, a cloud [ll. 57–63, 75] representing the same elemental variety we noticed in 'I Wandered Lonely as a Cloud'), initiates one of the 'severer interventions' that in *The Prelude* is attributed to nature (I, 355). A figure who is seen as partly human being, partly natural object, partly divine messenger, he raises the man-nature interchange to a new level of complexity. But the narrator to whom he provides such a necessary complement is just as original a creation, and one that would prove decidedly unsuitable for most of Wordsworth's other major poems.

EXERCISE IN INTERPRETATION

No discussion of Wordsworth as 'maker,' and as chronicler of the creative interchange between the human and natural worlds, can conclude without a consideration of the story of Margaret. Indeed, a good case could be made for regarding 'The Ruined Cottage,' later incorporated into Book I of *The Excursion*, as the most significant achievement in the whole of Wordsworth's work. In saying this, I am not merely reiterating F.R. Leavis's pronouncements on the poem as 'the finest thing that Wordsworth wrote,' as the all-important creative juncture after which 'we can say: "Wordsworth becomes a great poet here".'[14] I am also suggesting that it provides – contains within itself – a classic example of the interpretation of a Wordsworthian poem. It would be impossible to do anything even approaching justice to 'The Ruined Cottage' at this point. Fortunately, however, the poem has recently attracted a good deal of attention, notably from Leavis and from Jonathan Wordsworth who, in his book-length study, *The Music of Humanity*, has offered a minutely detailed examination of the writing of the poem and printed reliable and convenient texts of the two poems, 'The Ruined Cottage' and 'The Pedlar,' that Wordsworth later combined. I can therefore limit my remarks to the aspects most relevant to my own theme, presenting reasons why, as it seems to me, Wordsworth felt impelled to introduce the story of Margaret with the biographical account of the character who, in *The Excursion*, is known as the Wanderer.

Wordsworth's focus here is less on the facts of Margaret's story than on human responses towards it. Far from giving us the account from her own lips, and thus ensuring the utmost immediacy, he sets up a number of barriers or filters between Margaret and the reader. In the first place, she is never described directly and is seen indirectly only for brief, static moments. The story of her decline and death is told obliquely through reference to the condition of her cottage, and that of its adjoining garden, which faithfully reflect Margaret's own situation. I have not the space to illustrate in detail, but the following description by the Wanderer, at a time when decay has become only too evident, is representative:

> I withdrew,
> And once again entering the garden saw,
> More plainly still, that poverty and grief
> Were now come nearer to her: weeds defaced
> The hardened soil, and knots of withered grass:
> No ridges there appeared of clear black mold,
> No winter greenness; of her herbs and flowers,
> It seemed the better part were gnawed away
> Or trampled into earth; a chain of straw,
> Which had been twined about the slender stem
> Of a young apple-tree, lay at its root;
> The bark was nibbled round by truant sheep.
>
> (*Excursion*, 1, 832–42)

Cottage and garden are employed, then, as objective correlatives for Margaret's physical and emotional state.

Moreover, between Margaret's experience and the reader's response stand two intermediaries – the Wanderer, wisest and most sympathetic of Wordsworth's traveller figures, and the Poet, the narrating 'I.' The Wanderer tells the story as he has pieced it together from his own brief and sporadic visits to her cottage in his role as itinerant pedlar, and from what he has heard of her fortunes from other sources. He recounts the story to the Wordsworthian 'I' on the site of the cottage which has long since reverted to nature (Margaret is described as 'last *human* tenant of these ruined walls' [l. 916, my italics]). This splitting of the interpreter-figure into two is, perhaps, the most original stroke in the whole poem. The narrator (like Wordsworth's readers) never knew Margaret, and is dependent upon the Wanderer for both the facts of the case and advice about the proper reaction to it. In consequence, the importance of the Wanderer is such that the lengthy account of his biography, a *Prelude* in miniature, can extend to well over three hundred lines and is almost as long as the story of Margaret herself.

The explanation for this is, of course, Wordsworth's extreme concern that the import of his poems should be properly understood, and it is here that the unique significance of 'The Ruined Cottage' becomes evident. At one level, I suggest, it can be read as a model of mature critical interpretation, as if Wordsworth, provoked by the controversies surrounding earlier poems such as 'The Old Cumberland Beggar' and 'The Thorn,' were offering a detailed example of how his poetry ought to be read. For this purpose he has split his own experience between the Wanderer and the narrator, the latter combining Wordsworth's own sensitivity with the reader's situation as he tries to come to terms with the story. The main emphasis falls, however, on the Wanderer, whose natural education bears resemblances to – is, indeed, an idealized version of – Wordsworth's own. The insight he has derived from 'natural wisdom' (l. 601) qualifies him as an authoritative guide. He is a teacher to the narrator and, via the narrator, to ourselves.

This accounts for the general function of the framework to Margaret's story, but it is much too simple an explanation of the subtle balance that exists within the poem. As Leavis has demonstrated, the 'I' plays a far more complex role than mere transmitter between the 'official' response of the Wanderer and a reader expected to take over this response without question. 'The avowed "I" and the Wanderer,' Leavis writes, 'are both Wordsworth. The "I" is the actual Wordsworth for whom the thought of the poor woman's suffering is not a matter of "emotion recollected in tranquillity." The Wanderer ... is the ideal Wordsworth he aspires, in an effort of imaginative realization, to be.'[15] The narrator's sympathetic reaction, his ability to respond so completely to the Wanderer's account that Margaret seems 'one / Whom I had known and loved' (ll. 613–14), prevents a too ready acceptance of the Wanderer's 'easy cheerfulness' (l. 607) – a state which, in its reaching toward the superhuman, runs the risk of appearing *in*human. By his reluctance to accept a facile comfort, the 'I' represents, indeed, just that kind of sensitive questioning the absence of which proves a stumbling-block in interpreting such poems as 'Lines Left upon a Seat in a Yew-Tree' and 'The Old Cumberland Beggar.'

'The Ruined Cottage' is important in the history of nature poetry not only because Margaret's plight is reflected through the imagery of natural objects, but because natural objects play an influential part in the Wanderer's response, and indirectly in our own. The famous passage about the 'weeds, and the high spear-grass on that wall' (ll. 943ff.), the virtual identification of sleep 'in the calm earth' (l. 941) and the sense of peace at the site of the cottage with a 'natural wisdom' and 'natural comfort' (ll. 601, 602) transcending the never-underestimated facts of Margaret's suffering, go far towards reconciling the narrator to the Wanderer's philosophic serenity, though he remains uncomfortably and honourably aware of 'the impotence of grief' (l. 924). It is tempting to suggest that, by the end of the poem, Margaret has *become* a natural object, but although this may be true for the Wanderer, it is not true for the 'I,' whose achievement is to trace

> That secret spirit of humanity
> Which, 'mid the calm oblivious tendencies
> Of nature, 'mid her plants, and weeds, and flowers,
> And silent overgrowings, still survived.   (ll. 927–30)

The narrator's uncertainty is beautifully caught in the rich ambivalence of 'oblivious,' which holds perilously balanced within the context the seemingly opposed meanings of 'uncaring' and 'calming' (i.e. tending to oblivion). Something of Margaret's humanity remains, though she herself, like Lucy, is

> Rolled round in earth's diurnal course,
> With rocks, and stones and trees –

another strikingly ambivalent statement. The significance of 'The Ruined Cottage,' then, over and above its supreme success as a complete and self-sufficient work of art, lies in the suggestive clues it offers towards an approved interpretation of other Wordsworthian poems.

Before we proceed to consider the work of other nature poets, one or two related points should be made to round off the discussion of Wordsworth. I hope that what I have written will help to reconcile two different and at first sight totally opposed ways of reading Wordsworth – as nature poet on the one hand and as celebrator of the human mind on the other. The latter position cannot be ignored. At the end of *The Prelude* Wordsworth rises to a climax in proclaiming

> how the mind of man becomes
> A thousand times more beautiful than the earth
> On which he dwells,   (XIV, 448–50)

and in the introductory poem to the incomplete *Recluse* he writes of 'the Mind of Man – / My haunt, and the main region of my song' (*PW* v. 4). My consideration of Wordsworth in the preceding pages, as a 'human nature poet,' should have offered some clues to the way in which we should view these statements. Both need to be seen within the context of the wholes of which they form parts. *The Prelude* illustrates, in the words of the title to Book VIII, 'Love of Nature Leading to Love of Man'; the introduction to *The Recluse* goes on to marvel

> How exquisitely the individual Mind
> (And the progressive powers perhaps no less
> Of the whole species) to the external World
> Is fitted: – and how exquisitely, too –
> Theme this but little heard of among men –
> The external World is fitted to the Mind.   (*PW* v. 5)

The stress, even here, is on interchange. As in 'Tintern Abbey,' where Wordsworth learns to 'look on nature' and hear 'The still, sad music of humanity' (ll. 89,91), or in the 'Immortality Ode' where the emphasis on thought, human suffering, and the philosophic mind is not offered in any way as a renunciation of the natural world ('And O, ye Fountains, Meadows, Hills, and Groves, / Forebode not any severing of our loves!' [ll. 191–2]), so here man and nature are bound one to another. I would only add that the ways in which they interrelate differ widely, and that the best illustration of this is to be found, not in Wordsworth's abstract generalizations, but in the abundant variety of his intricately structured poems.

This leads me to my final point. I shall be arguing in the course of this book that Wordsworth's poetic example had a considerable, though varied, effect on poets such as Clare, Barnes, and Hardy who may reasonably be described as 'countrymen' while Wordsworth himself can be admitted less readily into such a company. He occupies a poetic and intellectual eminence apart from the world of which he writes that makes such a classification both inappropriate and incongruous. He is not intimately knowledgeable about the minutiae of the countryside like Clare, nor capable of imaginatively placing himself within a simple rural community like Barnes. We might say that Wordsworth was in the countryside but not of it, and it is a commonplace of criticism to observe that, at least in his adult life, there was a great gulf fixed between himself and the rural population that figures so prominently in his verse. 'Well you see,' said a local countryman to Canon Rawnsley, 'there's pomes and pomes, and Wudsworth's was not for sec as us.'[16] Moreover, the Wordsworthian 'philosophy of nature,' whether asserted by himself or abstracted by his commentators, did not prove acceptable to many of his poetic successors (Hardy's name immediately springs to mind here). But his experiments in structure and perspective were taken over by later poets even when the 'message' embodied in their work was fundamentally anti-Wordsworthian. There can be no more convincing proof of Wordsworth's specifically *poetic* legacy to an important strain in English verse.

THREE

John Clare

CLARE AND WORDSWORTH

Wordsworth I love, his books are like the fields,
Not filled with flowers, but works of human kind.[1]

In these words John Clare pays a paradoxical, even ambiguous tribute in an indifferent sonnet to the poet he admired but hardly resembled. It would be strange indeed if Wordsworth's original poetic presentation of the natural world had not attracted Clare, and De Quincey has preserved a record of Clare's 'rapturous spirit of admiration' at the mention of Wordsworth's name.[2] But although Clare occasionally imitated Wordsworth in the way that he imitated so many earlier poets in his lesser moments, we should not see him as a Wordsworthian disciple. His most detailed reference to the older poet, in a journal-entry of 1824, is curious and revealing:

Read some poems of Wordsworth; his 'Lucy Gray, or Solitude,' 'The Pet Lamb,' 'We are Seven,' 'The Oak and Broom,' 'The Eglantine and the Fountain,' 'Two April Mornings' are some of my greatest favourites. When I first began to read poetry I disliked Wordsworth because I heard he was disliked, and I was astonished when I looked into him to find my mistaken pleasure in being delighted and finding him so natural and beautiful. In his 'White Doe of Rylstone' there is some of the sweetest poetry I ever met with, tho' full of his mysteries.[3]

There is an attractive honesty about this, but the choice of poems is independent – one is tempted to say idiosyncratic. With the possible exception of 'The

Two April Mornings,' none is generally included among Wordsworth's major achievements, and Clare significantly ignores all the poems dramatizing a human confrontation with the natural world that I examined in the last chapter. But we can learn much from Clare's choices. 'Lucy Gray,' 'We are Seven' and 'The Two April Mornings' all derive from the ballad tradition that loomed larger and more directly in Clare's poetic inheritance than in Wordsworth's; 'The Pet Lamb' is a childlike song of innocence which recalls many of Clare's, the overrated 'Little Trotty Wagtail' being perhaps the best known; 'The White Doe of Rylstone' is less easy to fit into the pattern of Clare's particular poetic interests, but its basis in local tradition would appeal to the poet so fond of recalling stories told by village parents to their children on winter nights. But 'The Oak and the Broom' and 'The Waterfall and the Eglantine' (to give the poem its correct title) are the most interesting selections. Few besides Clare would rank them as Wordsworthian favourites, but they are among the very few Wordsworthian poems in which natural objects are allowed the powers of speech. This is a fancy which Wordsworth handles rather clumsily, but one which Clare, though he uses it sparingly, puts to good effect in such moving poems as 'The Lamentations of Round Oak Waters' and 'The Lament of Swordy Well,' both of which I shall discuss shortly. Clare's praise for Wordsworth, then, while honestly acknowledging what he could learn from him, is indirect testimony to the profound differences between the two poets' approaches to the world of nature.

The most obvious and at the same time most crucial difference between them was one of class. It is fashionable nowadays to profess to ignore the 'peasant-poet' aspect of Clare which so fascinated his contemporaries, but the matter is too central to pass over without comment. We have no right to gloat complacently over his disadvantages and wonder at the miracle of his appearance in 'polite letters'; at the same time, we should realize how Clare's position as an agricultural labourer enabled him to gain a knowledge of, and develop a viewpoint towards, the countryside that was totally different from Wordsworth's. This obviously has profound implications for the kind of poetry that he was to write. Although Wordsworth's poems are full of humbly born countrymen and countrywomen of all class-gradations from the independent 'Statesmen' like Michael through Margaret to such figures as Martha Ray and the old Cumberland beggar, they are presented from the outside – and generally from above. Wordsworth wrote about these people and expressed a genuine concern for them, but despite his theoretical principles about 'low and rustic life,' he could never be as one of them. Clare, by contrast, was himself 'the Northamptonshire peasant'; he knew from first-hand experience the world of rustic labour that Wordsworth portrayed with sincere but none the less detached sympathy in *Lyrical Ballads*. Above all, he spoke – and wrote – the rustic dialect, and the country people and things that form the staple of his poetry are thus presented vividly and accurately in an appropriate language.

It would be impossible to over-emphasize the significance of these social differences upon the kinds of poetry that each was capable of producing. Because Clare was younger and came under the influence of earnest and often misguided well-wishers who tried to mould him into an educated poet, we can find a number of Wordsworthian echoes and imitations within his verse. But these should not be mistaken for any basic similarity. The true test is not to look in Clare for resemblance to Wordsworth but rather to look in Wordsworth for anything that sounds like Clare. The only example of the latter that I have been able to find occurs in 'The Vale of Esthwaite,' an early poem significantly unpublished in Wordsworth's (or Clare's) lifetime:

> The ploughboy by his gingling wain
> Whistles along the ringing lane,
> And, as he strikes with sportive lash
> The leaves of thick o'erhanging ash,
> Wavering they fall; while at the sound
> The blinking bats flit round and round.   (PW i. 274)

These lines could have come from Clare's 'Shepherd's Calendar,' and they recall a number of passages from his early work – for instance:

> From the hedge, in drowsy hum,
> Heedless buzzing beetles bum,
> Haunting every bushy place,
> Flopping in the labourer's face.[4]

What is unusual in the Wordsworthian quotation is that, for a moment, the ploughboy is being looked at as if by another ploughboy – directly, horizontally, not from above, and without a trace of condescension. The viewpoint is very close to Clare's but notably unlike that of 'typical' Wordsworth.

Although it is not difficult to point to characteristics which the two writers share – a liking for simplicity in subject and language, a fascination with the theme of childhood vision and its loss in adult life – these should not obscure the profound differences that extend even to the treatment and tone of poems written on comparable subjects. Clare's vision, as genuine as Wordsworth's, is unconnected with the paraphernalia of Romantic theorizing. When he is at his most characteristic, Clare is content with nature as it is. The mind of man is decidedly not his haunt and the main region of his song; his poems are 'filled with flowers' rather than with 'works of human kind.' Moreover, he makes no attempt to probe beyond experience towards a mystical or metaphysical superstructure (which is what Clare surely refers to in his remark, already quoted, about Wordsworth's 'mysteries'). It is absurd to speak, as Harold Bloom does, of 'Clare's dialectic' (CCH, 429); such terminology is inappropriate, not (one hastens to add) on account of any snobbish assumptions about the quality of Clare's education or the capacity of the rustic mind, but because his very real poetic intelligence is simply not conducive to any kind of abstract categorization. Clare has to be protected from those on the one hand who would see him as a primitive and untutored peasant and those on the other who would romanticize him into a natural philosopher.

He had to contend with both extremes in his own time. The crass insolence of the 'dandified gentleman' who asked him about rustic habits of copulation (PJC, 72) is shocking, but the gratuitous advice of his well-wishers was scarcely less impertinent. His correspondent Mrs Emmerson considered him 'capable of higher subjects than – talking of birds & flowers' (CCH, 199), while even John Taylor, his publisher, wrote in connection with The Shepherd's Calendar: 'Your Poetry is much the best when you are not describing common Things, and if you would raise your views generally, & Speak of the Appearances of Nature each Month more philosophically ... you would greatly improve these little poems' (CCH, 197–8). Charles Lamb even exhorted him to write like Shenstone (CCH, 175)! It is a remarkable tribute to Clare's intelligence and integrity that, faced with such supposedly expert advice (not to mention the pressures arising from his financial dependence), he so seldom injected a fashionable Wordsworthian moralism into his poems.

A less obvious, but no less important, difference between Wordsworth and Clare, ultimately determined by their differing angles of social viewpoint, is to be found in their attitudes to the local. Wordsworth, as I have shown, only occasionally wrote (as in 'Michael') as a local poet. Clare, by contrast, was local to the core. There can be no poetic tension between traveller and native in Clare's poems, and his move from Helpston to Northborough in 1832, a distance of only three miles, proved a seriously disorienting experience. Indeed, John Barrell has recently argued that Clare is closest to Wordsworth after his removal from Helpston, that he fell back on Wordsworthian attitudes when his own original material failed.[5] Wordsworth looked through the local or the immediate; Clare, by virtue of his comprehensive knowledge of a confined locality, saw much that Wordsworth could never see. Living in a less 'picturesque' countryside, Clare is rarely concerned with the larger scenic qualities of the landscape. Northamptonshire provided no opportunities for flirtation with the Sublime. Clare is never tempted into 'a comparison of scene with scene,' to quote Wordsworth's confession in The Prelude (XII, 115); as he notes in his sonnet to Wordsworth,

> I love to stoop and look among the weeds
> To find a flower I never knew before.

There may be a sly allusion here to Wordsworth's 'Small Celandine,' but the lines offer an image of Clare peering into the minutiae of nature and finding his own world in a grain of local sand that is profoundly characteristic.

If Wordsworth's poems about the effect of the natural landscape upon man are more varied and more profound than Clare's, Clare's poems about individual birds and flowers are decidedly superior to Wordsworth's. John Middleton Murry has discussed these differences in relation to Wordsworth's attitude towards Peter Bell. Clare, he wrote, 'was someone to whom a primrose by the river's brim was in a sense, just a primrose; but it was wholly a primrose, not "something more" indeed, but altogether itself. ... If Wordsworth had seen a primrose as Clare saw it – and he did occasionally see things thus – he would have felt that he was "seeing into the heart of things," whereas Clare – who seems always to have seen in this way – felt that he was merely seeing things' (*CCH*, 360). 'Merely' is, I think, a mistake, but otherwise the comment is admirable, not least because it recognizes that the difference is fundamentally one of perception. If Wordsworth is a towering monument to the dignity to which nature poetry can attain, Clare, who once claimed that he kicked his poems out of the clods, presents not a humbler but a less intellectualized alternative: a nature poetry in which the emphasis remains on the natural object.

The difference can be seen most clearly if we turn to 'The Lamentations of Round Oak Waters' (i. 70–4) and 'The Lament of Swordy Well' (i. 420–2). While neither poem shows Clare at his best, both bear eloquent witness to his close association with local landmarks. In the first he imagines that, while lamenting his own unhappy lot, he hears Round Oak Waters express a similar complaint 'in grievous murmurs':

> Unequall'd tho' thy sorrows seem –
>   And great indeed they are –
> Oh, hear my sorrows for my stream,
>   You'll find an equal there.

When they are articulated, we recognize these sorrows as one of Clare's recurring preoccupations (in 'Remembrances' and elsewhere), his disgust at the changes brought upon the landscape by Enclosure:

> Oh, then what trees my banks did crown!
> What willows flourished here!

> Hard as the axe that cuts them down
> The senseless wretches were.

The complaint is direct and the tone bitter; significantly, the poem remained
unpublished in Clare's lifetime. But the directness and bitterness shared by man
and place create an effect outside Wordsworth's range. Clare is able – and this
becomes even more evident in 'The Lament of Swordy Well' – to subsume his
own character into that of the locality. While it is easy to retort, with partial
truth, that he merely imposes his own attitudes on to his subject, the fact
remains that he varies the extent to which the man is comparable to the place. In
the first poem the whole argument depends upon the balanced comparison: the
forces threatening the labouring class are equally threatening to the landscape.
In the second, Clare develops the possibilities of the idea and is able to reproduce
Swordy Well's unique viewpoint:

> The muck that clouts the ploughman's shoe,
> The moss that hides the stone,
> Now I've become the parish due
> Is more than I can own.

The final pun may suggest Hood, but the muck is Clare's original, unromantic
contribution, and it provides a context for the mossy stone that firmly distinguishes it from Wordsworth's in 'She Dwelt Among the Untrodden Ways.' The
Clare who can project himself into Swordy Well looks forward, as we shall see,
to the Clare who can view the world from the perspective of a ladybird in
'Clock-a-clay.' But it is not yet an *imaginative* projection. Because Helpston is
so intimate a reality for him, Clare can pass from his own folk-mind to the mind
of the locality without any apparent sense of strain.

Because Clare's outlook was more rustic than Wordsworth's he showed little
interest in the latter's technical experimentation. Suspicious of artifice, Clare
mistrusted formal considerations as alien to his unbounded vision. The nature
he loved was above 'Form'; he delighted in Thomson's 'rural confusion'
('Summer,' l. 486). The following passage from 'Cowper Green' is relevant
here:

> Some may praise the grass-plat whims,
> Which the gard'ner weekly trims,
> And cut hedge and lawn adore,
> Which his shears have smoothen'd o'er:
> But give me to ponder still
> Nature, when she blooms at will,

In her kindred taste and joy,
Wildness and variety.   (i. 175–6)

In these lines Clare not only explains his preferences in landscape (which go far towards explaining his aesthetic as distinct from socio-political objections to Enclosure) but also indicates his dislike of artificial moulding and structuring. Because he liked his nature unbounded, he preferred his poetry formless. 'Pleas'd I list the rural themes,' he announces in 'Summer Morning' (i. 67), and so leads on to another natural catalogue. The frequently anthologized 'Summer Images,' impressive as it is stanza by stanza, is a list rather than a poem; there is no logical reason why it should have sixteen stanzas or sixty. When gathering materials for a new collection of poems in 1832, Clare proposed to call it *The Midsummer Cushion*, and explained the title as follows: 'It is a very old custom among villagers in summer time to take a piece of green sward full of wild flowers and place it as an ornament in their cottages which ornaments are called Midsummer Cushions.'[6] This is a pleasant practice, but Clare's motives for employing it as a title are only too obvious: the poems, he knew, were themselves a collection of field flowers gathered together with no sense of an overall pattern or structure.

Similar reservations have to be made, I believe, even about a poem as fresh and appealing as 'The Shepherd's Calendar.' Individual lines are superb, individual images unforgettable; as a whole, however, it exists only as a succession of keenly observed and precisely etched pictures. It lacks 'appropriate form,' and because we find in Clare comparatively little of the conscious technical experimentation so conspicuous in Wordsworth, we are tempted to formulate a distinction between artlessness in the former and the illusion of artlessness in the latter. But such categorizations are too neat to be just. After all, Wordsworth has his poetic disasters and these, though recognized and deplored, are not allowed to detract from his obvious creative achievements. It is true that Clare fails sufficiently often to raise doubts whether his successes are due to happy accident or to deliberate design; but there is no doubt that he also achieves artistic excellence sufficiently often to be worthy of serious (and discriminating) critical attention. I shall be concentrating in the following sections on poems which combine his characteristic poetic strengths with a formal discipline and control. These poems, I am convinced, represent his most effective contribution to rural poetry.

VILLAGE BOY AND VILLAGE MINSTREL

Clare would have agreed with Wordsworth that the child is father of the man, and his boyhood experience in the as-yet-unenclosed village of Helpston provided the all-important foundation for his subsequent poetic achievement. This being so, there is no more suitable poem through which to approach the central pattern of Clare's work than his sonnet 'The Village Boy' (ii. 129):

> Free from the cottage corner, see how wild
>   The village boy along the pasture hies,
> With every smell and sound and sight beguiled,
>   That round the prospect meets his wondering eyes;
> Now stooping eager for the cowslip-peeps,
>   As though he'd get them all; now tired of these,
> Across the flaggy brook he eager leaps
>   For some new flower his happy rapture sees;
>   Now tearing mid the bushes on his knees,
> On woodland banks for bluebell flowers he creeps;
>   And now, while looking up among the trees,
> He spies a nest, and down he throws his flowers,
>   And up he climbs with new-fed ecstasies –
> The happiest object in the summer hours.

The village boy will grow into Lubin, 'the village minstrel,' observer and recorder of local life and customs; but he will also develop into the adult John Clare, eager to escape from the oppressiveness of human society into the recesses of the non-human world, and transmitting his most intimate revelation of the mysteries of life in a series of poems about the nests of birds. Moreover, the village boy's carefree and abrupt changes of interest and direction, though controlled within the poem by the unifying focus upon the boy himself, are indicative of the formal problems of a poet intent, like Clare, upon chronicling the manifold variety of nature rather than, like Wordsworth, imposing his own vision and interpretation upon the external world.

'The Village Boy' is, of course, yet another index of the poetic distance between the two poets. The emphasis on freedom and joy can legitimately be seen as a Wordsworthian characteristic, but the boy exists in what is, for Wordsworth, a pre-poetic state of consciousness; as the categories are set up in 'Tintern Abbey,' this poem is a record of 'The coarser pleasures of my boyish days / And their glad animal movements,' or at most represents the period of 'thoughtless youth' (ll. 73–4, 90). Since many of Clare's nature poems seek to preserve this childlike innocence of wondering response, it is important to remember that the Wordsworthian hierarchies are not sacrosanct. Instead of condescending to Clare as a poet who has failed to achieve the Wordsworthian profundities, we might be better advised to view him as one who has never relinquished the glory and the dream of childhood.

Although there is no 'I' in 'The Village Boy,' it remains unquestionably a 'human nature poem' in so far as the centre of interest falls upon the actions of the boy rather than upon the natural world that he is exploring. The poem is at once personal and detached, and in this respect resembles Clare's much more ambitious poem, 'The Village Minstrel,' where the blend of original attitude and standard poetic procedure is uneasy but, in my view, ultimately successful. The figure of Lubin, the poetic peasant, though he may at first sight appear a stereotype, is in fact an extremely flexible, not to say subtle, creation. One of the traditions which Clare derived from his reading was the eighteenth-century convention of the poet-spectator. This explains, at least in part, why when describing village life here and in such poems as 'Helpstone' and 'The Shepherd's Calendar,' he is observing rather than participating, solitary rather than communal. As a consequence we find a curious double focus in much of his verse. While ostensibly describing what he sees in an objective manner, he employs the 'inside' detail and the dialect-words derived from the villager's own language to convey the immediacy of a personal viewpoint without actually employing the first-person singular.

But although the role of spectator is dominant, he is decidedly not *'Spectator ab extra,'* which, according to Coleridge, was Wordsworth's 'proper title.'[7] Clare and his created Lubin are both spectators from within. Lubin *is* Clare, but a Clare observed by himself, a member of the village community but separated from it by his exceptional interests and responses. He is far more individualized than James Beattie's 'Minstrel' or Robert Bloomfield's 'Farmer's Boy'; he enables Clare to present both the realities of peasant life, which all labourers but few poets could offer ('every child of want feels all that Lubin feels' [i. 139]) but also to record details 'unnotic'd but by Lubin's eye' (i. 137) that depend upon the heightened awareness of the poet. His carefully plotted situation places him close to the villagers yet separated from them. Thus

> He lov'd 'old sports,' by them reviv'd, to see,
> But never car'd to join in their rude revelry.   (i. 137)

At the harvest-supper, he 'knew all well, a young familiar there, / And often look'd on all' (i. 145); the role of spectator is dominant. By the same token, he can himself be looked on sympathetically (when his special gifts are acknowledged) or, as here, scornfully by some of the uncomprehending villagers:

> A more uncouthly lout was hardly seen
> Beneath the shroud of ignorance than he;
> The sport of all the village he has been,
> Who with his simple looks oft jested free;

And gossips, gabbling o'er their cake and tea,
Time after time did prophecies repeat,
How half a ninny he was like to be,
To go so soodling up and down the street
And shun the playing boys whene'er they chanc'd to meet.   (i. 141)

Again, he deliberately avoids company ('Sequester'd nature was his heart's delight' [i. 136]), yet we are told later, as if regretfully, that 'there's few to notice him, or hear his simple tale' (i. 138). This is not contradictory; it is the direct result of Clare's shifting but flexible approach, which allows us to see Lubin from continually varying angles and viewpoints.

In creating the figure of Lubin, then, Clare is able to draw upon his own experiences and at the same time, by virtue of the 'persona,' to detach himself from them. This gives his report on village life an unusual authority. Lubin's is no idealized rural community; it is, on the contrary,

a village full of strife and noise,
Old senseless gossips, and blackguarding boys,
Ploughmen and threshers, whose discourses led
To nothing more than labour's rude employs,
'Bout work being slack, and rise and fall of bread,
And who were like to die, and who were like to wed.   (i. 140)

By the same token, the accounts of rustic festivals, that might otherwise be discounted as retrospective romanticism, take on an impressive authenticity. Lubin, through Clare, knew at first hand

The freaks and plays that harvest-labour end,
How the last load is crown'd with boughs, and how
The swains and maids with fork and rake attend,
With floating ribbons 'dizen'd at the end;
And how the children on the load delight
With shouts of 'Harvest home!' their throats to rend.   (i. 145)

Because of this double focus, the poem contains one of the most rounded portraits of a village that we possess.

'The Village Minstrel' is an important poem not only because Clare's viewpoint is of particular interest, but also because of the comprehensiveness of its themes; it encompasses virtually all the subjects (one might almost say all the poems) that Clare offers in his first two volumes. Although it might be possible to describe the poem as presenting the growth of a rustic poet's mind, any resemblance to Wordsworth stops at this point. Content simply to record what he saw instead of analysing its effects upon his consciousness, Clare was able to find poetic material in details which Wordsworth either never knew or deliberately excluded. Until we read Clare we are unlikely to realize how much natural detail is sacrificed by Wordsworth to the egotistical sublime:

> And he could tell how the shy squirrel far'd,
> Who often stood its busy toils to see;
> How against winter it was well prepar'd
> With many a store in hollow root or tree,
> As if being told what winter's wants would be:
> Its nuts and acorns he would often find,
> And hips and haws too, heaped plenteously
> In snug warm corner that broke off the wind,
> With happy nest made nigh, that warm green mosses lin'd.   (i. 147)

Wordsworth could no more have written that than Clare could have manipulated the poetic intricacies of 'Tintern Abbey.' What Wordsworth would have dismissed as trivial and beneath his notice, Clare describes with loving interest and also with recognition of its worth in poetic record:

> No insect 'scap'd him, from the gaudy plume
> Of dazzling butterflies so fine to view,
> To the small midgen that at evening come
> Like dust spots dancing o'er the water's blue,
> Or, where the spreading oak above-head grew,
> Tormenting maidens 'neath their kicking cow;
> Who often murmur'd at the elfin crew,
> And from th'endanger'd pail, with angry vow
> Oft rose, their sport to spoil with switch of murdering bough.   (i. 142)

So interrelated are Clare's views of the world of nature and of the village that the transition from midges to dairymaids can be made smoothly and without strain. And because the dairymaids are part of Clare's world, girls who are met with every day and have none of the romance of the unusual, he can present them without a trace of idealization.

One notices the difference most clearly when one encounters in Clare's verse his distinctive version of a recognizable Wordsworthian character. This discharged sailor begging at the statute-fair is a notable example:

> Here the poor sailor, with his hat in hand,
> Hops through the crowd that wonderfully stares
> To hear him talk of things in foreign land,
> 'Bout thundering cannons and most bloody wars;
> And as he stops to show his seamy scars,
> Pity soon meets the ploughman's penny then:
> The sailor heartfelt thankfulness declares,
> 'God blesses' all, and styles them 'gentlemen,'
> And fobs his money up, and 'gins his tale agen.   (i. 149)

Where Wordsworth makes his effect by converting such a figure into a subject for moral theorizing or social protest, Clare achieves an equally valid effect by refraining from such comment. The ploughman's generosity is no less evident for being underplayed, and the sailor's perfunctory flattery in no way detracts from our understanding of his plight.

Clare's success in 'The Village Minstrel' stems from the fact that he is able to create a situation in which squirrel and sailor can be viewed on equal terms. His presentation implies neither subjectivity nor detachment but a humane interest in all life. Towards the end of the poem, it is true, the all-important formal distinction between Clare and Lubin becomes blurred. A tone of self-pity intrudes; the poet himself enters, almost 'with his hat in hand,' and we are invited, rather too directly, to bewail the uncertainty of his lot. The poem, we might say, becomes a victim of Enclosure. As soon as the theme of Enclosure is introduced, with all the changes and deprivations attendant upon it, 'The Village Minstrel' falters. The poet despairs as he sees his accustomed way of life and the very subject-matter of his poetry undermined. But although it proves damaging to the aesthetic balance of this particular poem, the theme becomes the subject for some of Clare's later poetic triumphs when he finds the appropriate mode for its presentation. In the poems to be discussed in the following section, the persona is discarded and Clare speaks out for himself.

PERSONAL RESPONSES

The two most significant events in Clare's life were the enclosure of Helpston, with the subsequent destruction of so many of the landmarks which he had known as a child, and his move from Helpston to Northborough in 1832. Both have come to be seen as traumatic experiences probably contributing to his later madness but, however that may be, they also provided him with two of his most fruitful subjects for poetry: first, a psychical (or temporal) dislocation, the loss of a childhood world only to be recreated through memory and the poetic imagination; second, a physical dislocation that separated him from the place he knew as a native and set him in a locality that he could never know in quite the same way. Clare explored these themes in a series of intensely personal poems that maintain a formal coherence through the sheer force of deeply felt emotional response that flows through them.

'Remembrances' (ii. 257–9), which explores the first theme, is slowly but surely becoming recognized as one of the most moving and effective poems he ever wrote, and deserves detailed examination. One is tempted to describe it as Clare's 'Immortality Ode,' and there are certainly some thematic resemblances, but he does not develop the intellectual complexities of Wordsworth's poem, and the homeliness not only of the thought but of the language is unmistakably Clare's. There is a directness and authenticity of emotion here, a naked response to a human situation, that we do not find in the earlier poet.

Clare's tone and priorities are clearly established in the first stanza:

> Summer's pleasures they are gone like to visions every one,
> And the cloudy days of autumn and of winter cometh on.
> I tried to call them back, but unbidden they are gone
> Far away from heart and eye and for ever far away.
> Dear heart, and can it be that such raptures must decay?
> I thought them all eternal when at Langley Bush I lay,
> I thought them joys eternal when I used to shout and play
> On its bank at 'clink and bandy,' 'chock' and 'taw' and 'ducking-stone,'
> Where silence sitteth now on the wild heath as her own
> Like a ruin of the past all alone.

The names of the children's games (common knowledge to Clare but now so unfamiliar that even experts are not certain what they imply), the references to local names (Langley Bush here, Eastwell, Swordy Well, and Crossberry Way later) and colloquial phrases (like 'and never catch a thing' and 'have a soak' in the second stanza) contribute to an informal authenticity which in no way detracts from a basic seriousness and even profundity.

In the third stanza, after a succession of references to specific places and the memories associated with them, Clare exclaims:

> Oh, words are poor receipts for what time hath stole away,
> The ancient pulpit trees and the play.

'Stole' may seem a strong word, but it is deliberately chosen; Clare intends it literally, not metaphorically. The reference should be recalled later when Clare bitterly describes the effects of the Enclosure movement – something more specific than 'time' which stole away more than the 'ancient pulpit trees and the play.' Under the stress of intense personal emotion, words and images take on a developing, interlocking coherence that is not always evident in Clare's work. For instance, the picture of 'little mouldiwarps [moles]' as they 'hang sweeing to the wind' leads us neatly into the broader social questions. In the fifth stanza this image is extended:

> Here was commons for their hills, where they seek for freedom still,
> Though every common's gone and though traps are set to kill
> The little homeless miners.

The association broadens out irresistibly to include the whole 'culture' of Game Laws and man-traps. The break in the line after 'kill,' emphasized by its importance as a rhyme-word, lays stress on the harshness and holds up the less radical predicate, 'the little homeless miners' – though 'homeless' also suggests the dilemma of the landless agricultural labourers, while the first line of the stanza, with its allusion to 'freedom,' has a similar ambiguity of reference.

These indirect allusions to the injustices of the contemporary social process come to a climax in the superb line,

> Enclosure like a Buonaparte let not a thing remain.

Here the folk associations of Napoleon (which Hardy was to cull at a later date) link up ironically with the unstated but unmistakable charge that the peasantry is being conquered by its own ruling class. Implicit, too, in these lines is the assumption that the external forces invading Helpston are no less alien to the villagers than the concurrent French threat to England. And in the immediately succeeding lines –

> It levelled every bush and tree and levelled every hill
> And hung the moles for traitors –

the ironical associations with the French Revolution are surely deliberate, while 'levelling' takes on all sorts of overtones in the context in which the poem was written, which included the machine-breaking disturbances of 1830 and the un-levelling Reform Act of 1832.

The poem concerns itself with both the loss of childhood vision in later life and the loss of the unbounded freedoms of an unenclosed village after the transformations inaugurated by the local Enclosure Act. As John Barrell has demonstrated, the historical accident of both these events occurring at the same time in Clare's case (he was sixteen when the Act was passed, twenty-seven when the final award was published) inevitably associated the two in his mind. I use the word 'associated' deliberately. Some would write 'confused' – indeed, Barrell himself employs the word in this context, though with the acknowledgment that 'these two themes are confused ... more knowingly now.'[8] But this, I believe, undervalues Clare's artistry. In a more sophisticated or 'educated' poet we would assume that the two themes were consciously brought together, interwoven into the fabric of the poem so that the blending of the historical and psychological movements becomes a deliberate effect on the part of the poet. We can surely assume no less in Clare.

'The Flitting' (ii. 251–7), exploring the theme of physical dislocation, is a touching account of the effect that even a small move can have on a sensitive individual who has known the tradition of rootedness. In this poem, as in 'Remembrances,' the first person is truly equatable with the poet. Indeed, the poem depends for any unifying effect that it possesses on the developing but consistent response of the speaker. The Tibbles, though admiring 'The Flitting,' have called it formless,[9] but while it lacks the connecting discipline we expect of more sophisticated poetry (though in some respects it resembles the way Swinburne's stanzas pour out one after the other), it has its own logic and integrity. It would, admittedly, be possible to omit and rearrange stanzas without seriously damaging the effect of the poem, but the continual presence of Clare, with his characteristic attitudes and insights, prevents it from being formless in the sense in which the charge can be brought against a detached, purely descriptive poem.

The disorientation here recorded is moving in itself, but the terms in which Clare makes the point are both original and characteristic:

> The summer like a stranger comes,
> I pause and hardly know her face.

This occurs in the first stanza, and the seventh contains the famous lines,

> The sun e'en seems to lose its way
> Nor knows the quarter it is in.

This last observation has a long history. In his autobiography written in the 1820s, Clare records an incident which seems to have taken place in 1810. He had gone with a friend to find work at Newark-on-Trent (some thirty-five miles north-west of Helpston), and notes: 'I became so ignorant in this far land that I could not tell which quarter the wind blew from and I even was foolish enough to think the sun's course was altered and that it rose in the west and set in the east' (PJC, 28). The point I wish to emphasize, however, is the way the relative positions of Clare, the summer and the sun seem interchangeable. The summer comes 'like a stranger' whereas in fact the stranger is Clare; the sun is said to be disoriented because Clare is. This may, indeed, be no more than Clare's unconscious version of the egotistical sublime, but I suspect that the breakdown of distinction between human action and natural process, whether deliberate or not, has considerable significance, that it looks forward, in fact, to the dislocation that resulted both in his madness and in so startlingly brilliant a poem as 'Clock-a-clay.'

Even more important, perhaps, is the lack of human associations. As he writes in the twelfth stanza,

> Strange scenes mere shadows are to me,
> Vague impersonifying things.

In terms of poetic structure, the then/now distinction of 'Remembrances' has been replaced by there/here. Although he believed before the move that 'all the old associations are going before me,'[10] he now realizes that this is not so; however altered Helpston may be, it remains 'home.' In the earlier poems he obviously loved his immediate surroundings, but we find little of the 'personifying' or humanizing character of Helpston. Ironically – perhaps tragically – the qualities that belong to a localized spirit of place are not recognized until lost. In 'The Flitting,' as in 'Remembrances,' the places associated with childhood (Royce Wood and Langley Bush) are recorded as local names not, as in the earlier poetry, just because they were there but because they must now be remembered at all costs. In the process, it is true, Helpston has become idealized, a place

> Where envy's sneer was never seen,
> Where staring malice never comes.

We heard little when he lived there of the 'friends' whose loss he feels in the sixth stanza (in a letter written the previous January, in anticipation of the move, he states unequivocally: 'Other associations of friendships I have few or none to regret' [LJC, 258]), but the sentiment is true to his immediate feelings and so to this particular poem. The idealizing fancy is such that

> the very crow
> Croaks music in my native field.

The emphasis on human associations is worth stressing since this is later to become a major preoccupation in the work of Barnes.

The poem is brought to a close in muted fashion (I cannot agree with Barrell who considers it a 'triumphant ending')[11] when Clare recognizes a humble but familiar flower that *almost* reconciles him to his new lot.

                    Indeed
I feel at times a love and joy
    For every weed and every thing,
A feeling kindred from a boy,
    A feeling brought with every spring.

And why? this shepherd's purse that grows
    In this strange spot, in days gone by
Grew in the little garden rows
    Of my old home now left; and I
Feel what I never felt before,
    This weed an ancient neighbour here. ...

In Helpston the flower had been accepted but not recognized. As an unexpected
link with home it brings content. He finds that 'nature still can make amends' –
and Barrell is right to stress that this is, perforce, an abstract, unlocalized nature
closer to Wordsworth's. The homely shepherd's purse reminds him that 'the
grass eternal' will outlast the pomp that Clare presumably blames for his
enforced flitting.

'The Flitting' is important as a bringing-together, in artistically acceptable
form, of a number of Clare's favourite preoccupations. In it we are able to follow
the characteristic twists of his mind. A manifestation of the 'rural muse' (who
succeeds in eluding the deadening associations of learned pastoral), the likening
of the natural world – especially though not exclusively Helpston – to Eden
(which in Clare, I am convinced, carries with it little of the symbolic baggage
favoured by archetypal critics), the allusions to David (who is important not as
king or as the chosen of God but as poet), the conviction that 'passions of
sublimity / Belong to plain and simple things' – all these are familiar enough to
anyone who has read Clare at length. Too often they come and go within the
poetry in undisciplined fashion, but here the unifying theme is sufficiently
flexible to allow him a freedom of association that does not get out of hand.
Above all, the emotional force of Clare's situation holds the poem together. It is,
indeed, the earliest of his poems – perhaps the only one written before his entry
into the asylums – in which we are allowed a direct (and, from what we know of
his subsequent history, almost terrifying) glimpse into Clare's deepest being.

WILDNESS AND VARIETY

For Clare 'nature' had two overlapping but distinct meanings. In the first,
represented by such poems as 'The Village Minstrel,' man within a village
community is seen as part of the natural world, growing crops, tending cattle,
dependent upon the condition of the soil and the state of the weather. But there

was another nature outside the village boundaries, a feral world in which man was no more than an intruder. 'I long for scenes where man has never trod,' Clare observes in his best-known poem, 'I Am' (ii. 524). The expression may derive from the Byronic mask of his asylum years, but the longing to penetrate into nature's fastnesses, to discover the secrets of an essentially non-human life, to participate in the alternative world of unspoilt 'nature' is a recurrent element in his work. We find it, for example, in 'To the Snipe' (i. 337–9), where the bird is addressed as

> Lover of swamps
> And quagmire overgrown
> With hassock-tufts of sedge, where fear encamps
> Around thy home alone.
>
> The trembling grass
> Quakes from the human foot,
> Nor bears the weight of man to let him pass
> Where thou, alone and mute,
>
> Sittest at rest
> In safety.

Clare was fascinated by the natural world existing beyond the reach of human interference. Similarly he celebrates the reed-bird which lives

> in thickest shade
> Where danger never finds a path to throw
> A fear on comfort's nest.   ('The Reed-Bird,' ii. 244)

The bird is happy because 'man can seldom share / A spot so hidden from the haunts of care.' And the sand-martin is described as

> haunter of the lonely glen
> And common wild and heath – the desolate face
> Of rude, waste landscapes far away from men.   (ii. 243)

The terms in which this natural wilderness is presented explain Clare's bitter response to Enclosure. The Enclosure movement struck at both the natural worlds that he loved. The village was transformed, the ancient landmarks obliterated, the age-old traditions and practices expunged. And at the same time the wilderness was threatened; the snipe's quagmire would be drained, the reed-beds thinned, the 'rude, waste landscapes' fenced in and brought under human control.

Yet here, of course, we encounter a very human paradox. Clare loves the wilderness beyond man's range, but he wishes to probe its mysteries for himself. He needs to be free to go where other men do not go, to belong to that world in which he is by definition an alien. It is this impulse, I believe, that lies behind Clare's numerous poems about birds' nests. In observing the nesting habits of different species, he is discovering the most intimate secrets in nature. In mastering this knowledge he becomes, as it were, a part of this otherness; against it he can measure his own humanness – the 'I am' that became so crucial in the asylum years.

Most of the birds'-nest poems are short; indeed, the majority of them are fourteen-line near-sonnets. Before looking at some of these, however, I wish to discuss 'The Nightingale's Nest' (ii. 213–16), untypical in its length and consciously controlled formal discipline, but important because of the lesson it offers in the arts of natural observation. On a first reading, it is tempting to classify the poem as one of Clare's imitations, derived from Coleridge's 'Conversation Poems' – especially, though not exclusively, that entitled 'The Nightingale.' 'Come, we will rest on this old mossy stone!' begins Coleridge. 'Up this green woodland-ride let's softly rove,' begins Clare. The spontaneity produced by the demonstrative adjectives is noticeably similar, but the general resemblance soon fades. In Coleridge's poem the song of the nightingale is the starting-point for a series of personal thoughts and recollections, and his companions are specifically identified as Wordsworth and Dorothy. For Clare, however, the nightingale remains at the centre of the poem. The speaker here is not his usual first-person narrator but a highly selective Clare in his role as local ornithologist and guide. The persons addressed are left uncharacterized and unidentified so that they may include the reader.

We happen to know that in this poem Clare is using material that he originally wrote down in prose as part of a series of letters intended to form a *Natural History of Helpstone* that was unfortunately never completed. Clare was here obviously imitating the method of Gilbert White of Selborne; the local observations, written in the form of letters, were to be recorded in an informal style that would communicate not merely the facts themselves but the circumstances under which they were collected. He has carried over the same idea into the poem. The subject is not so much the nightingale's nest itself as the care that has to be taken in order to find it. Whereas in 'The Village Minstrel' we are told how Lubin

> Encroach'd upon the stockdove's privacy,
> Parting the leaves that screen'd her russet breast,   (i. 141)

in this poem we are invited to share the experience:

> There! put that bramble by –
> Nay, trample on its branches and get near.

The sense of immediacy is transferred from poet to reader.

This poem, though not perhaps outstanding in Clare's work, is one of the more memorable because its singleness of purpose and controlled dramatic form combine to isolate the experience. The conflicting interests of other natural objects are here suppressed, and our whole attention is focused on the nightingale. Again, the refreshingly low-keyed tone of the poem sets it apart from the more enthusiastic nature poems of the period. In this respect, it is an interesting anticipation of the quietly personal manner of Robert Frost, Edward Thomas, and Clare's admirer and editor, Edmund Blunden. Admittedly the strain is only fitful in Clare.

> Hush! let the wood-gate softly clap, for fear
> The noise might drive her from her home of love.

The colloquial ease of this is impressive until jarred by the sentimental poeticism of the last phrase, and the clash of two apparently separate stylistic modes is felt throughout the poem. But such lines as

> and her renown
> Hath made me marvel that so famed a bird
> Should have no better dress than russet brown

would not be out of place in Frost's 'Oven Bird.' Without quite mastering the full potentiality of a mode of poetic discourse which Clare gives every indication of having stumbled on accidentally, he none the less offers yet another possible way to chronicle the human connection with wild nature.

Most of Clare's birds'-nest poems are sonnets or, rather, what I have called 'near-sonnets' to indicate his adaptation of the form to his own purpose. Such poems are generally though not invariably fourteen lines in length and focus upon a particular incident, but they are not confined to the traditional rhyme-schemes nor to the unity of thought and balance of octet against sestet usual in the literary convention. Clare evidently wanted a form that imposed a gentle discipline upon him without being unduly constraining or inhibiting. It allowed him a variety of approach yet prevented him from rambling aimlessly from image to image. Three of these sonnets, 'The Thrush's Nest,' 'The Fern-Owl's Nest' and 'The Wryneck's Nest' will give some indication of the effects he could achieve in this form.

'The Thrush's Nest' is the most deliberately controlled of the three:

> Within a thick and spreading hawthorn bush
>   That overhung a mole-hill large and round,
> I heard from morn to morn a merry thrush
>   Sing hymns to sunrise, while I drank the sound
> With joy; and, often an intruding guest,
>   I watched her secret toils from day to day –
> How true she warped the moss to form a nest,
>   And modelled it within with wood and clay;
> And by and by, like heath-bells gilt with dew,
>   There lay her shining eggs, as bright as flowers,
> Ink-spotted-over shells of greeny blue;
>   And there I witnessed, in the sunny hours,
> A brood of nature's minstrels chirp and fly,
> Glad as that sunshine and the laughing sky.   (ii. 245)

Clare records the whole process from the courtship song in spring through nest-building and egg-laying to the eventual departure of the young. His capacity as a naturalist is evident from his meticulously accurate description of the nest. The seventh and eighth lines should be compared with W.H. Hudson's description in *British Birds*: 'The nest is built of dry grass, small twigs, and moss, and plastered inside with mud, or clay, or cow-dung, and lined with rotten wood. This is a strange material for a nest to be lined with, and is not used by any other bird.'[12] Yet the poet's concision of language is also noticeable ('How true she warped ...') and the poem is much more than a field-naturalist's report. We are conscious of the presence and response of the observer ('I heard,' 'I watched,' 'I witnessed'), but he is scrupulous in presenting himself as 'an intruding guest' in a natural world which is essentially separate. Yet the poem is further held together by the interrelation established between bird and man. Clare's description of the 'merry' thrush is not just standard sentimentalism. Hudson's account is worth quoting once again: 'It is pre-eminently cheerful, a song of summer and love and happiness of so contagious a spirit that to listen to it critically ... would be impossible.' Clare develops this anthropomorphism with deliberation as a structural device within the poem. The 'merry thrush' sang hymns to sunrise while Clare as narrator 'drank the sound / With joy.' And the same natural gaiety reappears at the close of the poem when the nestlings are represented as 'Glad as that sunshine and the laughing sky.' Here there are various elements (the joy in particular) that could be described as Wordsworthian; indeed, in its modest way the poem connects man and nature in the manner of 'I Wandered Lonely as a Cloud.' But the natural detail is beyond Wordsworth's scope.

'The Fern-Owl's Nest' (ii. 242) is very different in both structure and organization. No 'I' appears, but instead the poem has been placed within a human context. A 'weary woodman, rocking home beneath / His tightly banded faggot' is surprised by the nightjar's cry, unaware that 'he tramples near its nest.' The emphasis then turns to the bird's 'jarring noise' that continues until morning when the lonely spot which it inhabits is disturbed once again by human beings, this time by 'the herding boys' whose cries replace those of the bird. The detachment here may well have a biographical origin. Clare writes in the draft for his *Natural History of Helpstone*: 'I never found a nest of these birds in my life so I cannot say where they build' (*PJC*, 177). He is therefore unable to offer the details (the number and colour of the eggs, etc.) usual in these poems. But this accidental factor led to an artistic benefit. Clare succeeds in writing a poem that, in recording the woodman's failure to locate the nest, catches the elusive quality so characteristic of nightjars.

In 'The Wryneck's Nest' (i. 524) Clare once again prefers to suppress his own presence and record another human incident that illustrates the unique qualities of the bird in question. 'When peeping idlers stroll / In anxious plundering moods,' they notice some white eggs in a hollow tree. Unlike the narrator, they are unaware of the wryneck's habits. On being approached by the most adventurous of the idlers, the bird 'waves her head in terror to and fro' and emits 'a hissing sound.' The terror is then (quite specifically) transferred from bird to intruder:

> Quickly, with hasty terror in his breast,
> From the tree's knotty trunk he sluthers down,
> And thinks the strange bird guards a serpent's nest.

Again a comparison with Hudson's description in *British Birds* is useful: 'When taken in the hand he twists his neck about in [a most singular] manner, and hisses like a snake, as he also does when disturbed during incubation; and on this account he has been called snake-bird.'[13] Clare's poem, we might say, explains the rustic name. While purporting to narrate an amusing rural incident, the poem communicates an accurate sense of the wryneck's awkward and distinctive habits.

Many of Clare's rural poems, then, are either sonnets or, like the well-known 'Badger,' series of sonnets, and at his best Clare takes up an appropriate perspective for the needs of the individual poem. What may appear at first sight as 'pure' description often involves a deliberately detached stance. In 'Badger' the brutality of the badger-baiters links them with the wildness of their quarry and by the end of the poem the distinction between human and animal is effectively blurred. When, as in 'The Mole-Catcher,' Clare employs the same method to describe a human being that he has used elsewhere for a wild creature, a related effect is achieved. And occasionally the impact of an incident upon the observer becomes, as in so much of Wordsworth, the central concern.

'Mouse's Nest' (ii. 370) is a supreme instance. No one but Clare could have written it, and despite the humbleness of its subject it has strong claims to be considered a masterpiece. It begins:

> I found a ball of grass among the hay
> And progged it as I passed and went away.

Robert Frost could not have asked for a couplet closer to the rhythms of ordinary speech. The dialect verb admirably suits the word to the action, and the essentials of the scene are briefly but vividly established:

> And when I looked I fancied something stirred,
> And turned agen and hoped to catch the bird –
> When out an old mouse bolted in the wheats
> With all her young ones hanging at her teats.

The perfunctoriness of that initial gesture is indicated in the regularity of the metre and the expectedness of the rhyme on 'bird,' and this gives added force to the surprised discovery that it was *not* a bird. There is an irresistible sense of gruff rustic shock in the phrase 'When out an old mouse bolted' as the countryman-speaker relates a natural but unusual rural incident.

> She looked so odd and so grotesque to me,
> I ran and wondered what the thing could be,
> And pushed the knapweed bunches where I stood;
> Then the mouse hurried from the craking brood.

The narration is crisp and unsentimental, yet the unstated pity felt for both mother and 'craking' (fretting, quavering) brood is communicated in the speaker's decision, once his curiosity is satisfied, to refrain from interference:

> The young ones squeaked, and as I went away
> She found her nest again among the hay.
> The water o'er the pebbles scarce could run
> And broad old cesspools glittered in the sun.

At first reading, we may be disturbed by the final couplet. It almost looks as if Clare had finished his poem too early, 'among the hay' echoing the opening line and, as it were, rounding off the experience. But the last two lines, by separating us from the intimate little scene, place it within a wider natural context. Moreover, they suggest that the experience with the mouse has jolted the speaker into 'vision' – not in the transcendent Wordsworthian fashion, but more quietly, though not less deeply – so that he notices the details of the natural scene as if for the first time. Even the cesspools glitter in the sun; everything he looks upon (to adapt Yeats) is blest. The poem is ostensibly factual, straightforward, direct, yet Clare has succeeded in making an elaborate statement without employing anything that could be glibly elevated into a 'symbol.' 'Mouse's Nest' is supreme in its clarity, its wholeness, and (an unusual quality in Clare) its eloquent economy.

NATURE'S VENTRILOQUIST

In 'The Nightingale's Nest' and the other poems about birds written at approximately the same time (c. 1830–2), although Clare demonstrates an intimate familiarity with the natural world, a clear separation is maintained between observer and object. Such discrimination is, of course, the usual concomitant of sanity, but as Clare's mind gave way in his later years the distinction was not always maintained. Just as he entertained the delusion that he was Nelson or Byron or Burns or Ben Caunt the pugilist, so he developed a capacity (which, however dangerous for the man, had some remarkable implications for the poet) for breaking down the psychological barrier between man and nature.

An intermediate stage may be noted in the remarkable poem 'Song's Eternity' (ii. 266–8), apparently written soon after the departure to Northborough. The poem does not begin to reveal its full force until, as the Tibbles note, we realize that the language and stanzaic pattern form an imitation of the song of the 'bluecap' or blue tit. The first stanza reads (one should, perhaps, write: sings) as follows:

> What is song's eternity?
>   Come and see.
> Can it noise and bustle be?
>   Come and see.
> Praises sung or praises said
>   Can it be?
> Wait awhile and these are dead –
>   Sigh, sigh;
> Be they high or lowly bred
>   They die.

It may be helpful to set against this Hudson's description of the blue tit's song:

> The language of the blue tit resembles that of the oxeye [great tit]. Its voice is not
> so powerful, but the various sounds, the call and love notes, or song, composed of
> one note repeated several times without variation, have similar sharp, incisive,
> and somewhat metallic qualities.[14]

Clare has here steeped himself in the blue tit's world, writing as it were the libretto to the bird's score, and attempting to view the human world from the bird's perspective instead of vice versa. Such attempts always run the risk of becoming merely fanciful, but Clare manages to avoid making the effect too conspicuous.

He is also careful not to make the mistake of burdening the blue tit with an elaborate philosophy, and we must be on our guard against imposing an external system of thought upon it. I believe the Tibbles go too far in their commentary. 'Someone has remarked,' they tell us (it was, in fact, Robert Lynd), 'that Clare was more interested in the bird than in eternity. Not true: the bird is there because Clare hears in its song, untroubled by the thoughts of yesterday and tomorrow, a symbol of that eternity which man, by inventing Time, forswears, and then allows himself to be driven to reinvent.'[15] But that is to turn Clare into Keats. For Clare the song (like all other poetic manifestations) is not a symbol of eternity, but eternity itself:

> Nature's glee
> Is in every mood and tone
> Eternity.

> The eternity of song
> Liveth here,
> Nature's universal tongue
> Singeth here.

Clare offers not 'philosophy' but natural wisdom. The emphasis is upon 'here' (with a voiced pun on 'hear' lurking in the background), and eternity is not an abstract concept but the Now of immediate experience. One recalls Richard Jefferies in *The Story of My Heart*: 'I cannot understand time. It is eternity now. I am in the midst of it. It is about me in the sunshine; I am in it, as the butterfly floats on the light-laden air ... Now is eternity; now is the immortal life.'[16] Jefferies (whom some have considered mad on the evidence of this impassioned spiritual autobiography) makes the connection with the butterfly only through simile. In 'Song's Eternity' Clare strives to maintain the dramatic logic of his poem by speaking through the blue tit, but cannot keep up the distinction completely. The lines I have just quoted continue:

> Songs I've felt and heard and seen
> Everywhere.

It is the only first-person pronoun in the whole poem. Momentarily, it seems (though eternity and the moment may no longer be separable), Clare has blended his consciousness with that of the blue tit; the 'I' stands for both.[17] 'Song's Eternity' is shot through with a preternatural lucidity which is characteristic of Clare's finest poems. Faced with his obvious genius, it is a bold critic who would deny categorically that Clare is offering a conscious, deliberate effect at this point in the poem, but from what we know of his subsequent history it is not unreasonable to speculate that in this final stanza his ability to distinguish between subject and object begins to break down. And that way madness lies.

I do not intend to say very much about the asylum poems. They have already attracted sufficient attention, and have to some extent been over-emphasized. I sympathize with Donald Davie, who wrote in 1964: 'Anyone who goes to poems for poetry and not another thing will prefer the sane Clare of *The Shepherd's Calendar* to the lunatic Clare whose late poetry can be painfully deciphered from pathetic manuscripts in Northampton, the Bodleian and Peterborough' (*CCH*, 440). The statement provided a necessary corrective in its time, but the matter is not quite so simple as Davie suggests. A distinction needs sometimes to be made between the official mental state of the poet and the nature of the poems he produced; in the asylum, in fact, Clare paradoxically wrote some of his sanest verse. Much of it, however, does not qualify for consideration in a discussion of rural poetry. The asylum poems are full of natural imagery, sometimes of a searing brilliance. Thus the following lines from 'Mary Byfield' (ii. 495–6),

> Bluecaps [cornflowers] intensely blue,
> Corn-poppies burnt me through,
> Seemed flowers among the weeds,

while grammatically uncertain, possess the piercing visionary quality of late Van Gogh. But for the most part, these later poems, when written on rural themes, are reflections of earlier material. There is, however, one outstanding exception – 'Clock-a-clay.'

Clock-a-clay is one of the dialect-names for the ladybird. In an early sonnet, 'Sabbath Walks' (i. 279), Clare refers to the

lady-cow, beneath its leafy shed,
Call'd, when I mix'd with children, 'clock-a-clay,'

and it is worth noting, perhaps, that a variant, 'Lady-clock,' occurs in *Jane Eyre* (ch. 23). Clare's poem could, I suppose, be classified as a dramatic lyric, but the vivid immediacy of its non-human viewpoint places it, surely, in a class of its own. Here all separation between man and nature has been expunged.

> In the cowslip's peeps I lie
> Hidden from the buzzing fly,
> While green grass beneath me lies
> Pearl'd wi' dew like fishes' eyes,
> Here I lie, a clock-a-clay,
> Waiting for the time o' day.[18]

The obvious echoes from Ariel's songs in *The Tempest* ('In a cowslips bell I lie,' 'Those are pearls that were his eyes') at first suggest the kind of literary imitation that, when off-form, Clare was quite capable of perpetrating. We soon realize, however, that he is in full control of his material here, that the allusions are deliberate, and that he is using the Shakespearean imagery as a starting-point for his own poem. 'Where the Bee Sucks' is a celebration of Ariel's non-human freedom, 'Full Fathom Five' a song about miraculous transformation. Both themes are important to Clare. The word 'free' rings through the asylum poems like a bell, and he consoles himself with the conviction that, while the authorities can imprison his body, they can never shackle his imagination. 'Clock-a-clay' is itself a token of the free range of his mind, and the facility with which he can imaginatively transform himself into a ladybird may even be said to surpass Ariel's powers. For Clare is, in fact, less fanciful than Shakespeare here. Ariel not only lies in a cowslip's bell but flies on a bat's back, the images proving assertions of protean ability; Clare's clock-a-clay is a real insect in a real cowslip. In Ariel's metaphoric fancy, eyes become pearls; the equivalent line here ('Pearl'd wi' dew like fishes' eyes') is a valid simile based on visionary observation. It is as if the Shakespearean allusions work by means of contrast to underline the earthy reality, the supernatural naturalism of Clare's poem.

Since the poem demands to be quoted in full, I now reproduce the last three of its four stanzas:

> While grassy forests quake surprise
> And the wild wind sobs and sighs,
> My gold home rocks as like to fall
> On its pillar green and tall;

When the pattering [puthering?] rain drives by,
Clock-a-clay keeps warm and dry.

Day by day and night by night
All the week I hide from sight;
In the cowslip's peeps I lie
In rain and dew still warm and dry,
Day and night and night and day,
Red black-spotted clock-a-clay.

My home it shakes in wind and showers,
Pale green pillar topt wi' flowers
Bending at the wild wind's breath
Till I touch the grass beneath.
Here still I live, lone clock-a-clay,
Watching for the time of day.

The imaginative audacity of 'grassy forests,' 'my gold home,' 'pale green pillar topt wi' flowers' is supreme. Even more remarkable, perhaps, is the imaginative perspective, the impression left by the poem of a small creature surrounded by massive shapes and forces. Clare has succeeded in subsuming his own personality into that of the ladybird, yet this does not mean that he yields up poetic control. What at first sight seem slack repetitions prove to be disciplined and carefully manipulated. We may note, for example, the subtle variation in the first and fifth lines of the penultimate stanza, and the forceful substitution of 'watching' for 'waiting' in the last stanza as compared with the first. The poem is a rich mosaic of words and images beyond Wordsworth's scope, that looks forward in its artistic dexterity to the work of William Barnes, yet remains, triumphantly and unmistakably, a culmination of Clare's unique genius.

FOUR

William Barnes

BARNES, CLARE, AND WORDSWORTH

If this were a book about nature poetry in the more general sense, Barnes's verse might not have been selected for discussion. Though he is decidedly a rural poet, a local poet, a poet of the 'village community,' the natural world is not a subject of detailed concentration. The titles of his poems frequently involve rural people ('The Shepherd o' the Farm,' 'Naïghbour Plaÿmeätes'), rural places ('Be'mi'ster,' 'Melhill Feast') and rural buildings ('Mindèn House,' 'Leeburn Mill'), but less often natural objects ('The Clote' is perhaps the best-known exception). For the most part the natural world is the ever present but taken-for-granted background to human lives. Because Barnes wrote about people for whom all features of the countryside were familiar, there is none of the sense of surprised discovery that we encounter so frequently in the poetry of Wordsworth; and because he wrote primarily for a local audience, his poems contain little of the loving reproduction of detail so characteristic of the writings of Clare. At the same time, Barnes realizes the significance of the natural background for the village life that he celebrates. Although he does not over-emphasize those aspects of the natural world that initially attract the visitor, we must not underestimate their importance. They are, I would argue, integral to his verse, and for a study of 'human nature poetry' Barnes is an essential witness.

H.J. Massingham once asserted that 'William Barnes and John Clare may be justly called the most fundamentally rural poets *from within*' that England has ever produced.[1] The claim is valid, but it is obvious that *'within'* carries very different connotations in reference to the two poets. Although Barnes's origins were decidedly humble, he never knew the grinding poverty that was a continually haunting presence for Clare, and his subsequent vocations as schoolmaster and clergyman are sufficient indications of differing social and intellectual status. Although both writers could draw their inspiration from happy childhoods in an agricultural world that had passed into history by the time they came to write their mature poems, their diverging circumstances led inevitably to completely dissimilar attitudes to poetry and its function.

Clare, it may be admitted, possessed the greater poetic genius, but Barnes was able to rely upon a controlled and highly sophisticated artistry that Clare lacked. Every effect in Barnes is calculated; so much in Clare appears 'hit-or-miss.' Barnes made a deliberate and informed decision in confining most of his poems to a particular locality; Clare, by reason of his birth and circumstances, had no choice in the matter. While Clare used Northamptonshire words because they occurred to him spontaneously but was incapable (even if he had desired to do so) of writing in a consistent dialect, Barnes's use of the Dorset dialect was almost pedantically deliberate. Clare is often effective despite incorrect grammar and slapdash syntax, whereas Barnes is scrupulous in recording (one is tempted to say 'constructing') a variant English tongue in all its purity and according to its often complex linguistic principles. Whereas Clare lays claim to something close to untutored 'Romantic' inspiration ('I found the poems in the fields, / And only wrote them down' [ii. 384]), Barnes relies on a controlled and classic discipline.

But the difference involves not only upbringing and situation but temperament and sensibility, and these in turn result in a very different approach both to the natural world and to village life. Barnes has two poems entitled 'The Common a-Took In,' but neither offers anything like Clare's impassioned response to Enclosure. In one, an 'Eclogue,' he reverts to the classical form of the pastoral dialogue, and although he intends to express sympathy for the dispossessed, the convention distances his speakers and produces a disturbing sense of complacency. The second, a monologue spoken by a village boy to his sister, recalls Clare in its presentation of the child's freedom and inquisitiveness but substitutes gentle regret for Clare's bitter indignation:

> Ah while the lark up over head
> Did twitter, I did search the red
> Thick bunch o' broom, or yollow bed
>   O' vuzzen vor a nest
> An' thou di'st hunt about, to meet
> Wi' strawberries so red an' sweet,
> Or clogs, or shoes off hosses' veet,
>   Or wild thyme vor thy breast.[2]

Barnes was not indifferent to (still less unaware of) the plight of the poor, but it did not, at least in its overtly political manifestations, provide him with congenial subject-matter for poetry. He is a poet not of protest but of fulfilment. In consequence, he runs the risk of seeming excessively ideal and even idyllic, but he can, through his art, reproduce the communal voice of a village society in a way that Clare, with greater genius and less discipline, could not.

Barnes gives no hint of knowing Clare's poetry but is recorded as acknowledging Wordsworth, along with Robert Burns, as an influence upon his work.[3] In terms of my argument, this is as interesting and revealing as the negative evidence concerning Clare. When we encounter the 'Dissertation' introducing his first volume of dialect poems in 1844, it is impossible not to recall the 1800 Preface to *Lyrical Ballads*. Barnes writes:

> The author thinks his readers will find his poems free of slang and vice as they are written from the associations of an early youth that was passed among rural families in a secluded part of the country ... As he has not written for readers who have had their lots cast in town-occupations of a highly civilized community, and cannot sympathize with the rustic mind, he can hardly hope that they will understand either his poems or his intention ...
>
> The dialect in which he writes is spoken in its greatest purity in the villages and hamlets of the secluded and beautiful Vale of Blackmore. He needs not observe that in the towns the poor commonly speak a mixed jargon, violating the canons of the pure dialect as well as those of English.[4]

Barnes nowhere approaches the subtleties of Wordsworth's argument; there are some readers, I suppose, who will condemn his remarks as hopelessly 'provincial,' but he clearly depends upon similar assumptions concerning rustic situations and the language really used by men (though his later practice severely qualifies Wordsworth's theories about rural speech). Robert Burns, on the other hand, was obviously important as testimony to the fact that dialect poetry could be read with pleasure and profit by readers outside the region from which it sprang, though this is not Barnes's prime concern. To quote once more from the 'Dissertation':

> If his verses should engage the happy mind of the dairymaid with her cow, promote the innocent evening cheerfulness of the family circle on the stone floor, or teach his rustic brethren to draw pure delight from the rich but frequently overlooked sources of nature within their sphere of being, his fondest hopes will be realized.[5]

Since the learned dissertation and elaborate glossary which frame the poems are hardly designed for 'rustic brethren,' Barnes was clearly not uninterested in a wider audience, but it remains true that the poems were originally written without the idea of a cosmopolitan readership in mind. At least at first, Barnes was a regional writer in the sense that he wrote not only about but for his limited local community. His daughter records in her biography that he once remarked of his poems as originally published in the *Dorset County Chronicle*: 'I did not look, as I sent them to the press, to their going beyond the west of England.'[6]

Barnes differs from Wordsworth (and, indeed, from Clare) in rarely venturing into *wild* nature. For him the natural world is primarily agricultural country, cultivated, humanized. Natural objects are celebrated not because they provoke sudden, impulsive, individual responses but because they are recognized as habitual and recurring. Barnes praises not so much the unique experience as the gentle beauty of the accustomed scene. His is less a poetry of natural encounter than one of natural assimilation. He could subsume his own character into the larger consciousness of the community as Wordsworth could not; a travelled man, he could still speak as a native. Yet despite all these differences, Barnes was able, I believe, to learn much from Wordsworth. Above all, he was in a position to develop in his own way Wordsworth's experiments with varied narrators and 'dramatic' speech. He found a means of retaining Wordsworth's poetic sophistication without needing to separate himself from the villagers about which he wrote. While Wordsworth could only occasionally offer himself as the poet of Grasmere, Barnes wrote almost invariably as the poet of Blackmore Vale.

HALLOWED PLACES

Barnes is often described as 'the Dorset poet' or 'the Wessex poet,' but the boundaries of his poetic domain are in fact more limited than either of these terms might suggest. For the most part, the topographical references in his verse are confined to two areas – the Blackmore Vale in which he was born and (to a lesser extent) the environs of Dorchester in which he lived for the greater part of his life. These are the tracts of country described by Hardy in *Tess of the d'Urbervilles* as the Vales of the Little and the Great Dairies respectively. Barnes was born, indeed, only a few miles from Marnhull, which appears in Hardy's novel as Marlott, Tess's birthplace, and it is interesting to note that Hardy took over the description of Blackmore Vale that appears in the second chapter from a passage which he had originally written as part of a review of Barnes's poetry.

Hardy's description itself seems to have been influenced by the pictures Barnes paints in his poems. 'This fertile and sheltered tract of country,' he tells us, 'is bounded on the south by [a] bold chalk ridge'; in this valley 'the world seems to be constructed on a smaller and more delicate scale' (ch. 2). A few lines earlier (in the novel but not in the review) Hardy calls it 'an engirdled and secluded region, for the most part untrodden as yet by tourist or landscape-painter.' These are precisely the terms (I am not at present concerned with perspective) in which Barnes describes the Blackmore Vale. 'Oh! small the land the hills did bound,' exclaims the speaker in a poem appropriately entitled 'The Little Worold,' and the locality is described as one

> Where vew vrom other peärts did come,
> An' vew did travel vur vrom hwome.   (*PWB*, 468)

The idea of a small, self-contained community, protected by a natural formation of encircling hills, is one which recurs again and again in Barnes's poetry. As he notes in 'Childhood,'

> our worold did end wi' the neämes
> Ov the Sha'sbury Hill or Bulbarrow,   (*PWB*, 259)

and the same point may be found in 'The White Road up Athirt the Hill,' a poem I shall discuss a little later. It is an area in which a small town like Sturminster Newton appears as an important centre, and Shroton Fair (referred to in several poems) becomes a significant event in the local calendar. In such poems as 'Pentridge by the River' (which refers not to the place of that name in Cranborne Chase – Tess's Trantridge – but to the farm near his own birthplace owned by his uncle and aunt), 'Lydlinch Bells' (the only Barnes poem that actually mentions Bagber, the hamlet in which he was born), and 'The Water-Spring in the Leäne' (the specific references in which can be readily identified on the appropriate large-scale Ordnance Survey map as features of his immediate local landscape when a boy), Barnes was recording with minute and loving fidelity the lineaments of the local scene for the enjoyment and satisfaction of the native inhabitants.

Such poems record the ordinary lives, customs, and practices of the cottagers of the vale, and therefore have a value, beyond their intrinsic poetic merits, as records of what might be called living history. Rolf Gardiner has described Barnes and Hardy as 'the great [Wessex] remembrancers of the nineteenth century,'[7] and this is, indeed, one of the most important points of connection between them. Barnes was a noted antiquary, and his learned discussions of the historic and prehistoric past of this area of Dorset may be found in numerous contributions to (among others) the *Gentleman's Magazine* and the *Proceedings of the Dorset Natural History and Archaeological Field Club*. But his love of the old is equally apparent in his verse. Just as he recorded the details of the local language academically in such works as his *Glossary of the Dorset Dialect*, so he demonstrated its creative possibilities in his poetry. Similarly, his interest in folklore had both scholarly and poetic results. A historic account of harvest practices contributed to *Hone's Year Book* is balanced by a series of poems on 'Harvest Hwome' that present such customs in action; and we find poems like 'Leädy Day, an' Riddèn House,' 'Whitsuntide an' Club Walkèn' (both of which clearly impressed the future author of *Tess of the d'Urbervilles*), 'Guy Faux's Night' and 'The Drevèn o' the Common' that provide admirable glimpses into the life of the rustic past. Such occasions, like many of the dialect-words, were not of course confined to the Blackmore Vale, but they often survived there in purer and more complete form. H.J. Massingham has written well about this aspect of Barnes's work. He notes that, by virtue of this subject-matter and his habitual treatment of it, Barnes was 'the only post-peasant poet who wrote peasant poetry,' and he argues (rightly, I think) that 'his poetry and his scholarship were gropings into the depths of organic being.'[8]

Sometimes, however, Barnes offers not so much a contemporary record as a literary preservation of what has already passed. 'Harvest Hwome' begins:

> Since we were striplèns naïghbour John,
> The good wold merry times be gone:
> But we do like to think upon
> What we've a-zeed an' done.   (*PWB*, 137)

I shall be discussing the dramatic nature of Barnes's poems in a later section; it will suffice here to note that, by putting the poem into the mouth of an aged and reminiscent countryman, Barnes at once eludes the charge of personal nostalgia, comments on the fact of historical change, and records the human reality of a constant looking-back to the past. The reminiscence at the present Harvest Home is as much the subject as the recollection of earlier times. Typically Barnes places the emphasis not on the rustic occasion in general but on particular (though representative) incidents at such gatherings. This is no reconstruction of moribund folk-practice but a vigorous account of a living event. Above all, it is a *communal* experience, and it is this feature that distinguishes Barnes not only from his contemporaries but from most poets (even nature poets) in other ages. 'Out a-Nuttèn' and 'Slidèn' are useful instances to cite here, since even a cursory comparison with Wordsworth's 'Nutting' or the account of skating in Book I of *The Prelude* shows the radical difference between the two poets. In the former poem, the Wordsworthian speaker is characteristically a solitary, while in the latter, although it begins as a communal activity ('We hissed along the polished ice in games / Confederate' [I, 434–5], the poet soon separates himself from his companions. Such a separation would be unthinkable in Barnes's poems, which are essentially social in attitude. The unique personal experience in nature, so important to Wordsworth, is absent here. A comparison with Clare might seem useful at this point, but although Clare often makes poems out of local festivals (Helpston Statute, etc.), and although he writes from the village viewpoint, his temperament and interests separate him from the community in which he dwells. Similarly (and this is perhaps a historical point rather than a psychological one) in 'Vellèn the Tree,' which, as several commentators have noted, is virtually identical in subject with Hardy's 'Throwing a Tree,' Barnes's community speaks, as it were, through his verse, while in Hardy's poem any kind of communal rapport is conspicuous by its absence.

For Barnes the association of human beings with the natural settings in which they have lived and died is integral to the form of many of his poems. Such localities become humanized, and are all, to quote the title of one poem, 'Hallowed Pleäces.' The point is made specifically in 'A Wold Friend':

> What tender thoughts do touch woone's soul,
>   When we do zee a meäd or hill
> Where we did work, or plaÿ, or stroll,
>   An' talk wi' vaïces that be still;
> 'Tis touchèn vor to treäce, John,
> Wold times drough ev'ry pleäce, John.   (PWB, 198)

The 'meäd or hill' is not, as it would be in Wordsworth, unique or influential; no 'interventions,' severe or otherwise, are to be expected. On the contrary, human experience projects feeling into nature. Thus, when he refers in another poem to 'The paths our fathers trod avore' (PWB, 274), he is employing a living image, not a dead metaphor; the paths are real, and they call up memories of friends and ancestors as surely as the gravestones in the churchyard. Of all the rural poets, Barnes is perhaps the most sensitive to what he calls 'the landscape's harmony with man's life.'[9]

Similarly, the traditional village tasks are 'hallowed' by the historical continuities they involve. The point is made movingly about the bell-ringers in 'Lydlinch Bells':

> There sons did pull the bells that rung
> Their mothers' weddèn bells avore,
> The while their fathers led em young
> An' blushèn vrom the church's door.[10]

And so, it is implied, others will ring for their weddings, and their sons will carry on the tradition when they themselves are dead. In 'Our Fathers' Works,' a poem considered sufficiently central to be read at Barnes's funeral, he draws attention to the benefits derived from ancestors:

> They clear'd the groun' vor grass to teäke
> The pleäce that bore the bremble breäke,
> An' draïn'd the fen, where water spread,
> A-lyèn dead, a beäne to men;
> An' built the mill, where still the wheel
> Do grind our meal, below the hill.   (PWB, 270)

He goes on, of course, to exhort his hearers to continue the process for the benefit of their descendants. He succeeds in catching within these poems the realization that one is taking part in a continuous historical process, a realization that can turn even the humblest occupation into 'work a-blest' (PWB, 271).

From this we can understand why the voice of the community is so prominent throughout Barnes's poetry. He is more conversational than Wordsworth or even Clare, and also more social; we notice this especially when a poem comes to us not through a first-person singular but through a first-person plural. Such a poem is 'The White Road up Athirt the Hill' (PWB, 90–1), worth discussing in some detail not only because it is an excellent example of the poem that speaks for a local community but also because it displays many of Barnes's most characteristic poetic qualities at their best.

The setting and circumstances are firmly established in the first stanza:

> When hot-beam'd zuns do strik right down,
> An burn our zweaty feäzen brown;
> An' zunny slopes, a-lyèn nigh,
> Be back'd by hills so blue's the sky;
> Then, while the bells do sweetly cheem
> Upon the champèn high-neck'd team,
> How lively, wi' a friend, do seem
>   The white road up athirt the hill.

'Our zweaty feäzen [faces]' indicates a poetic viewpoint as far removed as possible from the Wordsworthian 'Spectator ab extra.' The countryside is indeed presented 'from within' – more so, indeed, than in most of Clare, where the viewpoint is generally that of a detached observer and recorder, however rustic. Here the voice comes from within the process of rural labour, but (and here the contrast with Clare is most specific) Barnes is able to achieve this without sacrificing the sophisticated artistic resources that he has developed in his own person. This is evident from the deceptively smooth-flowing third and fourth lines which convey a subtly graded sense of perspective and the phrase 'so blue's the sky' which combines the effect of oral formulaic (Barnes employs it elsewhere – in 'Waÿfeärèn' for example) with a painter's eye for colour-combination and tonal composition. The communal foundation of the poem is underlined by the team of horses and the deliberately inserted phrase, 'wi' a friend,' both indicative of a concern for company. Also worthy of attention is the striking adjective 'lively,' which, I assume, is not a dialect usage (it does not appear in either Barnes's *Glossary of the Dorset Dialect* or Wright's *English Dialect Dictionary*) but a bold poetic usage meaning 'attractive, full of life.'

The second verse extends the scene portrayed in the first to include a description of what lies beyond the sheltered home valley. Within the 'zwellèn downs' are to be found 'green meäds an' zedgy brooks, / An' clumps o' trees wi' glossy rooks,' but natural beauty, though recognized and appreciated, is secondary to human society. The hollows in the downs also contain

> hearty vo'k to laugh an' zing,
> An' parish-churches in a string,
> Wi' tow'rs o' merry bells to ring,
> An' white roads up athirt the hills.

The emphasis is on human celebration (we are not surprised that the next stanza is concerned with a feast) and connection (even the churches are seen as linked, 'in a string'), and the poet has imposed an additional association by setting off the church-bells against the harness-bells in the equivalent place in the first stanza.

The two central stanzas record a rural festival, and need to be quoted in full:

> At feäst, when uncle's vo'k do come
> To spend the day wi' us at hwome,
> An' we do lay upon the bwoard
> The very best we can avvword,
> The wolder woones do talk an' smoke,
> An' younger woones do plaÿ an' joke,
> An' in the evenèn all our vo'k
>   Do bring em gwaïn athirt the hill.

> An' while the green do zwarm wi' wold
> An' young, so thick as sheep in vwold,
> The bellows in the blacksmith's shop,
> An' miller's moss-green wheel do stop,

An' lwonesome in the wheelwright's shed
'S a-left the wheelless waggon-bed;
While zwarms o' comèn friends do tread
The white road down athirt the hill.

The reference to 'uncle's vo'k' is of some interest, since a biographically minded critic would lay stress on the fact that Barnes spent much of his childhood at Pentridge Farm, the home of his uncle and aunt almost two miles from his own home at Bagber near Sturminster Newton, and that a number of his poems contain specific references to his uncle and aunt; this poem too, it could be argued, has its personal element. I stress the point because it offers an excellent example of the way in which Barnes adapts autobiographical experience to general ends. 'Uncle's vo'k' here are both his own relations and any villager's relations, and the occasion, though not lacking in particulars, is solidly representative. The actions are commonplace and unremarkable, but all the more human for that. The activity on the village green ('so thick as sheep in vwold,' an apparently simple image that proves profoundly appropriate on reflection) is effectively contrasted with the rest in the craftsmen's workshops, and the line of friends descending the hills to join in the festivities is balanced (like the church- and harness-bells) with the courteous accompanying of visitors on their way home in the evening.

The two final verses vary the theme of the human associations of locality by focusing upon personal memories of the past and hopes for the future. The winding road is especially dear when it leads to 'pleäzen, east or west / The vu'st a-known, an' lov'd the best,' and the uninsistent symbolic application of the 'zunsheen's glow' and the 'sheädes' of clouds, suggesting that the memories of the past are tinged with both joy and sorrow, displays Barnes's characteristic signature on a well-known Wordsworthian pattern (compare, for example, the opening of *The Excursion* and the close of the 'Immortality Ode'). The poem ends on an apparently quiet, almost anticlimactic note, but the emphasis on

Young blushèn beauty's hwomes between
The white roads up athirt the hills

is presumably intended to suggest, for a young man, the discovery of a future wife, or, for an old man, a comforting token of human continuity.

Like so many of Barnes's poems, 'The White Road up Athirt the Hill' makes significant use of the refrain which also gives it its title. In this case, Barnes takes special trouble to vary the wording so that, although the principle of expected repetition is maintained, no two concluding stanza-lines are identical. Once again we find the sophisticated poet transforming a traditional effect to his own purpose. But Barnes's frequent use of refrain has an additional significance; it is more than a mere technical device for rounding off the poem. Here, and more emphatically in poems in which the repeated refrain employs a local place-name (e.g. 'Blackmwore Maïdens' or 'Lindenore'), it underlines the fact that the locality is itself the boundary of the lives recorded within it. The poem exists within the repeated framework just as the village is sheltered by the encircling hills; the containing refrain parallels the containing landscape of the poem.

THE LANGUAGE OF THE COMMUNITY

No discussion of Barnes's poetry can proceed very far without facing up to the problem of his use of the Dorset dialect or, to employ the phrase Hardy coined later and Barnes would have preferred, 'the venerable local language.'[11] Since he is often classed, erroneously, with the 'peasant poets' as if he were himself an untutored genius warbling his dialect woodnotes wild, the historical record needs to be set straight, especially since it has profound implications for his approach to rural poetry. Although he naturally grew up speaking the dialect of Blackmore Vale, as an adult he seems to have taught and preached in 'National English,' and as Geoffrey Grigson has noted he used this same National English 'in his reading, in his letters, and, I suppose, in his thoughts.'[12] Later in life he allowed himself to ride his philological hobbyhorse to extremes, and his prose then becomes cluttered with revived archaisms and idiosyncratic neologisms, but his earlier correspondence is written in a smooth-flowing, precise, though recognizably nineteenth-century English which bears no resemblance to the style and language of his dialect-poems.

Why, then, did he employ the dialect, which he seldom used in everyday circumstances, for the major part of his creative work? It is always a mistake with questions of this kind to assume a *single* answer. Doubtless a number of motives combined. One point that should be made immediately is that Barnes certainly did not think he was doing anything eccentric or unprecedented in using the dialect. On the contrary, he believed that the Dorset speech was, in Hardy's words, 'a tongue, and not a corruption' (*SPB*, viii) and that its use was appropriate to the sanctioned tradition in which he worked. As he wrote in the 1844 'Dissertation': 'The Dorset dialect is a broad and bold shape of the English language, as the Doric was of the Greek. It is rich in humour, strong in raillery and hyperbole, and altogether as fit a vehicle of rustic feeling and thought, as the Doric is found to be in the Idyllia of Theocritus.'[13] Where earlier poets in the pastoral tradition imitated Theocritean structures and tropes and various conventions of pattern and reference, Barnes went further to reproduce similar linguistic tensions to those which Theocritus had been able to exploit in his own time.

In this connection it is interesting to consider A.S.F. Gow's comments on Theocritus' language with Barnes's situation in mind:

> Theocritus lived in an age when Greek as spoken by educated people was rapidly becoming standardised all over the Greek world, and though he himself must have been familiar with the Doric of his native Sicily and of Cos, it is not likely that he spoke Doric among his literary friends in Alexandria; and it is certain that, if he did so, it was not the Doric he employs in his poems … His Doric is an invented dialect.[14]

Gow makes a brief comparison with Robert Burns, but the resemblance to Barnes is surely much closer. Like Theocritus, Barnes was able to create a personal language purer and more flexible than the dialect as heard in common speech, and one that enabled him to introduce complex and sophisticated literary devices – 'verbal gymnastics,' as Gow labels some of Theocritus' effects – without incongruity (see pp. 86–7 below). Both were able to turn the linguistic standardization of their times to advantage by forging a distinctive literary language out of the remnants of a vanishing speech.

In 1862 Barnes wrote in his preface to the third collection of *Poems of Rural Life in the Dorset Dialect*: 'To write in what some may deem a fast out-wearing speech-form may seem as idle as the writing one's name in the snow of a spring day. I cannot help it. It is my mother tongue, and is to my mind the only true speech of the life that I draw' (*MLB*, 33). This seems clear enough, though Geoffrey Grigson, in his otherwise admirable introduction to the Muses' Library edition, makes curiously heavy weather of it. Noting that Barnes's 'first promptings were to write poems in plain English, which he did until he was thirty-four, and continued to do, at intervals, all through his life,' Grigson goes on to comment: 'In other words he could perfectly well help it, and often did' (*MLB*, 10). But what Barnes 'cannot help' is not his writing in dialect, but the judgment of his contemporaries that such writing is 'idle.' Nor, I believe (though this is more speculative), is the remark about Dorset being his 'mother tongue' a *reason* for employing it, but a factual statement bearing witness to his intimate and extensive knowledge of its usage.

Grigson then proceeds to make out an argument for Barnes's poetry arising as a by-product of his linguistic and philological interests, and goes on to describe his choice of the dialect as a 'learned perversity' (*MLB*, 11). This is surely unjust; I am prepared to believe that Barnes experimented in writing dialect as a test of his mastery of the language and its principles, but such a stage (if it ever existed) certainly didn't last for long and is indiscernible in the earliest dialect poems that we have. That poems like 'The Spring,' 'Haÿ-Carrèn' and 'The Clote' should have been written in what might be called philological cold blood seems to me inconceivable.

If, as literary critics, we approach the matter from what is surely the right direction, trying to explain the dialect from the viewpoint of the poetry rather than vice versa, we shall see that a far more likely explanation is forthcoming. Barnes makes it himself, indeed, in the statement from which this part of the discussion began: 'It ... is to my mind the only true speech of the life I draw.' The phrasing is admittedly contracted, as if an intermediate step had been omitted from his argument. What Barnes means, I think, is that Dorset speech is the actual language of the region, and that a poet who is to present the life and society of that region 'from within' can only do so adequately by drawing upon the unique resources of this language. In this way Barnes was able to write poems remarkable for what Gerard Manley Hopkins, with his own idiosyncratic but exact vocabulary, called 'their Westcountry "instress"' (MLB, 48). This could no more be achieved by a simplified National English like Wordsworth's than it could with a detached Wordsworthian viewpoint. Barnes's choice of the dialect was made, then, on strictly poetic grounds.

Grigson goes astray because he underestimates the dramatic quality of most of Barnes's poems – an aspect I shall consider in detail in the next section. In arguing (rightly, of course) that Barnes was not compelled to use dialect, he observes that 'it was in plain English that he wrote a poem to Julia Barnes after her death in 1852' (MLB, 10). The reference is to 'Plorata Veris Lachrymis,' but as the poem is written in his own person, National English is as proper and to be expected in this instance as is the dialect when he employs a rustic persona. But my argument has another, related consequence. If I am correct in what I have suggested in the preceding paragraph, it is obvious that the majority of Barnes's dialect poems cannot be satisfactorily 'translated' (by Barnes or anyone else) into National English. This I believe true, granted some exceptions where the subject-matter is not integral to either the region or the language; Grigson, however, insists unequivocally that 'Barnes does translate, and without a great loss.' The example he chooses to illustrate his argument is, to my mind, curious:

There are two lines I keep among the furniture of memory, and keep in this form:

The cuckoo over white-waved seas
Do come to sing in thy green trees.

Barnes wrote:

The gookoo over white-weäved seas
Do come to zing in thy green trees.   (MLB, 12)

The variants appear slight, but the difference in effect is surely considerable. First of all, 'do come' is artificial in modern standard English, while the use of the 'Present Habitual' tense, as Barnes calls it in his *Glossary of the Dorset Dialect*, with the '*do* unemphatical ... pronounced as *de* in French,'[15] is common and accepted idiom in the language Barnes used. A similar objection could be made to 'thy,' which seems falsely archaic or poetical in Grigson's 'translation.' More important, however, is the way Grigson's version implies a different kind of speaker. His suggests a formal naturalist-observer, while Barnes's speaker is unmistakably a countryman. Far from illustrating the minimal loss involved in translation, this example pinpoints the peculiar qualities of Barnes's carefully chosen and controlled poetic language – qualities that do not transplant. Grigson's couplet could only form part of a totally different poem; I believe that it would prove decidedly inferior to Barnes's own.

My point can be reinforced, I think, by an examination of 'The Woodlands' (*PWB*, 72), one of Barnes's poems that come closest to the form of traditional nature poetry. The first stanza reads as follows:

> O spread ageän your leaves an' flow'rs,
>   Lwonesome woodlands! zunny woodlands!
> Here underneath the dewy show'rs
>   O' warm-aïr'd spring-time, zunny woodlands!
> As when, in drong or open ground,
> Wi' happy bwoyish heart I vound
> The twitt'rèn birds a-buildèn round
>   Your high-bough'd hedges, zunny woodlands!

Again the rural speaker is integral to the effect. The dialect not only contributes to the dominant tone (the slow intonations proving appropriate to the leisurely paced nostalgia of a village speaker) but draws attention to an essentially rural attitude to the natural world. The woodlands are acknowledged as a sustaining but customary background to human life, not celebrated emphatically as either exceptional or 'other.' Natural objects are mentioned without fuss; there is no attempt, for instance, to identify the different species of trees or flowers. They are loved not because they are excitingly unfamiliar but, on the contrary, because they are comfortingly habitual.

Nor is the landscape offered as a changeless Arcadia. Indeed, the natural process of change and loss lies at the heart of the poem:

> An' boughs o' trees that woonce stood here,
> Wer glossy green the happy year
> That gie'd me woone I lov'd so dear,
>   An' now ha' lost, O zunny woodlands!

Certain trees have either fallen or been felled, and these recall human beings who once walked in the woods but are now dead, especially the speaker's beloved. Human life is recognized as part of the natural cycle, and the natural continuity manifest in the woodlands upholds him in his grief:

> An' where the missèn trees woonce stood,
> Or tongues woonce rung among the wood,
> My memory shall meäke em good,
>   Though you've a-lost em, zunny woodlands!

Memory, the human quality not shared by other natural species, provides solace. Whereas in Cowper ('The Poplar-Field') or Clare ('Langley Bush'), the disappearance of natural objects is lamented as a disaster, Barnes characteristically offers a more positive response. The shared loss of man and woodland brings a muted comfort. Because he sees himself as part of an organic community, itself part of a larger natural environment and subject to the same natural laws, the unindividualized speaker is able to discover, in Wordsworth's phrase, 'strength in what remains behind.'

If 'The Woodlands' were translated into National English, the poem would lose much of its effect because the words and usages that identify the speaker as a local villager would be obliterated. As a result, the balance of the poem would be tipped in the direction of the sentimental and the conventional. Both the sounds and the associations of the dialect are requisite for the poem's success, and the same holds true for most of Barnes's verse. In particular his eclogues ('A Bit o' Sly Coortèn' and 'The Veäiries,' for instance) and such poems as 'A Lot o' Maïdens a-runnèn the Vields' are dependent on the sounds and rhythms they reproduce. Without the dialect they are nothing, yet this in no way implies that Barnes produced anything that could be termed 'pure poetry'; on the contrary, while providing the appropriate – indeed, the only – speech in which such poems could exist, the dialect at the same time roots the poetry firmly in the local earth. Barnes is thus able to be artistic without ever running the danger of becoming aesthetic, which, given the tendency of his times, can be considered an achievement. Above all, the dialect, linked inevitably to the inflections of the spoken language, requires a dramatic delivery, even when the poems are not written (as the eclogues are) in dialogue form. Barnes's poems demand to be spoken, and even acted; it is therefore the dramatic quality of his work to which we must now turn our attention.

VILLAGE VOICES

The dramatic or impersonative aspect of Barnes's poetry is so central to his achievement that it cannot possibly be over-emphasized. Yet, because he uses his dramatic devices with such aplomb, they all too often pass unrecognized. It is therefore worth insisting with some force that, since Barnes did not habitually speak in dialect himself, whenever he employs it he is also, willy-nilly, employing a persona. All the dialect poems are deliberate constructs, and the poet who produces them is invariably a conscious 'maker.'

Samuel Hynes has observed that the 'conception of the poem-as-drama is ... the one thing for which Hardy is directly indebted to Barnes,'[16] and appropriately enough Hardy lays the greatest stress on this feature of Barnes's work. 'The assumed character of husbandman or hamleteer,' he writes shrewdly, 'enabled him to elude in his verse those dreams and speculations that cannot leave alone the mystery of things ... and helped him to fall back on dramatic truth, by making his personages express the notions of life prevalent in their sphere' (SPB, xi–xii). Hardy also claims, however, that Barnes 'often used the dramatic form of peasant speakers as a pretext for the expression of his own mind and experiences.' He is obviously thinking of the stanzas containing moralistic and religious sentiments (many of which Hardy silently omitted from his own selection), stanzas which reflect the didactic attitudes of the Dorchester schoolmaster and the unquestioning pieties of the rector of Winterborne Came. There is clearly some truth in this, but we get a better insight into Barnes's poetic art if, instead of watching Barnes impose his own attitudes on the villagers, we see him imagining himself in their situations. In the use of the dialect he found a simple means of separating the 'I' of the poem from the autobiographical circumstances of the poet, a means that had not been available to Wordsworth and that Hardy himself (though he learnt from Barnes's practice) only employed sparingly.

A convenient example will be found in 'The Wife a-Lost' (PWB, 333–4), a poem first published in Barnes's second dialect-collection in 1859, seven years after his own wife's death. The first two stanzas read as follows:

> Since I noo mwore do zee your feäce,
>   Up steaïrs or down below,
> I'll zit me in the lwonesome pleäce,
>   Where flat-bough'd beech do grow;
> Below the beeches' bough, my love,
>   Where you did never come,
> An' I don't look to meet ye now,
>   As I do look at hwome.

> Since you noo mwore be at my zide,
>   In walks in zummer het,
> I'll goo alwone where mist do ride,
>   Drough trees a-drippèn wet:

Below the raïn-wet bough, my love,
Where you did never come,
An' I don't grieve to miss ye now,
As I do grieve at hwome.

The emotion is obviously Barnes's own, and we can be sure that he wrote it as a personal tribute to his wife. But by 'transferring his experience to a poor Dorset countryman,' in Giles Dugdale's words, [17] he has enlarged his own response to speak for all men who have lost their wives. Because we know that the speaker who in the third stanza chooses to 'eat the bit I can avvword, / A-vield upon the ground' is decidedly not equatable with William Barnes, we can accept him as a representative figure no closer to the poet than to ourselves. In a curious way, by expressing his feelings in the 'limiting' dialect, Barnes has succeeded in universalizing them. In terms of poetic success, 'The Wife a-Lost' compares favourably with 'Plorata Veris Lachrymis,' the National English poem which in its original version opened with the line 'My Julia, my dearest bride' (see *PWB*, lii), and which even in the printed text contains numerous personal details, including the fact that Julia Barnes died on June 21, the longest day of the year. By contrast, 'The Wife a-Lost' employs aesthetic distance not to lessen the effect of the grief but rather to distil it.

From 1859 onwards, Barnes endeared himself to thousands of his fellow-countrymen by giving public readings of his poems across the length and breadth of the county and even farther afield. The overwhelming success of these readings suggests that they provided more than an echo of Dickens' solo performances of his novels (which he had first attempted in 1853) or a mere Dorset variant of Charles Kingsley's 'Penny Readings.' For one thing, they had a sociological significance which Barnes's daughter sensed when she observed: 'It was the first time a Dorset audience had heard its feelings, language, and daily life portrayed in its own common speech.' [18] Nor is their success wholly explicable by reference to the personality of the performer. The poems themselves are uniquely fitted to oral delivery; they require a dramatic, vocal presentation. However alien the phonetic marks on the page may seem (at least at first sight), they have the merit of perpetually reminding us that the sound of the words is a quintessential part of the effect. The emphasis is consistently on the voice, and lines which look unremarkable on the printed page come alive with the right intonation and stress. Hardy, indeed, goes further than this, and extends the poetic territory to the physical actions that create speech: 'Gesture and facial expression figure so largely in the speech of the husbandmen as to be speech itself; hence in the mind's eye of those who know it in its original setting each word of theirs is accompanied by the qualifying face-play which no construing can express' (*SPB*, viii).

The requisite dramatic accompaniment, of course, can never be more than hinted at in print, but a discussion of 'The Leäne' (*PWB*, 306–8) may none the less be useful at this point. This is a dramatic monologue in the strictest sense, since it implies a specific listener as well as a specific speaker, and the poet is able to convey not only the countryman's speech rhythms but also his appropriate intonations and gestures. The opening stanza offers a good foretaste of the variety of tone and rhythm that Barnes can achieve:

> They do zay that a travellèn chap
>   Have a-put in the newspeäper now,
> That the bit o' green ground on the knap
>   Should be all a-took in vor the plough.
> He do fancy 'tis easy to show
>   That we can be but stunpolls at best,
> Vor to leäve a green spot where a flower can grow,
>   Or a voot-weary walker mid rest.
> 'Tis hedge-grubbèn, Thomas, an' ledge-grubbèn,
>   Never a-done
> While a sov'rèn mwore's to be won.

Although the pattern of the stanza is quite rigorous, Barnes has no difficulty in subsuming it to the seemingly spontaneous conversational rhythms of the Dorset speaker. The sheer ease with which he carries off this effect may well prevent us from noticing it, but where else, it may be asked, has Robert Frost's principle of the 'sound of sense' been achieved so effortlessly and exquisitely before Frost's own example? The tone of confidential gossip is struck immediately ('They do zay ...') and this evolves naturally into exasperated wonder as the utilitarian suggestion is related. Accompanying grunts and nods are built in to the superficially redundant line, 'He do fancy 'tis easy to show,' and the tone rises to indignation at the word 'stunpolls,' which is at once emphatic because of the unfamiliarity of the dialect usage, and telling since it is obviously so much more appropriate a word than any which the sophisticated 'travellèn chap' could offer to express his complacent scorn. The extended seventh line (constant in length throughout the poem) enables Barnes to speed up the verse at this point, and an argument that might otherwise sound excessively sentimental is strengthened by the bubbling annoyance of the speaker. This leads up to the staccato bitterness of the last three lines, which force home the moral failing that is at the root of the problem. Only a master-poet could so control the implications of his vocabulary as to instil the maximum possible effect of contempt into the word 'sov'rèn.'

The poem is too long to analyse in full, but throughout its seven stanzas we find the same tonal variety and poetic control. Virtually the whole gamut of the speaker's emotions is encompassed within the poem. In the second stanza, for example, he can provide a comically grotesque illustration of the possible consequences:

> He would leäve sich a thin strip o' groun',
>   That, if a man's veet in his shoes
> Wer a-burnèn an' zore, why he coulden zit down
>   But the wheels would run over his tooes.

This is more of a joke than an argument, but the social implications of the proposal are serious ('As if all that did travel did ride'), and the speaker has succeeded in overturning the conventional moral evaluations so that the humble walker is exalted and the advocate of wheels and roads ('a travellèn chap') lowered in stature to suggest nothing more than a tramp.

The irrepressible high spirits are later extended in the notion that

> the goocoo wull soon be committed to cage
> Vor a trespass in zomebody's tree,

but again the implications of social disruption ('Men mussen come nigh woone another') are genuine and deeply felt. Barnes can pass from such arguments to earnestly pathetic ones, like the picture of the restrained children with 'a thin musheroom feäce' and 'bodies so sumple as dough,' where the comparisons are brilliantly apt and thoroughly rustic. And after a bitter condemnation of fox hunting and its double standard ('Trample noo grounds / Unless you be after the hounds'), all the more forceful (and radical) by being put into the mouth of a simple villager, the poem ends on an effectively quiet note with a reference to the old squire's humane treatment of trespassers:

> An' he zaid, 'I do fear you'll catch cwold in your veet,
>   You've a-walk'd drough so much o' my grass.'

The quiet dignity of the speech (in context) achieves, as it were, a climax in anticlimax. Barnes the poetic technician must have been pleased by his ability to slow up the verse at this extended line which up to this point in the poem has resulted in increased speed. Unostentatious in its dexterity, 'The Leäne' is in fact a triumph of verbal control and an essentially dramatic technique.

THE ART OF THE POET

Much has already been written (too much, I believe) about Barnes's technical virtuosity. A good deal of the emphasis derives, of course, from the sheer unlikelihood of finding Persian, Norse, and Friesian poetic effects (not to mention those of geographically closer languages like Welsh and Irish) in the work of a 'provincial' – all the more so when the poems are presented not directly from a learned speaker but through the mouths of ordinary country-men. As Hardy noted, 'his ingenious internal rhymes, his subtle juxtaposition of kindred lippings and vowel-sounds, show a fastidiousness in word-selection that is surprising in verse which professes to represent the habitual modes of language among the western peasantry' (*SPB*, ix). Historically, we know that Barnes's experiments aroused the admiration (perhaps, indeed, the practical emulation) of Gerard Manley Hopkins, but for our purposes the existence of these erudite effects is of less interest than the reasons Barnes must have had for employing them.

Here in particular the difference between Barnes and Clare is most evident. Barnes must surely have realized the danger of formlessness incurred by any writer of verse that is primarily descriptive. In Clare, as we saw, stanzas or couplets can often be omitted without any noticeable loss to the poem as a whole, and although the same can occasionally be said of Barnes (Hardy made quite drastic cuts in his own selection, though not without loss), the matter is far less serious. This is partly because Barnes deliberately kept his poems much shorter than Clare's, but more, I think, because he was careful to introduce a self-disciplining formal structure (involving elaborate rhymes and/or a con-cluding refrain) that encouraged or even forced him to keep to the main point.

Barnes is extraordinarily attentive to the formal aspects of his art. W.T. Levy has shrewdly noted of 'The Geäte a-Vallèn To' that 'the poem makes use of the gate's sound as the gravitational center around which the contents of all the stanzas rotate – a mode of Barnes's thinking which gives unity to a number of his poems.'[19] Title, refrain, and central image are all important in this respect. I have already shown how he frequently employs the encircling hills of Blackmore Vale as a topographical frame. Similarly, the ideals and attitudes of Christianity provide a moral frame (ruthlessly dismantled by the agnostic Hardy), while the complicated stanza-forms and exotic verbal devices (and often, especially in the National English poems, experiments in alliteration) all have their technical part to play in the formal discipline of his art.

Geoffrey Grigson has drawn attention to a central statement on the subject of artistry in one of Barnes's obscurer essays, 'The Old Bardic Poetry,' first published in *Macmillan's Magazine* in 1867. Barnes wrote: 'When ... a man writes with a skill that conceals skill, and his lines while they keep all the strict rules of verse, yet flow as if they were wholly untied ... we cannot but feel that kind of pleasure which is afforded by the easy doing of a high feat, besides that which is offered by good writing' (*MLB*, 33). It is a curious remark, since he talks about 'a skill that conceals skill' while at the same time assuming that the skill will be recognized, but this paradox lies at the heart of Barnes's writings. The point can best be made through examples where passages of natural description are strengthened by complicated technical effects. Here are stanzas from two of Barnes's most conspicuous stylistic triumphs. The first is from 'Trees be Company' (*PWB*, 312–13):

> Though downs mid show a wider view
> O' green a-reachèn into blue
> Than roads a-windèn in the glen,
> An' ringèn wi' the sounds o' men;
> The thissle's crown o' red an' blue
>   In Fall's cwold dew do wither brown,
> An' larks come down 'ithin the lew,
>   As storms do brew, and skies do frown –
>   An' though the down do let us free,
>   The lowland trees be company.

And this is from 'The Flood in Spring' (*PWB*, 381–2):

> But, oh! so cwold below the darksome cloud
>   Soon the night-wind roar'd,
> Wi' raïny storms that zent the zwollèn streams
>   Over ev'ry vword.
> The while the drippèn tow'r did tell
> The hour, wi' storm-be-smother'd bell
> An' over ev'ry flower's bud
> Roll'd on the flood, 'ithin the dell.

Barnes himself must have derived considerable personal satisfaction from introducing and manipulating the half-rhymes, internal rhymes, chain-rhymes, alliteration, parallelism, and all the other rhetorical effects crowded with extravagant ease into these verses. A reader who has not studied the theoretical intricacies of such devices will, on reading the stanzas aloud, be able to recognize their presence even if he cannot put a technical name to the individual effects. Their extent is in fact staggering, but it is sufficient to respond to the art being demonstrated, just as one need not be able to name the finger-combinations of a pianist to appreciate a bravura performance. The classification of metrical effects can be left to the specialist scholars; as literary critics, however, we may note how Barnes has succeeded in containing the formless beauty and power of the natural world within the discipline of a highly assured and sophisticated art.

'My Orcha'd in Linden Lea' (*PWB*, 233–4) is one of Barnes's best-known poems, usually quoted for the sake of its refrain where the Welsh device of *cynghanedd* – the repetition and interlacing of a limited series of consonants, 'Do leän down low in Linden Lea' – is introduced with such skill and delicacy as to constitute a poetic *tour de force*. This is certainly a remarkable line, and I would be the last to want to detract from the technical accomplishment that it represents. None the less, I believe that its success lies not so much in its phonological pyrotechnics as in its tasteful integration within the texture of the poem as a whole. It is the most conspicuous but by no means the only verbal effect in the poem. Even more admirable, in my opinion, is the way in which, in the first two stanzas, Barnes indicates the difference between early and late summer by the dexterous substitution of a few key words. The first stanza begins as follows:

> 'Ithin the woodlands, flow'ry gleäded,
>   By the woak tree's mossy moot,
> The sheenèn grass-bleädes, timber-sheäded,
>   Now do quiver under voot;
> An' birds do whissle over head,
> An' water's bubblèn in its bed. ...

The emphasis falls on luxuriance ('flow'ry gleäded,' 'mossy moot [stump]') and motion ('quiver,' 'whissle,' 'bubblèn'). In the second stanza, however, although the basic ingredients of trees, birds, and sky remain the same, the lively movement has been replaced by heaviness and stillness:

> When leaves that leätely wer a-springèn
>   Now do feäde 'ithin the copse,
> An' païnted birds do hush their zingèn
>   Up upon the timber's tops;
> An' brown-leav'd fruit's a-turnèn red,
> In cloudless zunsheen ...

'A-springèn' is cancelled by the heavy vowel-sounds as well as the meaning of 'leätely' and 'feäde,' 'zingèn' extinguished by 'hush,' the limpid water replaced by the solid fruit. By a few deft strokes, and without altering the major constituents of the landscape, Barnes has substituted the season of autumn for that of spring.

But the poem is not merely descriptive. It is spoken by a rustic yeoman, owner of a modest property, who is able to express through his description both the independence of his situation and his accompanying love for the land that he owns. By means of a smoothly managed but definite shift in tone, somewhat unusual in Barnes, the poem ends by focusing not so much upon the orchard as upon its owner:

> Let other vo'k meäke money vaster
> In the aïr o' dark-room'd towns,
> I don't dread a peevish meäster;
> Though noo man do heed my frowns,
> I be free to goo abrode,
> Or teäke ageane my hwomeward road
> To where, vor me, the apple tree
> Do leän down low on Linden Lea.

The dramatic stress here insists that the emphasis should fall on 'I' in the third line, 'my' in the fourth, and 'free' in the fifth, and the seemingly inevitable flow of the last four lines imitates the uninterrupted content of the speaker. The apple tree is the constant within the three stanzas; whatever the season, it remains a comforting emblem of security and of 'hwome.'

A similar analysis could be made of 'Woak Hill' (*PWB*, 378–9). These two poems are probably the best known of all Barnes's writings, but I suspect that their popularity resides more in their simple human truth than in their undeniable claims as exquisite examples of poetic art. The repeated, middle-rhyming refrain is a device that Barnes imported into English from his reading in Persian poetry, yet the identification of the metrical form is a trivial matter compared with the supremely moving way in which Barnes has adapted it to his local purpose. A poem embodying a universal emotion is thereby rooted in a dear perpetual Dorset place. As in 'The Wife a-Lost,' all the personal grief that he suffered at the death of his wife is transmuted into art through its transposition into an invented situation. The poetic discipline required to maintain the stanza-form (with its ten rhyming words in the refrain) provides a counterbalance for what might otherwise prove an excessively naked emotion. The expected pattern of every fourth line creates a lulling effect which detracts from the painfulness of the grief without in any way lessening its quality.

The memories of the dead wife are roused by the realization that the speaker is leaving scenes that were hallowed by her presence:

> The brown thatchen ruf o' the dwellèn
> I then wer a-leävèn,
> Had shelter'd the sleek head o' Meäry,
> My bride at Woak Hill.

Similarly, the 'goods all a-sheenèn / Wi' long years o' handlèn' (lines which so

impressed Hardy that he quoted them in *Far From the Madding Crowd* [ch. 56])
provoke recollections of those who have handled them. The conviction that the
wife's spirit haunts the place where she lived and died is conveyed so delicately
that we receive it without any sense of its being either quaint or morbid:

> I call'd her so fondly, wi' lippèns
> All soundless to others,
> An' took her wi' aïr-reachèn hand
> To my zide at Woak Hill.
>
> On the road I did look round, a-talkèn
> To light at my shoulder,
> An' then led her in at the door-way
> Miles wide vrom Woak Hill.

My reference a few lines earlier to Hardy was not idle. It is difficult to withstand
the belief that the genuine dignity of the emotion in this poem, linked with a
mature poetic control, profoundly influenced the later poet when he came to
write his 'Veteris vestigia flammae' poems on the death of his first wife.
Needless to say, in such a context 'influence' carries no sense of imitation.
While Hardy was clearly stimulated and helped by Barnes's example, the
resultant poems are as firmly Hardy's as 'Woak Hill' is unmistakably Barnes's.
Indeed, a sensitive response to the relationship between these poems can reveal
more about the nature of literary tradition than a shelf-full of scholarly commentary.

The last paragraph may seem to have digressed from my immediate technical
concern, but I do not believe that this is so. One of the most characteristic
qualities of Barnes is his emphasis upon the simple – in this case, an ordinary
countryman's heartfelt grief for a lost beloved – but he insists also that,
paradoxical as it may seem, the simple can be extremely complex, that the grief
in 'Woak Hill' is of such a quality that it demands all the sophisticated resources
of an unusually skilled poet to present it adequately. At this point, indeed, the
distance between Barnes and Wordsworth, for all their basic similarities, can be
seen most clearly; while Barnes concentrated, like Wordsworth, on 'the essential passions of the heart' (*Prose*, 1, 124), he would have had some reservations
about the language really used by men. His unabashed concern for the linguistic
possibilities of art stems from his conviction that poetry can express gradations
of experience beyond the scope of ordinary language. No countryman (no
non-poet, in fact) could express the love of freedom and home exemplified in
'My Orcha'd in Linden Lea' or the purity of continued grief manifested in
'Woak Hill.' But the poet's function, at once a personal challenge and a sacred

responsibility, is to perfect his art so that the communication of such states becomes possible. Hence Barnes's technical virtuosity, though impressive and even dazzling, invariably constitutes a means rather than an end.

This conclusion is reinforced, I believe, by the fact that 'dazzling,' however appropriate to his technical artistry, is not an adjective that anyone would apply to Barnes's poetry as a whole. On the contrary, his verse is marked by a solid sameness that can sometimes lapse into monotony, though it is best characterized in George Eliot's words as 'that sweet monotony where everything is known, and *loved* because it is known' (*The Mill on the Floss*, ch. 5). Unlike Wordsworth and Clare, who are notorious for the unevenness of their work, Barnes is remarkable for an impressively consistent standard of competence. If he seldom rises to poetic heights, he never descends to the equivalent depths; we do not find the 'two voices' in Barnes that J.K. Stephen identified in his parody of Wordsworth.[20]

This unostentatious consistence has been represented by some commentators as Barnes's appropriate equivalent to the level, natural sameness of the Blackmore Vale about which he wrote. H.J. Massingham, for instance, described Barnes's poetry as 'a song-book of the Vale not of the hills, nor the horizon, nor the depths of man's mind ... and you can quote from it almost anywhere, so level is it like the Vale itself.'[21] This is part but not all of the truth. Just as his natural descriptions are pleasant but unremarkable, so the speakers of his poems, though various, are similarly narrow in range. They share a family or, rather, a community likeness, and here we may recall that George Sturt came to the conclusion, after a meticulous study of folk-culture, that 'Folk' and 'Individual' are in fact antitheses.[22] Sturt's theory and Barnes's imaginative record bear each other out impressively. As W.T. Levy has written, 'Barnes was alert to the permanent village type which cloaked its individual members, as well as the way in which these very individuals merged into the type and found in it the daily pattern of their lives.'[23] Barnes gave this village community a distinctive voice; through the sophistication of his technique, the colloquial and the quotidian could be raised to the level of art without sacrificing the simplicity and ordinariness that made them so attractive. In Barnes and his verse, the poet and the countryman, man and nature, are for once happily united. As a result, the 'little worold' of Blackmore Vale in the nineteenth century, its woods and streams, villages and hamlets, encircling hills and encircled rustic life, are preserved for ever.

FIVE

Thomas Hardy

HARDY AND WORDSWORTH

Early in *Tess of the d'Urbervilles*, in his capacity as omniscient narrator, Hardy remarks: 'Some people would like to know whence the poet whose philosophy is in these days deemed as profound and trustworthy as his song is breezy and pure, gets his authority for speaking of "Nature's holy plan"' (ch. 3). And towards the end of the same novel he observes that

> to Tess, as to not a few millions of others, there was ghastly satire in the poet's lines –

Not in utter nakedness
But trailing clouds of glory do we come.   (ch. 51)

From such references it might reasonably be assumed that Wordsworth was anathema to Hardy, and it is therefore somewhat surprising to find Donald Davie accepting him (albeit with some reservation) as a 'devout Wordsworthian.'[1] Yet the biographical evidence backs up this view. As a young man he had recommended a reading of 'Resolution and Independence' as a cure for despair, and had reverently 'repeated some of Wordsworth's lines thereon' during a visit to Tintern Abbey, while in the month of his seventy-first birthday he made a Lake Country pilgrimage and dutifully visited Wordsworth's grave in Grasmere churchyard.[2] References to Wordsworth's poetry are in fact numerous throughout Hardy's work and the older poet is almost invariably treated, if not with devotion, at least with respect. Indeed, as I hope to demonstrate, Hardy's poetry often depends (though in ways that are, to say the least, oblique) upon Wordsworthian example. The critical references in *Tess*, primarily directed towards Wordsworth's 'philosophy,' were determined, I believe, by the tonal requirements of that novel, and suggest that, in his fiction as much as in his poetry, the sentiments of the 'implied author' are not to be slavishly equated with the habitual opinions of the writer himself.[3]

Only one instance is to be found of what might be called direct imitation of Wordsworth by Hardy, and this is, interestingly enough, the first Hardy poem to survive. The poem in question, 'Domicilium,' is little known since it did not appear in volumes of Hardy's poetry until the recent publication of *Complete Poems* (1976), but it was reproduced at the opening of the *Life* and was specifically described there, in words that are almost certainly Hardy's own, as 'some Wordsworthian lines' (*LTH*, 4). Much of the poem, in fact, reads like a series of initial drafts for 'The Ruined Cottage.' The rather slack, not to say limp, blank verse suggests off-form Wordsworth, while the introduction of 'a stunted thorn' verges on Wordsworthian parody. And who, confronted with the lines,

> Fifty years
> Have passed since then, ... and change has marked
> The face of all things,

would not attribute them to the author of 'Michael'? At the same time, the future author of *The Return of the Native* is discernible in the central lines of the last verse-paragraph:

> Snakes and efts
> Swarmed in the summer days, and nightly bats
> Would fly about our bedrooms. Heathcroppers
> Lived on the hills, and were our only friends.

It is this same curious blend of Hardyesque matter with Wordsworthian manner that we shall find recurring, much more subtly, in the mature verse.

The similarities between the two poets are manifold. In the *Biographia Literaria* Coleridge listed 'a *matter-of-factness*' as one of the characteristics of Wordsworth's poetry (ch. 22). The same phrase could be used of Hardy's, though to consider it with Coleridge a poetic defect would be as erroneous in Hardy's case as in Wordsworth's. Both poets needed the stimulus of an actual incident or scene to initiate the process of creation. Wordsworth's concern in his conversations with Isabella Fenwick with the places where his poems were composed recalls the topographical notes to the novels and stories which Hardy provided for his readers in a mood divided between annoyance and fascination. Both poets tended to begin (though not to end) with locality. Both were pleased if they could point to a factual origin for their work. As Hardy remarked on one occasion, 'I ... like best those [poems] which are literally true.'[4] Often enough, of course, they were able to rely on personal experience, but they were both willing to preserve local traditions by throwing the mantle of poetic narrative over the bare bones of historical record. Thus Hardy's 'The Lost Pyx,' like Wordsworth's 'Hart Leap Well,' dramatized a regional legend, both poems deriving an added solidity from their origins in specific places that could be visited. It is not surprising, then, that many of Hardy's poems have a distinctly Wordsworthian flavour, and that 'A Trampwoman's Tragedy,' described in the *Life* as 'based on some local story of an event more or less resembling the incidents embodied' (*LTH*, 311) and 'A Sunday Morning Tragedy,' to name only two, are as unquestionably 'lyrical ballads' as 'Goody Blake and Harry Gill' or 'The Thorn.' Even a poem as quintessentially Hardyesque as 'Voices from Things Growing in a Churchyard' ('These flowers are I, poor Fanny Hurd,' etc.) reads like a sardonic, literalizing commentary on Wordsworth's Lucy 'Rolled round in earth's diurnal course, / With rocks, and stones, and trees.'

But the resemblances penetrate beyond the mere choice of subject; they involve not only the poetic method but the artistic theory lying behind it. Hardy refers on a number of occasions to the Preface to *Lyrical Ballads* and freely acknowledges its influence.[5] His diction is not, perhaps, as close as Wordsworth's to 'the language really used by men,' but it similarly avoids the artifice of a high-flown vocabulary of 'poesy.' J.I.M. Stewart has made the point well in observing that 'there is no English poet since Wordsworth whose pedestrianisms are so frequently satisfactory to the habituated ear.'[6] These pedestrianisms pertain to both subject-matter and language. The ability to extract something poetically valuable from the undignified and the idiosyncratic, from what most conventional theories of poetry exclude, is common to both. Wordsworth's advocacy of rustic material was doubtless congenial to Hardy, though in this case it may have reached him most usefully through the filter of Barnes's poetic example. But Barnes's selective imagination tended to idealize the ordinary (though without seriously falsifying it). Hardy preferred the material that Barnes was likely to pass over. There is a curious notebook entry of 1868 quoted in the *Life*: '"Perhaps I can do a volume of poems consisting of the *other side* of common emotions."' To this Mrs Hardy (or, more probably, Hardy himself) has added the cryptic comment: 'What this means is not quite clear' (*LTH*, 58). The reference may well be to the kind of quirky situation-poem summed up in the later title, *Satires of Circumstance*, but whatever its meaning it surely implies a Hardyesque variant on Wordsworthian practice. Wordsworth had portrayed 'common emotions,' and

Barnes, as we have seen, carried on the tradition. So does Hardy, but with a difference. In Wordsworth's time, to treat incidents from rustic life in a straightforward manner was itself unusual; for Hardy, the angles and insights were unusual compared with those of Wordsworth and Barnes.

But it is time to be more specific, and examine the resemblances as they manifest themselves in individual poems. What is 'Neutral Tones,' we may reasonably ask, but a Wordsworthian 'spot of time' or, to employ Hardy's equivalent phrase, a 'moment of vision'? If we exclude 'Hap,' which belongs to the assertive, 'philosophizing' side of Hardy, it is the first of the poems stamped with Hardy's characteristic signature. In conception, in tone, and especially in diction ('starving sod,' 'bird a-wing,' 'wrings with wrong,' 'God-curst sun') it is unmistakably Hardyesque, but the three focusing images of pond, sun, and tree inevitably recall the naked pool, the beacon, and the girl with the pitcher on her head in Wordsworth's scene of 'visionary dreariness' in Book XII of *The Prelude*. Like so many of the Wordsworthian poems discussed in the second chapter, 'Neutral Tones' is a poem about memory, and the configurations of the natural setting enable the speaker to retain the scene in his mind and to recall it to consciousness through recollection of the surrounding natural objects. Here the depressing associations of the wintry landscape provide an appropriate correlative for the unspecified but readily imaginable human confrontation that takes place against it. While it would be critically irresponsible to describe the poem without qualification as Wordsworthian, it is doubtful if it could have been written without Wordsworth's example.

I do not wish to imply, however, that Wordsworth's influence on Hardy was an unmixed good. On the contrary, where it has been insufficiently assimilated and transformed, it results in the kind of poem that amounts to little more than a perfunctory gesture. When Hardy is too obviously employing a Wordsworthian manner for an expressly anti-Wordsworthian purpose, he produces squibs rather than poems. Both 'Yell'ham Wood's Story' and 'The Wind's Prophecy,' for example, exploit the Wordsworthian device of natural objects directly intervening in human life, but in each case the message ostensibly vouchsafed by nature is all too closely imposed by Hardy himself. There is no reason (as the Hardy of 'The King's Experiment' knew perfectly well) why Coomb-Firtrees should maintain 'that Life is a moan' nor why Yell'ham Wood's message should be: 'Life offers – to deny!' Nor is there any adequate point in the wind's knowing the speaker's amorous destiny in advance of himself. These belong to the category of Hardy poems in which, as R.P. Blackmur noted, the poet substitutes formula for form,[7] and the Wordsworthian undercutting, which constitutes a considerable part of the poems' *raison d'être*, in no way saves them from a facile and contrived obviousness.

None the less, the principle of questioning Wordsworth's teaching by turning his own habitual methods against him becomes an important feature of Hardy's poetry. 'The Darkling Thrush' is a poem that has been so exhaustively discussed by previous critics that it is almost an embarrassment to consider it here, but the Wordsworthian structure upon which it is built can bear some additional commentary. At first sight, to compare the poem with, say, 'I Wandered Lonely as a Cloud' would seem absurd, but there are in fact a number of resemblances. The time is winter instead of spring, and the natural world is desolate rather than dancing, but these effects can be seen as deliberate, almost systematic inversions of the Wordsworthian norm. More to the point, however, the basic situation of a human being finding himself drawn into the mood of his immediate environment (joining the natural dance of daffodils and waves in Wordsworth's lines, recognizing the other objects in the landscape as 'fervourless' like himself in Hardy's) is undeniably similar. Furthermore, the elaborate associations of sky, earth, and water by means of simile and metaphor in Wordsworth's poem (see my discussion on pp. 12–13 above) are paralleled here by the connecting musical images: the binestems like 'strings of broken lyres,' the wind as death-lament, the thrush's notes resembling evensong and carolling. Indeed, the psychological progress in the earlier poem from an enforced loneliness to a blissful solitude through the society of the daffodils is not all that different from the movement in 'The Darkling Thrush' from deadened, spectral depression to the possibility, however remote, of 'some blessed Hope.' John Peck has noted in the poem a 'grim parody' of a Wordsworthian situation,[8] and while he seems to me on the right track, in this instance I believe Hardy to be not so much parodying Wordsworth as qualifying him. The thrush represents – one is forced into a Hardyesque phrase to make the point – a minimal positive; the 'I' of the poem (and later the reader) must draw his own conclusion from the situation as he sees it. Is the bird right, or should we follow the ominous suggestions of the landscape? While nature's comfort is decidedly equivocal here, it is certainly not absent (as it is in 'Yell'ham Wood's Story'). The capitalized Hope in the penultimate line is not altogether cancelled by the speaker's being 'unaware' of it; the negative gets the last word, but the thrush's defiant positive sticks in the mind. It is almost as if Hardy were here employing the Wordsworthian method to test how far in all conscience he could venture along the Wordsworthian road.

Although Wordsworth liked to regard himself, especially in his later years, as a thinker, 'a Teacher or nothing,' Hardy did not. As he observed in the introductory note to his last, posthumously published volume, *Winter Words*, 'I … repeat what I have often stated on such occasions, that no harmonious philosophy is attempted in these pages – or in any bygone pages of mine, for that matter' (*CPH*, 834). Moreover, Hardy continually insists in the introductions to his books of poetry that the 'I' in his poems is not a fixed entity but a technical device enabling him to present an ever-shifting poetic perspective. The following extract from the preface to *Time's Laughingstocks* is representative: 'The sense of disconnection, particularly in respect of those lyrics penned in the first person, will be immaterial when it is borne in mind that they are to be regarded, in the main, as dramatic monologues by different characters' (*CPH*, 190).

Robert Gittings has recently suggested that these denials of personal reference in the poems were themselves highly personal in motivation, being inserted to placate Hardy's first wife.[9] Although there may well be an element of truth in this, the statements read as accurate accounts of the kind of poetry he wrote, and prove as valuable for the literary critic as they may be deceptive for the biographer. Most remarkable is the resemblance they bear to Wordsworth's practice (as distinct from his theory) in much of his most successful work. They suggest that Hardy instinctively recognized the essential nature of Wordsworth's poetic experiments in which, as I showed in the second chapter, he both imagines and presents a series of differing human responses to landscape. It would be foolish, of course, to claim that Hardy derives his procedures directly from Wordsworth or even indirectly through Barnes; I am here tracing one of the many tributaries that come together in the full spate of Hardy's genius, and any argument that tries to explain everything by reference to its own parochial stream proves self-defeating. Hardy's profound admiration for the poetry (though, again, not the philosophy) of Robert Browning is well known, and he obviously did not need to go to Wordsworth for initiation into the techniques of the dramatic monologue. None the less, when he came to write poems that explore the numerous, seemingly irreconcilable facets of man's relation to the natural world, in Wordsworth alone could he find a significant technical precursor.

HARDY AND BARNES

If Hardy considered that Wordsworth kept too wilfully to the sunnier side of doubt, we shall hardly expect him to respond with much sympathy to the general attitude of William Barnes. He respected Barnes and admired his poetry, but Barnes's way was not his way, and we find him voicing his qualifications quietly, indirectly, but firmly on various occasions. Barnes 'held himself artistically aloof from the ugly side of things – or perhaps shunned it unconsciously,' he writes in the introduction to his second selection of Barnes's poems,[10] and his habit of silently omitting stanzas of pious or moralistic comfort in his earlier selection of 1908 was itself an act of literary criticism.[11] But his dissatisfactions with Barnes's unquestioning idealization are to be found most subtly in his subjection of Barnes's poetic manner to the same process of ironical undercutting that we discerned in his reaction to Wordsworth.

Once again Hardy reworks a subject to turn the tables on the older poet. The process can be seen most clearly, perhaps, in the way Barnes's Poll in 'The Milk-maïd o' the Farm,'

> so happy out in groun',
> Wi' her white païl below her eärm
> As if she wore a goolden crown,   (*PWB*, 80)

is replaced in Hardy's 'The Milkmaid' by Phyllis, whose pastoral name belies her anti-pastoral stance. Her mind on 'her gay new gown' and the apparent fickleness of her lover, she is in fact no part of the essence of nature, which is what the narrator at first believes her to be. Similarly, Barnes's poem 'Went Hwome,' portraying the warm welcome accorded the return of a native, is upended in Hardy's ironically titled 'Welcome Home' in which the speaker is only faintly remembered and totally rebuffed. A deeper socio-historical contrast is to be found in the way Hardy's 'Throwing a Tree' repeats Barnes's 'Vellèn the Tree' but alters the tone by replacing a communal action with one of individual destruction. These parallels have been pointed out before;[12] what I wish to stress is the fact that in each case Hardy depends for his ironical effect upon the existence not specifically of Barnes's complementary poems (since Hardy's can be appreciated adequately, though not perhaps in their entirety, by readers unacquainted with Barnes) but of a system of values and a literary tradition that Barnes represents. Hardy is not an iconoclast attacking the conventions of his forefathers, nor a parodist poking fun at his innocent fellow Dorsetian. He is, rather, exploring 'the *other side* of common emotions,' using the tradition as he inherited it to illustrate the extent to which its assumptions are in need of qualification and to extend the possibilities of the tradition itself.

Many literary characteristics of Hardy have been traced by commentators back to Barnes, but by far the most important, I think, is the concern for human associations of landscape and everyday objects. It is generally agreed, for example, that the description of the chimney-corner in Keeper Day's house in *Under the Greenwood Tree* (Pt. II, ch. 6) is inspired by Barnes's 'The Settle an' the Girt Wood Vire.' Moreover, towards the end of *Far From the Madding Crowd* – significantly enough, in the scene that leads to their reunion – Gabriel and Bathsheba are seated among old furniture, and Hardy deliberately quotes the lines from 'Woak Hill': 'all a-sheenèn / Wi' long years o' handlèn' (ch. 56). A few years later, two of Hardy's diary-jottings make essentially the same point:

> An object or mark raised or made by man on a scene is worth ten times any such formed by unconscious Nature. Hence clouds, mists, and mountains are unimportant beside the wear of a threshold, or the print of a hand.   (*LTH*, 116)

> The beauty of association is entirely superior to the beauty of aspect, and a beloved
> relative's old battered tankard to the finest Greek vase.   (*LTH*, 120–1)

The last remark recalls a poem like Barnes's 'Grammer's Shoes,' while the 'object or mark raised or made by man on a scene' implies that such a scene becomes one of Barnes's 'hallowed pleäces.' The whole cluster of responses gets its supreme expression in an apparently late poem of Hardy, entitled (with a possible reference back to the scene in *Far From the Madding Crowd*), 'Old Furniture':

> I know not how it may be with others
>   Who sit amid relics of householdry
> That date from the days of their mothers' mothers,
>   But well I know how it is with me
>   Continually.
>
> I see the hands of the generations
>   That owned each shiny familiar thing
> In play on its knobs and indentations,
>   And with its ancient fashioning
>   Still dallying:
>
> Hands behind hands, growing paler and paler ...

'Each shiny familiar thing' is too close to the quoted passage from 'Woak Hill' to be coincidental, but, although the concept is thoroughly Barnesian, Hardy has as usual been able to set his own signature upon it. The fact that the poem is not in dialect separates it, as it were, from the rustic generations which, because of the speaker's detachment, become 'paler and paler' in a way that would be unthinkable in a Barnes poem. And the bold shift of tone in the last stanza, besides being a successful way of formally closing the poem, is itself symptomatic of a totally different attitude:

> Well, well. It is best to be up and doing,
>   The world has no use for one to-day
> Who eyes things thus – no aim pursuing!
>   He should not continue in this stay,
>   But sink away.

The poise that Hardy succeeds in maintaining here is remarkable. The Barnesian position is not dismissed; on the contrary, we are persuaded that it has both a steadiness and a moral value lacking in the 'progressive,' aim-pursuing world. Like the simple faith manifested in 'The Oxen,' it is congenial but doomed. Hardy cannot shut out the tendencies of the world into which he was born. He cannot avoid the destructive element, but he encounters it fully aware of its destructive quality.

Hardy's ultimate relation to Barnes is superbly presented in 'The Last Signal,' the poem he wrote as a tribute at the time of Barnes's death. Here Hardy pays Barnes the compliment of writing in his own style, and the ease with which he can manipulate the poetic devices Barnes had borrowed from Welsh ('an uphill road / That led from my abode to a spot yew-boughed'; 'The sudden shine sent from the livid east scene') is very remarkable testimony to his powers of technical assimilation. But the fact that, from the technical standpoint, the poem is unique in Hardy's work is itself indicative of the limits of Barnes's influence. Indeed, the poem can virtually be read as an allegory of the relation between the two poets. 'The Last Signal' portrays one of Hardy's 'moments of vision' (it was first collected in the volume of that title). The scene is characteristically Hardyesque: autumnal, dark, desolate. The reflection of the setting sun upon Barnes's coffin as it is carried to the funeral creates a 'brief blaze,' a 'sudden shine' in the otherwise dull, 'livid' scene. It represents a last manifestation of the general sunniness of Barnes's personality and the habitual tone of his poetry.

> Thus a farewell to me he signalled on his grave-way,
> As with a wave of his hand.

Ostensibly a physical parting, this is also a spiritual farewell. In his prose-obituary Hardy described Barnes as 'probably the most interesting link between present and past forms of rural life that England possessed.'[13] With his death, this link was snapped. Hardy was deeply attracted to the old ways, but he knew that his own genius led in other, more sombre directions. 'The Last Signal' is itself a farewell, Hardy's reciprocating 'wave of his hand.'

To discuss Hardy in terms of traditions and influences is fraught with peril. I must therefore stress that, when discussing his respective debts to Wordsworth and Barnes, I am neither attempting to force him into a preconceived and limiting pattern nor implying that his verse was in any way derivative. Hardy himself was eager to accept and quick to digest his literary legacies; he did not copy his predecessors, he *used* them, and the fact is an index not of artistic weakness but of artistic strength. Acutely sensitive to 'the hands of the generations' that have touched and used old tools and old furniture, Hardy was similarly aware of, and grateful to, those poetic ancestors who had evolved his stanza-forms, polished his rhymes, and moulded his language. Their existence was a stimulus, their success an inspiration; and out of the clash between *their* achievements and *his* temperament a new poetry was born.

HARDYESQUE STANCES

The technique of Hardy's poetry is in many respects similar to that of his fiction. In the Wessex novels the narrative viewpoint veers between an aloof, detached, omniscient presence and a wraithlike observer who watches the characters at a distance and follows them like a persistent but intangible shadow. Similar stances are taken up in the poetry. For most poets, the lack of a recognizable speaker (or the decision to dispense with one) results in a neutrally descriptive poem; for Hardy this becomes itself a technical effect contributing to a sense of discontinuity between man and his environment. In such poems, we might say, the narrator becomes paradoxically conspicuous on account of his apparent (but only apparent) absence. This is, of course, a notably unWordsworthian position. In my introductory chapter I juxtaposed Wordsworth's 'Written in March' with Hardy's 'Last Week in October' (see pp. 4–6 above), and the differences in effect illustrate my present argument. The opposed seasons, of course, typify the conflicting moods of the poets, but, more important, Hardy's withdrawal from the material about which he writes is integral to the point of his poem while it seems insignificant and accidental in 'Written in March.' In Wordsworth's poem the human implications of language associate man and nature; in Hardy's they subtly reinforce the separation.

The aloof Hardyesque stance is to be found in its quintessential purity in 'The Sheep-Boy,' a relatively neglected poem valuable for the imagistic clarity with which it presents (and embodies) this separation. The initial description of heathland may at first sight appear 'objective,' but the idiosyncratic Hardyesque vocabulary in which it is couched implies a detached yet specific observer:

> A yawning, sunned concave
> Of purple, spread as an ocean wave
> Entroughed on a morning of swell and sway
> After a night when wind-fiends have been heard to rave:
> Thus was the Heath called 'Draäts,' on an August day.

The ominous dialect-name for the Heath (glossed by J.O. Bailey as ' "drafts" or moist winds')[14] and the implication that someone has been abroad to hear the wind-fiends are the only evidences of human presence, though the language makes it clear that, whoever the observing consciousness belongs to, it is not the as-yet-unseen sheep-boy. The poem continues:

> Suddenly there intunes a hum:
> This side, that side, it seems to come.

From the purple in myriads rise the bees
With consternation mid their rapt employ.
So headstrongly each speeds him past, and flees,
    As to strike the face of the shepherd-boy.
Awhile he waits, and wonders what they mean;
Till none is left upon the shagged demesne.

The action of the bees seems mysterious, even menacing, although the principle of the bee-line is well known, and such habits, especially at the time of approaching storms, are well documented.[15] Yet more remarkable than the bees' behaviour is Hardy's in first introducing his sheep-boy as a mere obstacle that the bees have struck. It is a weird, disturbing incident, and even more odd in that it is virtually the last we see of him. The poem concludes:

To learn what ails, the sheep-boy looks around;
    Behind him, out of the sea in swirls
    Flexuous and solid, clammy vapour-curls
Are rolling over Pokeswell Hills to the inland ground.
    Into the heath they sail
    And travel up the vale
Like the moving pillar of cloud raised by the Israelite: –
In a trice the lonely sheep-boy seen so late ago,
        Draäts'-Hollow in gorgeous blow,
        And Kite-Hill's regal glow,
Are viewless – folded into those creeping scrolls of white.

That is all. As if in a Samuel Beckett playlet the sheep-boy, sole representative of mankind, appears in order to be struck in the face by an indifferent bee, and then is enveloped in the storm-cloud – to all intents and purposes, for ever! Nature and man could hardly be more separated from each other. There is no question of hostility. The bees' behaviour is a natural sign (like the signs warning Gabriel Oak of the approaching storm in *Far From the Madding Crowd*), but here the sheep-boy's ability to read it makes no difference to his fate. The mist resembles the pillar of cloud in Exodus, but serves not to protect but to blot out.[16] The phrase 'seen so late ago' draws attention to an observing narrator, but he is not characterized, and the implication from his emotion-free description is that he is distant and uncaring. The pastoral figure of the sheep-boy is transformed (in poetic, not philosophical terms) into a lonely and bleakly ephemeral cipher for modern man.

The same principle of separation works to very different effect in the justly celebrated 'During Wind and Rain.' There is no need to repeat the detailed and convincing analyses of this poem that already exist;[17] I will merely note here that the structure of each stanza effectively separates the human beings ('He, she, all of them') from the natural realities to which they are subject. In each stanza the first five lines are concerned with human activities, particularly those involving art and order: making music, tidying the garden, the ritual of breakfast out-of-doors, moving house. But the varying refrains emphasize 'the years' and the inevitable passing of time that dooms all human effort. Yet the image that rounds off each stanza with a depressingly apt finality refers not to time but to nature: falling leaves, storm-birds, a dying rose, rain eroding gravestones (presumably *their* gravestones). Moreover, each of the concluding lines *specifically* counters the development of its stanza: the domestic candle-flames burn upward, but the sick leaves reel down before an extinguishing wind; a shady seat is built, but it cannot provide shelter from the destructive tempest that blows the storm-birds across; the pet fowls come voluntarily to the hand, but the rose is forcibly ripped from the wall; finally, the 'brightest things' are spoiled, even obliterated, by the erasing rain-drop. Thom Gunn notes in the poem 'an almost complete omission of social and historical context,'[18] but Hardy's main point, surely, is to demonstrate that the works of nature inexorably prevent any permanent human context.

When Hardy employs first-person narrators in his poems, they are similarly detached from the natural world in which they move or haunt. 'Overlooking the River Stour' (whose title draws attention to a favoured Hardyesque perspective) documents this in a convenient if unusual way, since this poem begins in an 'impersonal' manner but introduces a distinctly characterized narrator at the close. The opening three stanzas present successive natural images of swallows, moorhen, and kingcups; these are offered as if for their own sakes, meticulously selected and faithfully recorded. In the final stanza, however, the poem drastically changes direction:

> And never I turned my head, alack,
>   While these things met my gaze
>   Through the pane's drop-drenched glaze,
> To see the more behind my back. ...
> O never I turned, but let, alack,
>   These less things hold my gaze!

The whole poem depends upon the irony that the natural objects, ultimately evaluated as 'less things,' continue to dominate the reader's attention as well as the narrator's. None the less, although the rain-washed window efficiently separates narrator from landscape, anticipating Robert Frost's emblematic fences and walls, what began as a nature poem ends as a 'human nature poem.'

A narrator anxious to set human values above natural processes but unable or unwilling to do so is a recurrent figure in Hardy's poetry. He may bring the complexities of his personal situation into an unresponsive but appropriate landscape, as in 'Neutral Tones,' or the natural features of the landscape may, as here, distract him from his individual concerns, but in either case the relation between man and nature is responsible for much of the tension in the poetry. More often than not, the renowned Hardyesque 'rootedness,' if present at all, is a rootedness of the poems rather than of the speakers. One thinks of the 'I' in 'The Darkling Thrush' or the wanderer following the ghost of his dead wife in the 'Veteris vestigia flammae' poems. 'Wessex Heights' offers an excellent example of the spectral narrator who, though based on Hardy himself, exists as an independent creation; however, as the poem has been treated exhaustively by J. Hillis Miller,[19] I will concentrate on the equally remarkable 'In Front of the Landscape.'

Here the 'I' of the poem seems lost in a fog which proves not so much an actual meteorological phenomenon (like the mist in 'The Sheep-Boy') as an external image of his mental state:

> Plunging and labouring on in a tide of visions,
>   Dolorous and dear,
> Forward I pushed my way as amid waste waters
>   Stretching around,
> Through whose eddies there glimmered the customed landscape
>   Yonder and near
>
> Blotted to feeble mist. And the coomb and the upland
>   Coppice-crowned,
> Ancient chalk-pit, milestone, rills in the grass-flat
>   Stroked by the light,
> Seemed but a ghost-like gauze, and no substantial
>   Meadow or mound.

At first sight, the last quoted lines may seem to contradict my point, but in fact the 'customed landscape' is real enough, and the landmarks only *seem* insubstantial to an observer whose 'tide of visions' prevents him from noticing the quite specific natural features. In the third stanza he admits that these are visions from memory 'Hindering me to discern my paced advancement,' his daytime experience transformed as if to a night of haunting dreams. These memories, 'scenes, miscalled of the bygone,' come between the speaker and the landscape, blotting it out. And henceforward he is preoccupied with an inner landscape in which the 'headland of hoary aspect,' recalled in 'the intenser /

Stare of the mind' is more real than the natural features through which he is struggling (an ironical dimension in the poem's title manifests itself at this point). The poem ends, daringly, with a shift of perspective in which the speaker imagines how he must seem to others:

> Hence wag the tongues of the passing people, saying
> > In their surmise,
> 'Ah – whose is this dull form that perambulates, seeing nought
> > Round him that looms
> Whithersoever his footsteps turn in his farings,
> > Save a few tombs?'

They assume that he sees nothing, while in fact they cannot see what he sees.

It appears as if we have come a long way from Wordsworth, and in many respects we have. Nothing could be less Wordsworthian and more Hardyesque than the intricate stanza-pattern and deliberately cluttered vocabulary; the elaborate system of alliterating consonants, assonantal effects, and link-rhymes creates a verbal *tour de force* that would have aroused the admiration of Barnes, although it is readily distinguishable from Barnes's own technique. Yet Wordsworth is not, I think, wholly displaced. 'In Front of the Landscape' is a poem about memory and its effects, about different ways of seeing, and about the relation (albeit negative) between a traveller and the landscape through which he passes. All these are characteristic Wordsworthian themes, and Hardy can be credited with a deliberate reworking of the earlier poet's preoccupations transformed by a tone and idiom that are uniquely his own. Here, we might say, is a classic example of the working relation between tradition and the individual talent.

TRAVELLING AS A PHANTOM

Hardy's poems are full of travellers in both time and space. In 'My Cicely' and 'The Revisitation,' for example, narrators describe journeys that are primarily geographical, though the historical associations of the landmarks indicate a strong temporal preoccupation. Above all, memories enable Hardy to journey into the past, and these are often, as in 'Wessex Heights,' stimulated by places and landscapes; in his famous autobiographical poem 'When I Set Out for Lyonnesse' (interestingly balanced by the later poem written from the perspective of his first wife, 'A Man Was Drawing Near to Me'), Hardy recreates an all-important journey in his own early life. Most of his first-person narrators are memory-haunted, and the supernatural element, so strangely characteris-

tic of his poetry, frequently involves figures from the past recalled to the mind
so strongly that they seem visible as spectral presences. Words like 'ghost,'
'phantom,' 'haunt' recur. 'The Ghost of the Past' is a typical title, and he claims
in another poem to see 'the ghost of a perished day' ('A Procession of Dead
Days'). Memory can recall the dead to a brief, fitful afterlife, and Hardy often
finds himself so preoccupied with the past that he must appear to others little
more than a ghost haunting the present. 'I travel as a phantom now,' he claims
in one poem, and in another imagines the spirit of his dead wife travelling
'memory-possessed' to the Cornwall of her childhood ('My Spirit Will Not
Haunt the Mound').

All these elements – the geographical journey that is also a journey into the
past, the ghost-like narrator, the associations of landscape, the comfort and pain
of memory – are prominent in the 'Veteris vestigia flammae' poems of 1912–13
written after the death of his first wife. Hardy succeeds in extracting the
maximum possible complexity from the situation in which the ghost of the dead
wife (half spirit, half *genius loci*) is followed into the area of north Cornwall near
Boscastle ('Castle Boterel') where she was living when he first met her. The
distinction between 'there' (Cornwall) and 'here' (Dorchester) provides a constant tension within the poems. The series is intensely personal, but the effect is
only communicable, the emotion only released, through the return to the
'hallowed places' in which their love first budded. I have already suggested that
Hardy may have been influenced by Barnes's poems on the death of Julia; not
only does 'Veteris vestigia flammae' recall 'Plorata Veris Lachrymis,' but the
possible associations between a dead woman and the places in which she lived,
which Barnes explored in 'The Wife a-Lost' and 'Woak Hill,' are here adapted
and transformed to Hardy's own unique purpose.

Hardy's subtleties are innumerable. As he presents the sentimental journey
he undertook in March 1913, the ghost is hardly less substantial than the
surviving husband or (if the angle is reversed) the living man hardly less spectral
than the ghost. In 'After a Journey' the husband re-enters her 'olden haunts,'
tracking her through 'dead scenes.' At last he realizes that the ghost is leading
him on 'To the spots we knew when we haunted here together,' where the
meanings of 'haunt' as verb and noun subtly coincide. In the present, however,
they haunt together in a different sense, the husband a stranger, almost an
intruder, in the landscape to which she belongs. Though she has become but a
'thin ghost that I now fraily follow,' the adverb reduces the speaker almost to
the ghost's status. In 'The Phantom Horsewoman,' on the other hand – and this
is a good example of the apparent inconsistency that has no effect on the tonal
congruity of the series – the ghost-girl-rider ('A phantom of his own figuring')
is triumphantly independent of the effects of time:

And though, toil-tried,
He withers daily,
Time touches her not,
But she still rides gaily
In his rapt thought
On that shagged and shaly
Atlantic spot. ...

Hardy is able to ring numerous changes on the basic situation, and claims the privilege of exploring the subject from all angles. In 'The Voice,' for example, the ghost is heard but not seen ('Can it be you that I hear? Let me view you, then'), while in 'After a Journey' she is visible but 'voiceless.' Although a majority of the poems present varying aspects of the man's response, 'The Haunter' and 'His Visitor' are written from the viewpoint of the female ghost, while 'The Phantom Horsewoman,' in a bold experiment that recalls Wordsworth's 'A Night Piece' (see pp. 19–21 above) but is notably more successful, involves an independent spokesman who watches the husband's movements from afar ('Queer are the ways of a man I know').[20] The emotion of the whole series is indisputably genuine, but its realization is dependent upon unparalleled artistic versatility and control.

One of the finest poems in the series, 'At Castle Boterel,' has recently been the subject of bitter critical controversy,[21] and deserves to be discussed in greater detail as an excellent example of Hardy's interweaving of human action and natural landscape. This particular 'moment of vision' occurs as Hardy (in so acutely personal a poem, no separation of poet and 'I' is either necessary or possible) is driving away from Boterel Hill, having completed his pilgrimage. The present is dull and rainy ('the drizzle bedrenches the waggonette') but it recalls, 'distinctly' while the visible scene is 'fading,' a memorable incident in his past that took place in 'dry March weather' (the month shared but not the meteorological conditions). The speaker is not reliving the previous experience; rather, he is seeing it from a detached viewpoint, separated in time and space, and discerns on the hill images of both himself and the woman ('Myself and a girlish form').

The brief walk up the hill, which might seem trivial to an observer who was emotionally as well as physically detached, had momentous personal consequences:

What we did as we climbed, and what we talked of
Matters not much, nor to what it led, –
Something that life will not be balked of
Without rude reason till hope is dead,
And feeling fled.

> It filled but a minute. But was there ever
>   A time of such quality, since or before,
>   In that hill's story? To one mind never,
>   Though it has been climbed, foot-swift, foot-sore,
>   By thousands more.

There is a curious double perspective here. Donald Davie properly insists on the positive nature of the incident ('a time of such *quality*'). The stress is demanded by the movement of the verse, yet it is modified to some extent by the admission in the following line that the importance is evident 'to *one* mind' – where the 'one' receives a similar, balancing emphasis. And how are we to interpret the first quoted lines:

> What we did as we climbed, and what we talked of
>   Matters not much, *nor to what it led?*

Hardy is, I presume, insisting on the personal nature of the experience. What they did would have no interest to most people, but to the mind that is now experiencing the vision (and creating the poem) the significance of the moment surpasses all others in the hill's long history.

This leads directly to the next verse, which is crucial:

> Primaeval rocks form the road's steep border,
>   And much have they faced there, first and last,
>   Of the transitory in Earth's long order;
>   But what they record in colour and cast
>   Is – that we two passed.

The 'primaeval rocks' are as permanent as anything we can imagine in this world. What they have 'faced' (and, by implication, 'outfaced') is a succession of vegetable, animal, and human forms that are, from the rocks' viewpoint, 'transitory' when compared with themselves. But the primaeval rocks are mindless, and they serve the imagining and discriminating human mind as aids to association. What they preserve for the speaker is a continuing reminder 'that we two passed.' From *his* viewpoint, the significance of the rocks is dependent upon the human drama to which they have been privileged to serve as background. They thus provide that 'beauty of association' which, Hardy tells us, 'is entirely superior to beauty of aspect' (*LTH*, 120).

In the penultimate stanza, the vision has been reduced from two phantom figures to one. The speaker no longer looks back upon his former self. Boterel Hill is part of her landscape, not his; within it he too is 'transitory,' but she 'remains.' Thus, in a paradox that throws light upon the previous stanza, the ghost proves more lasting than the living man. None the less, its status is questionable, as the final lines demonstrate:

> I look and see it there, shrinking, shrinking,
>   I look back at it amid the rain
> For the very last time; for my sand is sinking,
>   And I shall traverse old love's domain
>   Never again.

Whether the ghost is itself 'shrinking' or merely fading from sight as the speaker moves away from the hill is (I presume, deliberately) left unclear. The rain of the present returns, and he sees himself in terms of 'sand' in an emptying hourglass (a transitory mineral indeed compared with the primaeval rocks). He leaves the scene whose supreme meaning he alone can interpret 'for the very last time'; as the vision fades, the ending is negative, though – as so often – a faint positive still lingers. A connection between man and landscape is evident, but it is as frail as the departing speaker.

HARDY AS CAMERA

Although the number of Hardy's indisputably rural poems is comparatively (and surprisingly) small, towards the end of his life he published a series of short, fairly direct poems that, at least on the surface, attempt no more than the exact catching of a transient rural moment. Often they are baldly and impersonally descriptive; as other times an uncharacterized 'I' acts, so it appears, as little more than a camera reproducing the passing scene. Since these poems offer none of the conspicuous complexity of much of his better-known work, they are relatively neglected. As so often with Hardy, dating is a problem. Although they appear in the later volumes (the majority of them in *Human Shows and Far Fantasies* [1925]), there is no absolute proof in most cases that they were not written much earlier, though I consider this unlikely. As they bear certain superficial resemblances to the poetry of the Georgians, it is possible that they were influenced by some of Hardy's younger contemporaries. I intend to discuss them by way of introduction to the poets who made their reputations early in the present century, hereby registering the warning that, when I make comparisons with the work of other poets, the direction of any possible influence cannot always be clearly established.

One of the most hauntingly beautiful of these poems – as well as one of the most subtle – is 'The Fallow Deer at the Lonely House,' which first appeared in *Late Lyrics and Earlier*. It is short enough to quote in full:

One without looks in to-night
   Through the curtain-chink
From the sheet of glistening white;
One without looks in to-night
   As we sit and think
   By the fender-brink.

We do not discern those eyes
   Watching in the snow;
Lit by lamps of rosy dyes
We do not discern those eyes
   Wondering, aglow,
   Four-footed, tiptoe.

It would be easy to underestimate the delicate skill and control requisite for the successful communication of such apparent simplicity. We would do well to remember that these are the products of the poet of 'Afterwards,' the 'man who used to notice such things.' Much depends on the quality of the noticing, but even more on the economical and exact presentation. The subject of this poem would have attracted Robert Frost – indeed, it can profitably be compared with 'Two Look at Two' (discussed below, pp. 129–31) – but the lyrical, non-conversational manner converts it into a poem that could never be mistaken for one of Frost's. The resemblance lies in the deliberate separation of human and animal. The glistening white world of the deer impinges upon but can never blend with the artificial world of 'rosy dyes.' Yet the poet, who cannot even see the deer watching him, has been able, through the exquisite precision of the language (not the kind of phrase we expect to use of Hardy, but deserved and even demanded here) to catch in the last four words the timid stance of the graceful animal as it remains poised, watching but always ready to leap off into the darkness. The words 'watching' and 'wondering' applied to the deer are not examples of pathetic fallacy; they are the equivalent of the human 'sit and think.' Moreover, they are qualities shared by the poet, who watches though he does not discern, and whose poem is itself proof of his capacity to 'wonder.' The more we consider this pellucid and ostensibly simple poem, the more complex and admirable it appears.

   'A Bird-Scene at a Rural Dwelling' is less perfect but perhaps more representative. It recounts the gradual rising of the inhabitants of a rustic cottage in the early morning by reference to the complementary retreat of song-birds from window-ledge and door-step to codlin-tree. The poet is impressed not so much by the scene itself as by its significance as a daily ritual extending back into history:

I know a domicile of brown and green,
Where for a hundred summers there have been
Just such enactments, just such daybreaks seen.

This is an observation that would not seem out of place in a poem by Edward Thomas. Evocative of the world of 'Clare and Cowper, Morland and Crome,'[22] it represents the kind of inconspicuous, unostentatious, generally unnoticed, humble scene that, once recorded, becomes emblematic of the essential England that Hardy loved and Thomas died for.

More ambitious, and considerably more assured, is 'Life and Death at Sunrise,' the first of a remarkable cluster of accomplished poems deliberately placed together in *Human Shows*. I lay particular stress upon this one because of the (for Hardy) original use of language and emphasis that is entailed. Here is the first stanza:

The hills uncap their tops
Of woodland, pasture, copse,
And look on the layers of mist
At their foot that still persist:
They are like awakened sleepers on one elbow lifted
Who gaze around to learn if things during night have shifted.

There is a crisp, jaunty quality about the verse, and again the name of Robert Frost suggests itself. This time, however, it is because the staccato, conversational rhythms of the first four lines obey the requirements of the young poet's 'sound of sense' principle, while the chirpy ominousness of 'to learn if things during night have shifted' has a decidedly 'North of Boston' flavour. Once again I must insist that I am not arguing in terms of direct influence, one way or the other. I am merely demonstrating the variety of tone and approach possible when writing about the natural world, and noticing in this instance how Hardy, venturing outside his own more characteristic style and method, may be found approaching the more habitual manner of another poet.

The poem has a deceptively simple structure. A rural workman meets a man with a waggon on a deserted road, and they pause to exchange news. The pedestrian announces a birth, the waggoner a death. The conversation is brief, succinct, apparently inconsequential. The pedestrian's

'She's doing well. And we think to call him "Jack"'

is balanced by the waggoner's

'He was ninety-odd. He could call up the French Revolution.'

The poet-as-maker seems distant here, yet in fact he has so controlled and shaped the elements that make up the poem that all sorts of meanings, unsuspected by the countrymen, begin to emerge. Their brief meeting on the road represents Hardy's homespun but by no means unsubtle version of the still point of the turning world. The night dies, the day is born; an old man dies, a child is born. A representative of the past and representative of the future are poised together for a fleeting moment that is itself dignified, or at least dignifiable, within the poem as an eternal now. The humanized natural features of the first stanza gaze down upon a human continuity that, like the 'maid and her wight' in 'In Time of "the Breaking of Nations"'' or the two lovers in 'At Castle Boterel,' is more impressive – perhaps, even more enduring – than themselves. The concluding reference to the French Revolution not only indicates the awe-inspiring timespan of a single life that stretches back into history but with the last word suggests analogies with the revolving seasons and constellations. A simple rustic meaning is set, through the distinct but unostentatious craft of the poet, into an extending historical and even cosmic contest.

By contrast, 'I Watched a Blackbird' records no more than the single action of a nest-building bird, yet even this apparently trivial observation is seen to have wider implications. Again the poem is short enough to quote in full:

> I watched a blackbird on a budding sycamore
> One Easter Day, when sap was stirring twigs to the core;
>   I saw his tongue, and crocus-coloured bill
>   Parting and closing as he turned his trill;
>   Then he flew down, seized on a stem of hay,
> And upped to where his building scheme was under way,
> As if so sure a nest were never shaped on spray.

J.G. Southworth wrote of this poem, 'the quality of observation … is that of a trained naturalist,'[23] but such a remark, appropriate enough for one of Clare's simpler bird-poems, is hardly to the point here. What is important is the capacity of the skilled poet to raise a natural observation to the level of significant art. The poem is based on a recorded incident that, unlikely as it may seem, actually took place on Easter Sunday in 1900.[24] Hardy has, indeed, created the poem out of this 'coincidence.' 'Budding,' 'stirring,' and 'sure' all strengthen the direct allusion to the day of resurrection. Even 'building scheme,' with its bold shift of language-levels that succeeds through its sheer audacity, suggests constructive growth.

Indeed, the poem can legitimately be read as a companion piece to 'The Darkling Thrush,' written, however, in a very different key. (It is interesting, though perhaps coincidental, that both poems take their inspiration from events in the same year [1900], though it is unlikely that 'I Watched a Blackbird' was written so early.) A comparison between the two poems is peculiarly instructive, since similar natural observations result in poems that are tonally related but distinct, the qualified optimism of the present poem (with the shadowy doubt implied in 'As if so sure a nest were never shaped on spray') contrasting with the unexpected challenge to a basic pessimism in 'The Darkling Thrush.' The two poems together provide an excellent example of conflicting attitudes out of which Hardy was capable of writing equally effective and convincing poems, justifying his insistence that he possessed not a fixed and unchangeable view of life but (as he notes in the 'Apology' to *Late Lyrics and Earlier*) 'a series of fugitive impressions that I have never tried to co-ordinate' (*CPH*, 558).

In the well-known 'Afterwards,' Hardy wrote an epitaph for himself in his capacity as camera-like nature poet. An impressive achievement, the poem is often, I believe, appreciated for the wrong reasons. One frequently sees it cited as an example of 'the simple Hardy,' yet this simplicity is a sophisticated creation on Hardy's part. 'He wrote the poem,' J.O. Bailey asserts, 'to tell his neighbors how he wished them to remember him,'[25] but one doesn't write poetry for one's neighbours; Hardy is writing, as always, for readers wherever they may be, carefully constructing a definitive version of one prominent aspect of his personality. Bailey is right to point out that 'it says nothing of literary fame.' This is Hardy the countryman, the villager, not the established man of letters, and certainly not the Victorian sage. We are offered once again a portrait of the shadowy, observing, wraithlike figure that J. Hillis Miller has urged us to recognize as the implied author of the novels and especially of the poems.

'Afterwards' is a meditation on the circumstances of his own death, which manages to be whimsically realistic without ever becoming sardonic.

> When the Present has latched its postern behind my tremulous stay,
>   And the May month flaps its glad green leaves like wings ...

The first line is Hardy's rendition of Barnes's 'geäte a-vallèn to,' and if the tone suggests an elegy in a country churchyard, the second line (note the 'glad') makes it clear that he has no illusions about nature's response. Versed in country things, he knows that they will continue as before, unnoticing and undisturbed, yet this is one of the reasons why he loves them. The essential separation between man and nature, observer and observed, remains ('He strove that such innocent creatures should come to no harm, / But he could do little for them'). But what of the neighbours, his fellow-men? Each stanza takes the form either of a question or of a queried possibility. The axiomatic form of the refrain-lines shouldn't prevent us from noticing the manner in which they are introduced: 'will the neighbours say?', 'One may say,' 'will any say?' Hardy claims to be uncertain of their reaction, so he takes the precaution of writing his own epitaph. Characteristically, it is as much about the natural world he loved as about himself, and his love is expressed in that precise but oblique and idiosyncratic diction that he made his own.

> If I pass during some nocturnal blackness, mothy and warm,
>   When the hedgehog travels furtively over the lawn ...

He skirts but avoids the euphemistic clichés like 'pass on' or 'pass away'; he knows that he will pass from life as he passed through it, quietly, inconspicuously. 'Nocturnal blackness' sounds typical enough, but with 'mothy and warm,' in Ezra Pound's phrase, he makes it new. 'Mothy' is not a neologism, but Hardy commandeers it to evoke both the sight and feel of moths on summer nights, while the unexpectedness of 'warm' (Hardy's night-scenes are generally wintry) conveys a still and oppressive airlessness with magnificent economy. And only Hardy would think of applying the word 'furtively' to a hedgehog, though once he has done so we recognize it as indisputably right. We come to realize at this point that Hardy is demonstrating as well as asserting his method. The 'dewfall-hawk,' for example, almost as concise as Gerard Manley Hopkins' 'Fresh-firecoal chestnut-falls' in 'Pied Beauty,' is the result not merely of observation (noticing), but of a personal way of looking – a poet's way of looking. 'He was a man who used to notice such things' thus becomes much more than a casual remark about an eccentric who took an interest in natural details that others ignored. Under the guise of ironic self-deprecation, Hardy has in fact paid himself a rich and thoroughly deserved compliment. 'Afterwards' is thus a fitting epitaph not only on the countryman but on the poet.

HARDY AS PIVOT

Hardy emerges as a pivotal figure in the particular 'line' of poetry that I am considering in this book, and it is altogether fitting that this should be so. Chronologically he overlapped all the poets I am concerned with, and there is a sense in which he also overlapped their diverse creative preoccupations. But in terms of art an unusually long writing life can have its attendant disadvantages; the case of Wordsworth, physically surviving the death of his poetic genius, inevitably presents itself as a ghost from the past. Always sensitive to satires of circumstance, Hardy himself remarked, in his introductory 'Apology' to *Late Lyrics and Earlier* in 1922, on 'the launching of a volume of this kind in neo-Georgian days by one who began writing in mid-Victorian' (*CPH*, 556). To the modern reader, for whom the poetic revolution of the 1920s is a matter of established history, the oddity of Hardy's survival as a practising poet is even more pronounced. That poems like 'A Man Was Drawing Near to Me,' 'Voices from Things Growing in a Churchyard,' 'Last Words to a Dumb Friend' and 'Weathers' should first appear in volume form in the same year as Eliot's *The Waste Land*, Joyce's *Ulysses*, and Lawrence's *Aaron's Rod* seems grotesquely incongruous; even Hardy's admission in the last poem in the collection that he is an ancient speaking to ancients scarcely qualifies (at least in the minds of the less tolerant) as an excuse. Yet in *Thomas Hardy and British Poetry* – and the surprising thing is that this *doesn't* come as a surprise – Donald Davie has not only offered Hardy as the most telling influence on modern British poetry, but has presented very cogent arguments to justify his claim.

That Hardy, in Shelleyan phrase, 'look[s] before and after' is not, of course, a new discovery; we are all used to the tidy syllabus-division, 'nineteenth-century novelist, twentieth-century poet,' but it is important to insist that the two major aspects of his work cannot be separated so easily. For over half a century Hardy was a well-known man of letters, and the writing of his poetry (as distinct from its publication) covers the same broad timespan. The man who grew up and began writing in the world of Tennyson, Browning, George Eliot, and John Stuart Mill lived on and continued publishing in the world of T.S. Eliot, Pound, Joyce, and Lawrence. Not that he ever really belonged to this latter world; rather, he haunted it like one of the troubled personae in his more characteristic poems. He was a persisting but never dominating figure, not so much an influence as a continual presence; and he wrote what he called 'poems of the past and the present' (the specific volume-title applies equally to all his collections of verse) that, with a curious and rather disturbing delayed action, had a palpable effect on the poetry of what was for him the future. It is an odd record for one who appeared (and in many respects was) outside the mainstream. Yet, assenting to that, we immediately recall Matthew Arnold's classic Victorian dilemma,

> Wandering between two worlds, one dead,
> The other powerless to be born –

a state which fits Hardy's case exactly. In that sense he is central, and his poems embody the strength of that centrality.

When we consider Hardy as a poet of the natural world, the same Janus-like quality is evident. He obviously belongs (a part of him, at least) within the sanctioned tradition yet, as we have seen, surprisingly few of his poems fit easily into the category of rural poetry; moreover, their tone and attributes are essentially different from those of his predecessors. Although his literary debt to Wordsworth is considerable, it certainly doesn't manifest itself in poems celebrative of natural joy or addressed lovingly to daisies and small celandines.

As Joseph Warren Beach remarked, Hardy 'heralds the disappearance in English poetry of nature with a capital N.'[26] Yet the old beliefs are abandoned not with a brash revolutionary fervour but with reluctance and genuine regret. And the sentiments that accompany the beliefs obstinately, doggedly persist. Thus Hardy embraces agnosticism but remains 'churchy.' His rationalistic mind cannot entertain the superstition that oxen kneel in their stalls on Christmas Eve, yet he is prepared (or, to be more circumspect, he creates a persona who is prepared) to go in the gloom 'hoping it might be so' ('The Oxen'). Here Hardy can communicate the attitudes of a native, but he remains apart. Unmistakably if reluctantly he has outgrown a 'popular-Wordsworthian' sense of the beneficence of 'Outer Nature,' but he longs for 'a moment / Of that old endowment' in which the world seemed created by Love and designed for human pleasure ('To Outer Nature'). Preferring to abide in 'these ancient lands,' he shrinks from seeking 'a modern coast / Whose riper times have yet to be' ('On an Invitation to the United States'), and although the specific reference within the poem sets up England against the United States, it is surely not illegitimate to see the separation in historical as well as geographical terms – nineteenth century against twentieth, provincial rustic past against cosmopolitan urban present. At all events, both the burden and the example of the past weigh heavily upon him ('We two kept house, the Past and I' ['The Ghost of the Past']), and his emphasis upon the earlier traditions of both poetry and the countryside associate him intimately with the earlier rural poets. On the other hand, his characteristic poetic persona, throbbing painfully with the ache of modernism, is no unfamiliar figure in our troubled century.

SIX

Robert Frost

FROST AND WORDSWORTH

To avoid possible misunderstanding, I should state immediately that the presence of Robert Frost in this book implies no attempt to detach him from his American heritage and smuggle him into an English tradition. Frost is of course firmly rooted in the United States in general and New England in particular; he belongs (in so far as he can be placed at all) with such American figures as Bryant, Emerson, Thoreau, E.A. Robinson, and even, though Frost himself might protest here, Carl Sandburg. Frost was understandably touchy on this subject, and insisted that his poetry 'was American to the core, and didn't belong to England.'[1] The English critic Edward Garnett expressed similar sentiments more astutely when he characterized Frost in 1915 as 'a genuine New England voice, whatever be its literary debt to old-world English ancestry.'[2] The qualifying last clause is fair. It is not wholly coincidental that Frost's poetic reputation was first made with the publication, in England, of *A Boy's Will* and *North of Boston*; besides, he not only learned (as he has frankly acknowledged) from the poetic examples of Wordsworth and Hardy, but left his mark on the indisputably English tradition by his encouragement of Edward Thomas. To overstress Frost's English inheritance would be foolish; to neglect it would be provincial. Moreover, Frost's English interlude (from 1912 to 1915) gave him the necessary detachment by which he could define his 'Americanness.' As he observed himself, 'I never saw *New* England so clearly as when I was in Old England.'[3]

But there is another, more substantial reason why Frost should not be omitted here in the interests of what would prove to be a narrowly insular convenience. Because the influence of Wordsworth upon subsequent rural poetry has been so pervasive, it is only too easy to exaggerate and 'read in' Wordsworthian elements where they are not present. Although Frost's poetry needs, like Hardy's, to be seen in relation to Wordsworth's, it is most decidedly not dependent upon it. Indeed, much of Frost's strength derives from his not being overwhelmed by 'the Wordsworthian shadow,' though I shall argue that, in producing a body of work in which the angle of viewpoint is continually shifting, Frost was, consciously or unconsciously, working out his own inimitable version of a Wordsworthian pattern. Frost's poetry could only exist within the American grain, and this enables him to learn from Wordsworth without echoing him. Twentieth-century poetry is richer as a result.

From the first, Frost laid emphasis on his mastery of diction and rhythm. Writing to John T. Bartlett between the publication of *A Boy's Will* (1913) and *North of Boston* (1914), he claims to have conscientiously set himself 'to make music out of what I may call the sound of sense' (*FSL*, 79). Six months later, he made a similar comment to the same correspondent: 'In "North of Boston" you are to see me performing in a language absolutely unliterary. What I would like is to get so I would never use a word or combination of words that I hadn't *heard* used in running speech' (*FSL*, 102). He emphasizes the conversational, colloquial, and vernacular nature of his poetic language, and distinguishes between 'the hearing imagination' and 'the seeing imagination,' stressing the first (though not, of course, to the exclusion of the second).

In an interview with C. Day Lewis in 1957, he recalled that even in his early poems, before he had worked out the 'sound of sense' principle, he was sensitive to poetic archaism: 'You may see in some poems some lingering words like "fain" and "list" that I was getting rid of, that I was ashamed of to begin with ... I don't remember thinking much about style except that I was ashamed of "thee" and "thou" and "thine" and such things as that.'[4] Even more important, however, was the rhythm. He would often describe his poems as 'talk-songs'[5] in an effort to stress the conversational lilt of his lines; similarly, he insisted on 'saying' his poems rather than 'reading' them. He refused to accept a distinction between the ordinary and the poetic, whether in subject-matter ('all life is a subject for poetic treatment' [*IRF*, 14]) or in language. A remark to an interviewer in 1918 is typical: 'Poetic diction is all wrong. Words must be the ordinary words which we hear about us ... to which the imagination must give an iridescence' (*IRF*, 25–6).

That last remark should produce within us a shock of recognition: 'gaudiness and inane phraseology,' 'the real language of men,' 'a certain colouring of imagination.' While it would be naive to suggest that Frost is advocating in 1918 what Wordsworth had advocated in 1800 – literary history does not recur as neatly as that – none the less a similar linguistic effort was required. Once again vocabulary had been elevated into 'poetic diction'; once again the written language had become separated from the spoken language. Frost claims, indeed, to have been even more radical than Wordsworth in his practice. Of the poems to appear in *North of Boston* he wrote that he had 'dropped to an everyday level of diction that even Wordsworth kept above' (*FSL*, 83–4). The assertion is valuable in itself but of particular interest since it establishes beyond the possibility of controversy that Frost was aware of the Wordsworthian connection (cf. also *IRF*, 7). By deliberately following Wordsworth's example, by turning back in order to strengthen the poetry of his own time with a much needed infusion of vernacular speech and colloquial rhythms, Frost was exemplifying what he called, with characteristic impishness, the 'old-fashioned way to be new.'[6]

Although the pleasant, rambling talk he gave at Cornell University in 1950 to mark the centenary of Wordsworth's death[7] reveals little about Frost's personal debt to Wordsworth, the way in which Wordsworth's name crops up in approving contexts throughout his life bears witness to a continuing familiarity. It is clear, though, that Frost learns from Wordsworth's poetry rather than from his 'philosophy.' Indeed it is noticeable in a reading of Frost criticism that the commentators who minimize any Wordsworthian influence are almost invariably those primarily concerned with subject-matter and ideas. But, as his fellow-poet C. Day Lewis sensibly pointed out, 'Frost's most remarkable affinity with Wordsworth lies in the temper (or tempo or temperature) of his verse' (*RRF*, 299), and as early as 1914, in his review of *North of Boston*, Edward Thomas (as was his wont) had gone straight to the point by declaring that the book 'marks more than the beginning of an experiment like Wordsworth's' because Frost knows the life about which he writes more intimately and 'sympathizes where Wordsworth contemplates' (*RRF*, 29).

Only rarely do we encounter a poem which seems Wordsworthian in attitude. 'The Tuft of Flowers' is an example, an early poem in which the narrator attains an insight into mankind by way of nature (the 'bewildered butterfly' and the tuft of flowers itself). More often, however, in poems like 'The Most of It' and 'Desert Places,' the tone is more sombre, closer to Hardy, and George W. Nitchie has described 'A Boundless Moment,' in which a vision of spring proves illusory, as 'a half-serious parody' of the Wordsworthian position,[8] a remark recalling the technique of Wordsworthian undercutting which I demonstrated in Hardy's work. But we are constantly reminded of Wordsworth while reading Frost. Thus 'We love the things we love for what they are'[9] is unmistakably Frostian in accent but no less Wordsworthian in sentiment. Sometimes the resemblance is structural. Thus 'The Black Cottage' demands comparison with 'The Ruined Cottage,' and this comparison extends to the two spokesmen (the minister and the reporting 'I') and the way in which the dead woman is set so strongly before us although neither reader nor first-person narrator sees her directly. Occasionally, a connection suggests itself in most unlikely contexts; 'Brown's Descent,' for example, could hardly be more Yankee in character, yet it is not far removed from the grotesque effects in some of the *Lyrical Ballads*. And more generally, *North of Boston*, like so much early Wordsworth, is full of countrymen, some happy and fulfilled, some unhappy and lonely, who play out their humble and often poverty-stricken and monotonous lives against a background of natural beauty.

None the less, the contrasts tend to prove at least as significant as the comparisons. Frost is never as aloof as Wordsworth, and as John F. Lynen has pointed out, 'Frost is anecdotal where Wordsworth tends to be didactic.'[10] Although there is much to be learned from Frost's wisdom, and although many poems (particularly his later ones) proffer advice and are often assertive in tone, there is always a saving humour and familiarity in Frost. When in 'To a Thinker' he prods us to 'trust my instinct – I'm a bard,' we sense a mischievous glint in the eye which would be unthinkable in Wordsworth, who took his bardic role more solemnly – though not, perhaps, more seriously. Resemblances between the two poets certainly exist, but they are most worth discussing in order to show that, while he was prepared to learn from Wordsworth, Frost drew up his own personal declaration of independence. Indeed, the danger with some of Frost's poems ('The Mountain' is a good example) lies in the fact that we are likely to expect a Wordsworthian revelation and, when it doesn't come, may miss Frost's own unique effect. Like all other poets worth discussing, Frost must ultimately be appreciated on his own terms.

But the 'sound of sense' was by no means the only technical principle that occupied Frost during his poetic apprenticeship. His constant concern for the dramatic perspective may be considered equally important. For Frost this was not just a matter of aesthetic theory, though he made numerous pronouncements on the subject. 'Lyrics ought to be dramatic,' he told Sidney Cox,[11] and in the preface to *A Way Out* (1929) he wrote: 'Everything written is as good as it is dramatic. It need not declare itself in form, but it is drama or nothing' (*FSP*, 13).[12] The corollary to this is that the poet takes up a deliberate point of view from which to present his material and in so doing becomes a dramatic character within the work of art that he creates. For Lynen, this point of view is the perspective of pastoral; the poet 'casts himself in the role of the country dweller and writes about life in terms of the contrast between the rural world, with its rustic scenery and naive, humble folk, and the great outer world of the powerful, the wealthy, and the sophisticated.'[13] This formulation is valuable for all the poets I am considering here, though the extent to which they embrace its technical principles varies considerably. Wordsworth seems at times to have rediscovered the pastoral mode without ever quite mastering its complexities,

although it may be doubted if he could have fully subdued his extreme indi-
vidualism to its demanding discipline; Barnes is a pure if simple example of the
pastoral poet in Lynen's sense; Hardy employs pastoral techniques fitfully, but
his personae are in his own phrase 'so various' that the sense of a conscious and
sustained pastoral attitude is lacking. What makes Frost unique among nature
poets is the dramatic role-playing which is not confined to his poetry but was a
prominent feature of his life.

This distinction is of some importance. Barnes appropriated the persona of a
Dorset countryman when he wrote his dialect verse. This was the traditional
method of pastoral, and the impersonation was always temporary. Frost, by
contrast, rarely if ever discarded his mask. His life, we might say, was a
continual performance – on reading-platforms, in classrooms, at interviews –
and the persona that he projected was, one feels, deliberately constructed both
to fit and to further the cause of his poetry. I have referred to Frost's mask, but it
would be more accurate, in fact, to speak of his masks. Of these, the most
obvious, the most important, and the most suitable for his poetic purposes was
that of the New England farmer. The speaker in his long poem 'New Hampshire' remarks, 'I choose to be a plain New England farmer' (l. 408), and we
overlook the main verb at our peril. The farmer persona is a deliberate choice for
the purposes of this particular poem, and many others are written from the
same viewpoint, but Frost was technically a native of California, and although
he once claimed, 'I grew up on a farm and I like it quiet,'[14] the statement fails to
stand up under strict biographical scrutiny. It is a description not of the life but
of the role. Frost was never a farmer in the 'professional' sense; his own farm
was 'a place apart,' a retreat and a studio – a small-holding rather than a
productive agricultural enterprise. But it also provided him with the basis for a
convenient poetic myth.

Frost had a number of other, interlocking dramatic roles that could be
emphasized or underplayed according to the immediate circumstances; of these
the most notable are the rustic philosopher (who sometimes employs the rustic
stance in the tradition of pastoral to offer universal wisdom), the teacher (who
alternates with a sort of anti-teacher, the subject of another series of anecdotes)
and the sage-poet (who, paradoxically, offers at the same time the common-
sense attitudes of the ordinary man). The protean quality so characteristic of
Frost the man is constantly overflowing into his poetry. He is at one and the
same time intensely 'human' yet also detached, elusive, impossible to pin down.
Hence the seemingly unending stream of memoirs by people who knew him
that aim to present the 'real' Robert Frost but only succeed in adding one more
layer to the evolving myth.

The role-playing in life connects with the poetry because the dramatic quality
in the verse so often involves a first-person singular. Moreover, because Frost's

idiom was so recognizable and so obviously his own, and because his public readings inevitably associated his voice with his poetry, it was tempting to go on to make the unwarranted assumption that the 'I' of the poem was equatable with the poet on the platform. The same point has been made with regard to the earlier rural poets, but it is crucial here because, with the development of modern technology, these readings are now preserved and universally available on long-playing records. While we have to rely on such contemporary descriptions as Hazlitt's to learn how Wordsworth read his own poetry, we can actually hear Frost, and so distinctive is his rich, gravelly New England intonation that, once heard, it is difficult not to read all his poems with the same accent and so hear a personal and continuing voice instead of a series of distinguishable dramatic speakers.

It is important to guard against this tendency and equally important to avoid underestimating the seriousness and (without implying anything pompous) the profundity of Frost's work. The role-playing is his individual response to the problem of being a poet in a generally unpoetic world; it implies no lack of sincerity. Because Frost blends humour with his insights, it does not follow that what he has to say is any less valid than the offerings of more severe or ostentatiously intellectual writers. Certainly, he had no more of a fixed and considered 'philosophy' than Wordsworth or Hardy, and the charges that have sometimes been laid against him – Yvor Winters' 'poet as spiritual drifter,' for example – amount to no more than a hostile expression of this fact. Frost's so-called 'drifting' is better seen as a flexible, multi-faceted view of a complicated world, and his decision to present his impressions of this world puckishly and whimsically as well as seriously and sardonically may even be recognized as evidence of maturity. As he writes in a late epigram:

> It takes all sorts of in- and outdoor schooling
> To get adapted to my kind of fooling.

Despite the fact that, on first publication, this couplet appeared under the generalizing title, 'The Poet,' it is a perfect illustration of his own method; indeed, Frost's whole response to art and communication is contained potentially within the rhyme: instruction becomes pleasurable, fooling becomes wise. Seemingly simple poems require both knowledge and effort on the part of the reader if their full meaning is to be revealed. In the present context, the 'outdoor schooling' lays the major claim to our attention.

VARIETIES OF NATURE POEM

Frost sometimes denied that he was a nature poet for the rather simplistic reason that 'all but a very few [of his poems] have a person in them.'[15] More helpful are the following remarks made during an interview in 1921: 'We have had so much [nature poetry] during the last century that there is almost a revulsion against it at the present time ... There must be a human foreground to supplement the background of nature ... We have had nature poetry for a hundred years. Now we must have the human foreground with it' (*IRF*, 34–5). As the early chapters of this study will, I hope, have demonstrated, Frost here neglects the unquestionable human element that has been an essential ingredient of the nature poetry of his distinguished predecessors. None the less, Frost certainly accentuated the human foreground in his own work, and he did so, as we have seen, by emphasizing the human voice. Indeed, so strong is the voice behind Frost's verse that even his purest nature poem has an incorrigibly human dimension.

'Spring Pools,' which Frost liked to quote as an example of the presentation of nature without man, is of special interest since, despite its superficially deceptive 'natural' subject, it is humanized not only by the speaking voice but by the human metaphors that express its meaning. While the snow melts naturally enough into water, the water 'shivers' in the cold and the trees are soon to 'blot' it out, 'drink' it up and 'sweep' it away. Moreover, the trees are exhorted to think:

> Let them think twice before they use their powers
> To blot out and drink up and sweep away
> These flowery waters and these watery flowers
> From snow that melted only yesterday.

This seems curious advice since, if they *were* to think twice and act upon their thought, the whole natural process would come to an end. Clearly a human perspective exists within the poem but, compared with most of Frost's poetry, it is extraordinarily aloof – and aloof, we might add, not so much in a Wordsworthian as in a Lucretian sense.

At the same time, the poem is typical of Frost in isolating a limited number of images from the external world and combining them within the verse in such a way that they come to communicate the essence of a place, a season or an experience. Here as elsewhere in his poetry one hesitates to call the process symbolic. 'These flowery waters and these watery flowers' represent a concentrated perception too close to what Hopkins called inscape to be usefully defined by the catch-all term into which 'symbol' has now degenerated. We can, perhaps, penetrate a little further by observing that the process resembles, on a larger scale, that rhetorical device known as synecdoche in which a part is invoked to stand for the whole. Here 'spring pools' typify the Spring itself, and their transitory existence is an 'embodiment' (to use the striking word that Frost employs in 'The Most of It') of the fragile brevity that constitutes so much of the attraction of the spring season. And in noting this we come to realize that the exhortation to the trees, though both impossible and quixotic, is faithful to the mood that the poem conveys, a mood itself as fleeting as the season it celebrates.

Much the same can be said of 'The Oven Bird,' which offers the essence of late midsummer in fourteen lines. The bird concentrates into its song all the thoughts and emotions that belong to its season. The choice of this particular bird (which readers outside North America may need to be told is a species of wood-warbler with the appearance of a small thrush) is especially appropriate not only because its call is familiar and penetrating but also, as Reuben A. Brower was, I think, the first literary critic to point out, because the human translation of this call, 'teacher, teacher, teacher,' underlines a possible didactic function.[16] It is typical of Frost that he should play upon the ornithological fact without actually mentioning it in his poem. Indeed, the poem can be seen as Frost's somewhat whimsical but artistically serious way of tackling the problem of the didactic in rural poetry. How can a bird like the oven bird 'teach' us? Simply, so it would seem, by being itself. What its song 'says' is what we feel when we hear it: that 'early petal fall is past,' that 'the highway dust is over all.' It catches that poised moment between high summer and the coming of 'that other fall we name the fall' as exquisitely as Keats's 'To Autumn' catches the moment between fruition and the beginning of decay. But the teacher-bird asks one question for which neither he nor the poet has an answer:

> The question that he frames in all but words
> Is what to make of a diminished thing.

Without turning Frost's poem into naive allegory, it is reasonable, I think, to assume that, through the bird, the poet is referring not merely to a diminished season but to a diminished natural world. The tone of melancholy admirably evoked within the poem extends beyond the immediate 'simple' subject.

If we turn now to 'The Wood-Pile,' we encounter a very different kind of nature poem. Here, true to his principle of introducing a 'human foreground,' Frost presents a confrontation between man and the natural world that, as several commentators have suggested, at first sight bears notable resemblance to a Wordsworthian 'spot of time.' The first-person speaker 'out walking in the frozen swamp one gray day' on a sudden impulse follows a frightened bird and comes by chance upon a neglected wood-pile ('four by four by eight' – which must surely echo the notorious measurements of the pond in the original text of Wordsworth's 'The Thorn'). It is hardly a remarkable occurrence, but the speaker is impelled to ponder its origin and attempt to extract a meaning:

> I thought that only
> Someone who lived in turning to fresh tasks

Could so forget his handiwork on which
He spent himself, the labor of his ax,
And leave it there far from a useful fireplace
To warm the frozen swamp as best it could
With the slow smokeless burning of decay.

Here the poem ends, and if we approach it with too many Wordsworthian assumptions we shall be surprised and unsatisfied. Wordsworth, it is fair to speculate, would have observed, as in 'Michael,'

> And to that simple object appertains
> A story, –   (ll. 18–19)

and would then have proceeded to tell it. But Frost's story has already been told, and for all its Wordsworthian similarities, we shall not penetrate to its core unless we recognize in it the qualities that make it uniquely Frost's.

Its tone immediately distinguishes the poem from Wordsworth. The hesitant, irregular first line not only reflects the indecisive speaker ('I will turn back from here. / No, I will go on farther') but sets up a familiar connection between him and the reader. Instead of being impressed, even overwhelmed, by Wordsworth's confident didacticism, we find ourselves sympathetic to a man who appears as aimless as ourselves. (This, incidentally, is a characteristically 'modern' response, and provides a good example of the way in which Frost, despite his preference for traditional poetic forms, reflects the early twentieth-century consciousness at least as firmly as his more obviously 'up-to-date' contemporaries.) The speaker who cannot 'say for certain I was here / Or somewhere else: I was just far from home,' is sufficiently identified by his speech-rhythms to be accepted as an individual, but left essentially uncharacterized so that we can recognize in him a part of ourselves. Against him is the apparent hostility of the natural environment, 'frozen' and 'gray' and potentially treacherous since a foot occasionally goes through the surface of the snow. The small bird flies before him, recognizing in him a probable enemy, and this seems to point up the essential separation of man and nature. But, and the paradox is important, the bird is the means by which the speaker arrives, apparently by chance, at the wood-pile. (It is worth noting that this is a repeated Frostian device: the 'bewildered butterfly' leads the man to the experience in 'The Tuft of Flowers,' while the sought-for flower is discovered in 'The Quest of the Purple-Fringed' by following the path of the fox.)

In this case the speaker follows the bird and finds the abandoned wood-pile. Like the spared tuft of flowers it seems a message from man rather than nature, but once again we must beware of over-simplification:

What held it, though, on one side was a tree
Still growing, and on one a stake and prop,
These latter about to fall.

The man-made props will collapse before the growing tree. And the wood itself
is an example of what nature can provide for man's use. Yet the man who could
cut it and so make it available for use was the same man who could leave it and let
it go to waste. The haunting final line, 'With the slow smokeless burning of
decay,' paradoxically links man and nature in one sense by equating human
wastefulness with natural decomposition. At the same time, Lynen is justified
in describing the wood-pile as 'the symbol of man's creativity.'[17] Against the
line, 'Someone who lived in turning to fresh tasks,' Frost wrote in Elizabeth
Sergeant's copy, 'What I have most aspired to be,'[18] and in abandoning his
'handiwork ... far from a useful fireplace' the woodcutter has placed the wood-
pile, in David Jones's terminology, in the category of 'the extra-utile and the
gratuitous,'[19] thus converting it into a work of human art. The pile could only
exist through a combination of the abilities of man and nature, and it is tempting
to suggest that, by leaving it in the wood, the woodcutter has sacrificed it as an
offering to nature and to any sympathetic human being (the reader or the
indecisive speaker who is himself, one feels, always 'turning to fresh tasks') who
is able to penetrate its meaning.

HUMAN AND NON-HUMAN

For Frost 'the line where man leaves off and nature starts' ('New Hampshire,'
l. 379) is finely drawn, and the division is marked by the well-known Frostian
imagery of barriers, walls, and zones. But some of his finest poems are set on the
borderline between the two states, and explore what commerce there may be
between the human and the non-human. Two classic confrontations are to be
found in 'The Most of It' and 'Two Look at Two.'
    'The Most of It,' despite its unmistakable North American setting, offers
some interesting points of comparison with Wordsworth's 'There Was a Boy,'
but these have been brilliantly discussed by Brower and Poirier,[20] and I can
therefore leave the connections to emerge naturally while I concentrate on other
matters that have not received the attention they deserve. As in so many of
Frost's poems, the protagonist is an anonymous 'he' whose experience is related
with a mixture of detachment (we know nothing of his life or circumstances) and
empathy (his inner thoughts and aspirations are recorded). He stands at the
edge of a lake which, though he doesn't realize it at the time, marks the
boundary between the world of man and that of nature; it is significant,
however, that both shores are presented in the same terms ('boulder-broken

beach' and 'cliff's talus'). When he calls across the lake, he receives nothing back but a 'mocking echo,' without any sign of 'counter-love, original response,' until one day he is confronted with a response so mysterious and equivocal that it may not even constitute a response at all:

> And nothing ever came of what he cried
> Unless it was the embodiment that crashed
> In the cliff's talus on the other side,
> And then in the far-distant water splashed,
> But after a time allowed for it to swim,
> Instead of proving human when it neared
> And someone else additional to him,
> As a great buck it powerfully appeared,
> Pushing the crumpled water up ahead,
> And landed pouring like a waterfall,
> And stumbled through the rocks with horny tread,
> And forced the underbrush – and that was all.

The poem is triumphantly complete in itself, and any elaboration of its own statement runs the danger of appearing clumsy and inept. All a commentator can do is to indicate some of the ironies and intricacies that he has noticed in the hope that they may prove helpful to others. The ambiguous status of the protagonist is evident from the implication that he half wants to keep 'the universe alone' and half wants company. His yearning for 'someone else additional to him' is answered, but not in the way he hopes. He looks for a human response ('someone') but all he gets is a non-human epiphany (something) and he must make 'the most of it.' The buck certainly teaches him that he *doesn't* keep the universe alone, and perhaps one has to be versed in country things not to believe that it was an answer to his call. The speaker is free, moreover, to interpret it as an answer (to make the most of it, in fact) though he is apparently unable to do so because what he wants, in Nitchie's words, is 'something too explicit, too personal, too unequivocal.'[21] The buck is obviously not human, but instead of accepting him as neutral, the protagonist (and the casual – but only, I think, the casual – reader) seems likely to regard him as hostile and to be rejected. Although the buck crosses the barrier, he does so only to reinforce the fact of the barrier. The barrier, indeed (though this is perhaps interpreting too radically), is part of the price we pay for being human.

'The Most of It' might well have been entitled 'One Looks at One'; in any case, it can usefully be compared with 'Two Look at Two.' The poems share virtually the same theme, but here Frost has introduced, if not 'counter-love,' at least love, which claims (literally) both the first and the last word. A man and a woman are making their way in the fading light up a mountainside that, as so often in Frost, seems to mean more than itself without qualifying as a distinct symbol. Soon they meet the inevitable barrier ('a tumbled wall / With barbed-wire binding') and are rewarded with a borderland-vision – first a doe and later a buck that look at them across the wall. Whereas the tone of 'The Most of It' had been mysterious and threatening, the confrontation in this poem is gentle, almost whimsical. Frost is here prepared to blend the human and animal worlds; the buck is presented with human attributes ('He viewed them quizzically') and articulates his opinion 'as if' with human speech. We hear rather more of the animals' response to the human pair than vice versa; Frost plays, indeed, with the two viewpoints: 'She [the doe] saw them in their field, they her in hers,' 'Two had seen two, whichever side you spoke from.'

But what is the significance of the encounter? Frost's (or, at any rate, the narrator's) statement, after the two animals have finally departed, is richly ambiguous:

> 'This *must* be all.' It was all. Still they stood,
> A great wave from it going over them,
> As if the earth in one unlooked-for favor
> Had made them certain earth returned their love.

This seems to imply a very different relationship between the human and animal worlds from that posited in the previous poem, though Lynen is right to remind us that 'the words "This *must* be all. It was all" echo the grim conclusion of "The Most of It" – "and that was all."'[22] None the less, the theme is transposed into a different key, and we are being offered at least the possibility of rapport. I suggested while discussing 'The Most of It' that a distinction is to be made between the protagonist's reaction and the response that the poet encourages us to feel. Do we have any cause to accept the lovers' certainty here? Brower believes we have: 'The reader goes easily with them and accepts the wonder because in Frost's telling he is exposed to incitements of image and rhythm that mime the spellmaking experience of the lovers.'[23] I am not quite so sure. With Nitchie I set more weight on the doubting connotations of 'as if,' which suggests a deliberately open-ended conclusion (we have already encountered a similar instance in Hardy at the close of 'I Watched a Blackbird' [see p. 113 above]). And we know that Frost was well aware of its possibilities; he closes his introduction to Robinson's *King Jasper* with a serio-comic meditation on the phrase (*FSP*, 67).

The last lines of 'Two Look at Two' are maddeningly indecisive. What does 'return their love' really mean? What relation does it bear to the phrase 'its own love back in copy-speech' in 'The Most of It'? How can earth show that it returns their love just by producing two deer who betray no signs of fear? How can earth return their love in any sense? I ask these questions with no hostile intent. They are not questions that Frost could be expected to answer, but it is part of the experience of the poem that he provokes us into asking them. He has created a situation in which the possible connections between man and nature are finely balanced. While his poems are readily distinguishable from those of Wordsworth and Hardy, Frost approached the challenge of the natural world with a similar flexibility and open-mindedness.

THE HUMAN FOREGROUND

Frost described *A Boy's Will* as 'an expression of my life for the ten years from eighteen on when I thought I greatly preferred stocks and stones to people' (*FSL*, 158). His later work has often been seen as a conscious reaction against this extreme; Elizabeth Sergeant, for example, has described *North of Boston* as 'a book of people, not of nature.'[24] The distinction is not as clear-cut, however, as this would suggest. Again and again in the 'human nature poems,' we find human beings defined and characterized by their responses to the natural world, or using examples from the natural world to illustrate the terms of their own humanity. 'The Mountain' is a convenient example of the first, 'West-Running Brook' of the second.

I must admit to a special reason for selecting 'The Mountain' for extended discussion: it provides an unusually clear instance of a poem that is itself a variation on a Wordsworthian theme and later has variations played upon it by Edward Thomas. The tourist narrator ('When I walked forth at dawn to see new things ...' [l. 8]) is rare in Frost, and his encounter with 'a man who moved so slow, ... / It seemed no harm to stop him altogether' (ll. 16, 18) is structurally reminiscent of 'Resolution and Independence' while being wholly Frostian in language, tone, and treatment. At the same time it looks forward to a poem like Thomas's 'As the Team's Head-Brass,' where the structural parallel is even closer, and although 'The Mountain' is as quintessentially American as Thomas's poem is unmistakably English, there are further resemblances in mood and emotional pitch. The three poems provide a classic instance of the benefits of working within a tradition as opposed to the debilitating effect of abject imitation; in each case the individual poet has been able to derive strength from the example of his predecessor but has also succeeded in setting his own characteristic signature upon the common elements that all three poems share.

No useful purpose is served by discussing 'The Mountain' as if one had to define its subject-matter as either man or nature. The mountain that gives the poem its title is a dominating natural object. It forms the topic of conversation between the narrator and the farmer, and they are differentiated by their reactions to it. In human terms, it is an obstacle, an impediment:

'We were but sixty voters last election.
We can't in nature grow to many more:
That thing takes all the room!'   (ll. 25–7)

It is also, in line with the recurring motif in Frost's imagery, a barrier – a wall separating the human and non-human worlds. The narrator

felt it like a wall
Behind which I was sheltered from a wind.   (ll. 5–6)

Later, the image recurs in what at first seems pure description:

Pasture ran up the side a little way,
And then there was a wall of trees with trunks;
After that only tops of trees, and cliffs
Imperfectly concealed among the leaves.   (ll. 29–32)

To the farmer, however, this 'thing' that stands in the way, that takes up valuable space, also functions as a realm of wonder:

'There's a brook
That starts up on it somewhere – I've heard say
Right on the top, tip-top – a curious thing.
But what would interest you about the brook,
It's always cold in summer, warm in winter.
One of the great sights going is to see
It steam in winter like an ox's breath ...'   (ll. 45–51)

But the farmer himself has never seen it because he has never climbed the mountain. We get the impression, though the point remains unstated, that he deliberately avoids any exploration because he wants the possibilities of the unknown to be kept untested and so inviolate. The miraculous brook or spring or fountain in a landscape which betrays both signs of drought and evidence of the ravages of flood stands 'as a resource, as a recourse' for the imagination (*IRF*, 75), though the farmer is enough of a realist not to stretch his fancy too far:

'I don't suppose the water's changed at all.
You and I know enough to know it's warm
Compared with cold and cold compared with warm.
But all the fun's in how you say a thing.'   (ll. 101–4)

And he moves off with the observation that he had lived in the district ever since the mountain was 'no bigger than a –' (l. 106) but the narrator never hears the end of the sentence. A joke? A Paul Bunyan tall tale? A more serious delusion? Frost never tells us; we must make up our own minds.

This refusal to reveal or even to sum up is characteristic of Frost's dialogue poems. Wordsworth, though the favoured interpretations of his poems are sometimes ambiguous or uncertain ('We Are Seven,' 'The Idiot Boy' and 'The Thorn' provide examples), never leaves us in doubt about their subject-matter. Edward Thomas, by communicating a more limited and consistent tone of contemplative melancholia, can avoid an excessively neat resolution without causing the reader to wonder whether he is approaching a poem in the approved way. But Frost deliberately provokes such a response, especially in *North of Boston*. A poem is offered as an enigma, and the question it raises is not so much: what does it mean? as: what are we to make of it? This does not imply that Frost is less of a teacher than Wordsworth, but rather that he teaches by asking questions and not (at least in his earlier work) by providing answers. The poet insists on an active reader by bringing before him fragmentary incidents, occurring as they might in real life, and inviting him to puzzle out their significance.

'West-Running Brook,' though a more complex poem, need not be discussed in quite such detail here. Like 'The Mountain,' its title derives from a natural object and the speakers, in this case a married couple, come to an enriched understanding of themselves and of what it means to be human by using the brook as a starting-point for a philosophical discussion. The poem recalls Wordsworth in the sense that it fits the Wordsworthian category of 'Poems on the Naming of Places'; the brook's name derives from the human occasion that the poem celebrates – 'West-Running Brook men call it to this day' (l. 3) – but although no one except Frost could have written it, it can hardly be called typical of his work. Lynen has written: '"West-Running Brook" occupies a pivotal position in Frost's development. Though it seems to be set in New England, one senses that the sophisticate has replaced the Yankee speaker, and an interest in ideas the methods of pastoral.'[25] This is true enough, but it can also be argued that Frost is availing himself of a Wordsworthian privilege, and adjusting his viewpoint to the peculiar artistic needs of his subject.

Here two seemingly irreconcilable ways of looking at nature are contained within a single poem by the tolerant understanding fostered by a firmly based human love. The wife's assumption, presented as characteristically feminine, presupposes a natural world that is sympathetically aware of human actions (and even, it seems, of human puns):

> 'Look, look, it's waving to us with a wave
> To let us know it hears me.'   (ll. 16–17)

The husband, better versed in country things, knows that the phenomenon she refers to, a wave flung back upon the current by a sunken rock, is inevitable and automatic, that it has existed 'ever since rivers, I was going to say, / Were made in heaven' (ll. 28–9). But this is no mere juxtaposition of conflicting attitudes. The husband is led to ponder on the backward-turning wave not as an 'original response' from nature (to use the term from 'The Most of It') but as an appropriate analogy that helps to explain the universal process. Life is born out of the 'contrariness' of nature; the impulse towards death and nothingness is checked by 'some strange resistance in itself' (l. 58). While most of the brook runs away to an abyss, the destructive motion initiates a small but all-important creative counter-motion that persists in maintaining life. And the husband concludes, with engaging simplicity: 'It is from this in nature we are from' (l. 71).

Though ostensibly more didactic than the majority of Frost's dialogue poems, 'West-Running Brook' communicates its ultimate wisdom through its artistic structure. The framework is not just a setting for the husband's philosophic speech, nor does his masculine reason invalidate the wife's instinctive response. The wife first observes that the brook in question runs west when all the other brooks flow east, and it is her reference to 'contraries' (l. 7) and the backward-turning wave that provokes his meditation. The final line, 'Today will be the day of what we both said,' points to the essentially collaborative nature of the achieved insight. Although we cannot say that this couple, like the lovers in 'Two Look at Two,' have received an 'unlooked-for favor' making them certain that 'earth returned their love,' a natural object has none the less been an influence. A correspondence has been established between their own love and the process out of which life springs. Their love is felt as deep, enduring, and 'natural.' If 'he' and 'she' represent 'the human foreground' they are well aware of their ties (the marriage image is employed [ll. 12–13]) with the natural 'background.' The west-running brook is not one of Frost's impassable barriers; on the contrary (and this is, we remember, a poem about contraries), it can be bridged. But, as the wife is astute enough to realize, the bridge must be built by human endeavour, and upheld by human love and human understanding.

VARIETIES OF 'I'

Now that we have explored Frost's presentation of the natural world in a selection of very different poems, we are in a better position to consider the poet's relation to his material. Appropriately enough, we have encountered some poems in which no narrator is specified, and others in which the centre of attention has been 'I,' 'he,' 'they,' and even 'we.' Frost has always been conscious of the artistic possibilities of such variation, and one reason for the narrative variety clearly lies in the poet's reluctance to be identified too closely with the speaker of his poems. Frost discussed the matter with Louis Mertins while talking about the explanatory prose-notes that appeared in the first edition of *A Boy's Will*. He is recorded as saying: 'I rewrote the marginal notes, taking the capital "I" out, and stressing the third person, transferring them thus over to an imaginary individual. You can never tell which person I am writing under. "I" sometimes means "he," while "he," in this case, means "I." We'll leave "we" out of consideration.'[26] If this sounds like Frost's habitual puckishness, a playful smokescreen of whimsy to elude biographical inquiries, we should note that, in effect if not in tone, it recalls the shifts and adaptations in Wordsworth (and to a lesser extent in Hardy) between original conception and completed poem. Basically, I am convinced, Frost is to be taken seriously here. The angle of narration depends not on the reflection in subject-matter of autobiographical experience but, as in poets from whom he learned his trade, on the artistic needs of individual poems.

One has only to alter the pronoun in the first line of 'The Most of It' and read,

> I thought I kept the universe alone,

to begin to realize what is at stake. Although we tend to assume that the first person gives greater vividness and immediacy, and that vividness and immediacy are unquestionably desirable qualities, Frost's effect in this poem (notwithstanding the element of empathy already mentioned) clearly depends upon impersonality and detachment. We need to look down on the solitary human being by the side of the lake and watch the great buck blundering past him. So far as I am aware, there is no evidence that the poem was based on any autobiographical experience, but even if it were, Frost's point is not 'This is how I feel in relation to the natural world,' but 'This is every man's situation when ultimately faced with what is apparently the brute indifference of nature.'[27] Similarly, in 'Two Look at Two,' the logic of the poem demands that the angle of narration should be split between lovers and deer. Only a withdrawn, neutral observer can remark: 'Two had seen two, whichever side you spoke from.' If Frost had written 'we' instead of 'they,' narrating the poem from the viewpoint of the lovers, the scales would have been tipped in favour of the human pair and the all-important balance of the poem destroyed.

The well-known 'Mending Wall' offers a more complicated instance. Here, true to what is obviously a favourite Frostian pattern, one looks at one over a separating barrier. In this case, however, the 'I' is a participant, and this has caused some readers to assume (illegitimately, I think) that in the friendly disagreement that is the subject of the poem we are to take sides with the speaker against his more traditional and conservative neighbour. But although the speaker maintains that the tradition is kept up at the insistence of the neighbour, he initiates the ritual himself: 'I let my neighbour know beyond the hill.' One suspects that both men enjoy the annual duty, that the give-and-take of neighbourly argument is cherished on both sides. Even the two catch-phrases, 'Something there is that doesn't love a wall' and 'Good fences make good neighbors,' both occur twice in the poem and so help to maintain a balance. 'Mending Wall,' we might say, is poised between these two mutually exclusive 'right' attitudes.

But should we equate the 'I' of the poem with Frost? Surely not, despite biographical evidence suggesting that the poem derives from the Derry years when Frost used to repair his boundary-wall with the French-Canadian neighbour who also appears in 'The Ax-Helve.'[28] Just as the symbolic application of the wall needs to be kept flexible if the poem is to have the maximum effect, so the limitation that any specifically personal reference would imply needs to be avoided. Besides, Frost offered a valuable clue to the tensions behind 'Mending Wall' when he remarked during an interview: 'Maybe I was both fellows in the poem' (IRF, 257).[29] Though 'Mending Wall' has been the subject of numerous critical commentaries, the possibility of Frost's deliberately dividing his allegiance between the two speakers has not yet been given the attention it deserves. Yet much of the poem's appeal may be explained by the way in which this conflict of attitudes which intrigued the poet is carried over to his readers. The poem's universality derives from the split sympathy that the vast majority of us feel between the respective claims of 'traditionalism' and 'progress.'

'The Road Not Taken' presents even greater complexities. Although countless readers have taken it at its face value, although it stands as opening poem in *Mountain Interval* and in one of Frost's recordings (suggesting that the poet saw it as a direct introductory statement), and although Elizabeth Sergeant has pointed to an autobiographical origin in an incident when Frost sensed that he was going to meet his double at an intersection in the woods,[30] a strong case can be made for its not being about Frost at all. Frost claimed it to be a playful parody of Edward Thomas, whose hesitant indecision Frost found both amusing and appealing, and on different occasions he gave varying accounts of the poem's development and of Thomas's attitude towards it.[31]

It is perfectly justifiable, however, to see the poem as about both Frost and Thomas. Indeed, the incident in the woods (which took place in 1912) may well have become associated in Frost's mind with Thomas's poems 'The Sign-Post' and 'The Other.' Both these were written while Frost was in England and he most probably read them quite soon after they were completed.[32] The former is about choosing which direction to take, the latter about an *alter ego* who seems to dog Thomas's path. Frost, I suspect, saw in Thomas exaggerated manifestations of his own traits, and by the same token the poem appeals to a wide audience because it deals with the problem of choice in terms that are universally applicable. Once again, too much individualizing (whether with Frost or Thomas as model) would have limited the scope of the poem; as it is, the reader, faced with a poem that demands to be approached dramatically, has little difficulty in blending the 'I' with himself.

A study of Frost's spokesmen and the various angles from which he views his subjects could well extend to book-length proportions. Here I must be content merely to draw attention to this aspect of his craftsmanship. It is an important and, I believe, a neglected feature of his artistic achievement. Borrowing the accents of the farmer in 'The Mountain,' we can say that much of the art as well as the fun derives from 'how you say a thing.'

VERSED IN COUNTRY THINGS

In the course of his long poetic career Frost made a number of statements about rural life and rural poetry. In 1931 we find him asserting: 'Poetry is more often of the country than of the city ... Poetry is very, very rural – rustic. It stands as a reminder of rural life – as a resource, as a recourse' (IRF, 75). In 1934 he remarked: 'Deep down in me is a strong friendship in favor of basing imagination and judgment on a knowledge of country things.'[33] And twenty years later we recognize the same viewpoint: 'Sometimes I hear someone say that he does not like poetry about nature, the country, that it should be about the city and machines and man-made things. When he says that I know what's inside of him. He is as clear as can be to me then, and I know what he is, whether he does or not' (IRF, 132). Of course, we must consider the possibility that these statements either derive from one of Frost's personae (they fit the role of farmer-philosopher neatly enough) or are elaborated in the interests of the occasion (the 1931 statement occurred in an interview for the periodical Rural America). None the less, even after we have made allowances for the enthusiasm of the moment and the inaccuracies of reporting, there remains a sufficiently substantial record of testimony to justify our accepting Frost as a sincere advocate for the rural point of view.

Although this aspect of Frost is currently unfashionable in literary-critical circles, acknowledgment of his rural perspective is essential for a balanced view of his work. It can help us, for instance, to come to terms with the controversy that has been raging ever since Lionel Trilling startled the guests (and, rumour tells us, the guest of honour) at Frost's eighty-fifth birthday party by describing him as 'a terrifying poet.'[34] The tactic was doubtless justifiable at the time; it was (and is) only too easy to miss the deeper and often darker implications in poems that habitually look much simpler than they are. But Trilling's argument has often been carried further – I would suggest, too far. When we come to suspect that the darker poems are emphasized and recommended because Frost, recognized as an important and influential poet, must be proved to inhabit the waste land at all costs, it is time to protest. Indeed, his inestimable value lies rather in his insistence that a more positive response to the problems facing twentieth-century man is possible without underestimating the magnitude of the challenge. In Frost, man's position within the universe is set in an appropriate perspective. The husband in 'West-Running Brook,' for example, admits that existence

flows between us
To separate us for a panic moment,   (ll. 51–2)

but goes on to observe: 'It flows between us, over us, and *with* us' (l. 53). The sonnet 'Design' is an excellent example of 'a panic moment,' but within the context of his collected poetry it is, surely, only a moment. And at this point we remember Frost's poignant definition of a poem as 'a momentary stay against confusion' (*FSP*, 18), a definition that would have impressed Hardy. Frost does not deny or underestimate the confusion; he is well aware of what he called on one occasion 'the larger excruciations' (*FSP*, 106), but he refuses to be overwhelmed by them. Contrary to certain contemporary assumptions, this is neither a naive nor necessarily a complacent attitude.

So many commentators have warned us not to be seduced by Frost's comforting (or apparently comforting) assurances that it is refreshing to remember Frost's own view that his poetry told a very different story. As he remarked to a reporter in 1916: 'I shall always write about the country. I suppose I show a sad side of it too often. It only seems sad to those who love the city' (*IRF*, 14). The point is taken up later in his important poem, 'The Need of Being Versed in Country Things.' It begins with an indirect account of the burning of a homestead:

The house had gone to bring again
To the midnight sky a sunset glow.
Now the chimney was all of the house that stood,
Like a pistil after the petals go.

The indirectness is a way of avoiding an exclusively human perspective. The fire is not seen as a disastrous end to a human chronicle but rather as a neutral stage in a much longer process. Although a sunset glow at midnight is unnatural and the sight of a pistil without petals indicates the dying of a flower, both references are to recurrent cycles, diurnal and seasonal, and imply continuity. The next stanzas describe the barn that has been spared by the wind as a balancing contrast to the house destroyed by fire. The barn is bereft of horses but now provides an ideal nesting-place for the phoebes (a North American species of flycatcher) who use it undisturbed:

> The birds that came to it through the air
> At broken windows flew out and in,
> Their murmur more like the sigh we sigh
> From too much dwelling on what has been.

This is the first reference to human responses, but although the birds' murmur is likened to a sigh, the sigh is immediately recognized as inappropriate, an excessive retreat into the past rather than a resolute advance into the future. The phoebes, unaware of either past or future, flying through what had once been man-erected barriers between the human and natural worlds, are accepted, even at this stage in the poem, as neutral, healthily detached.

The penultimate stanza extends the possibilities of pathetic fallacy:

> Yet for them the lilac renewed its leaf,
> And the aged elm, though touched with fire;
> And the dry pump flung up an awkward arm;
> And the fence post carried a strand of wire.

The emphasis here is on renewal and the unchanging. Although the imagery suggests human associations, the viewpoint has shifted to the birds as the centre of interest. The whole scene exists 'for them,' and in the last stanza the two related themes that have dominated the poem – what is the proper response to the scene? how do the phoebes respond to it? – are combined and resolved.

> For them there was really nothing sad.
> But though they rejoiced in the nest they kept,
> One had to be versed in country things
> Not to believe the phoebes wept.

The phoebes 'rejoice' in their nest-building, creative present (one thinks of Wordsworth's 'Lines Written in Early Spring':

> The birds around me hopped and played,
> Their thoughts I cannot measure: –
> But the least motion which they made,
> It seemed a thrill of pleasure),

but this is no more an index to their response than the deceivingly mournful sound of their murmuring song. Frost agrees, I think, that 'there was really nothing sad,' that the natural continuities outweigh (or, at the very least, balance) the human setback. His viewpoint is brilliantly exemplified in the richly ambiguous last two lines. On the one hand, the pathetic fallacy is denied. The speaker rejects the fanciful conventions of urban-centred pastoral; the phoebes do *not* weep, and nature is sublimely indifferent to the human plight. But alongside this runs a balancing counter-assertion. To those not 'versed in country things' (and it is worthwhile, parenthetically, to draw attention to the pun in 'versed'), the emphasis is on the weeping, on an exaggerated sense of sadness from too much dwelling on what has been. 'It only seems sad to those who love the city.' The rural perspective, Frost asserts, enables one to achieve Matthew Arnold's ideal, to see life steadily and see it whole.

It is dangerous to generalize about Robert Frost. Like Hardy whom he admired (he is on record as describing him as 'one of the most earthly wise of our time'),[35] he disclaimed any pretence to a fixed philosophical system. Poetry, he observed when giving a talk at Bryn Mawr, offers 'tentatives, but not tenets';[36] more mischievously, he once said of himself: 'I've as many inconsistencies as a philosopher.'[37] These remarks are the Frostian equivalents to Hardy's more solemn pronouncements in which he disclaims any 'harmonious philosophy' (see p. 97 above). Frost, we may agree, had a less austere and more outgoing temperament than Hardy, but this only means that his range of tone and mood is even greater. In consequence, it is no more accurate to paint him as one who saw nature as separate and alien than to characterize him, with the more enthusiastic of his undiscriminating admirers, as an uninhibited singer of natural joy and gladness. Frost would have rejected the codification of the either/or. In 'The Figure a Poem Makes' he declared (and it is of vital importance not only to his own work but to all the poetry I am concerned with here) that 'the object of writing poetry is to make all poems sound as different as possible from each other' (*FSP*, 17). Frost's poems are indeed different from each other, and, as in the cases of Wordsworth and Hardy, this is an important indication of the kind of poet he was. We need only juxtapose 'The Pasture' with 'Design' or 'Mowing' with 'Desert Places' to see the variety not only of effect but also of approach that is involved. The poems I have discussed in detail in this chapter naturally emphasize the rural element in his work, yet even within this limited area of his total output the range is remarkable. Frost's genius put new vitality into a kind of verse that might well have seemed written out by the end of the nineteenth century. But to those acquainted with the virtually inexhaustible possibilities of rural poetry it will not appear paradoxical that a poet so memorable for his intensely human qualities should, by communicating these qualities, invigorate the literature of the natural world.

SEVEN

Edward Thomas

THOMAS, WORDSWORTH, AND FROST

Edward Thomas was born in 1878, but his poetic talents did not begin to blossom until December 1914; at that time, however, he brought to the writing of his verse an extensive knowledge of the earlier rural poets whom I have been discussing. He had already written with sympathy and insight on Clare, Barnes, and Hardy,[1] though it would be difficult to point to any noticeable imprint of these writers upon his own work. Frost was, of course, a personal friend whose early volumes of poems Thomas had reviewed sensitively and intelligently, and one, moreover, who had directly encouraged him to turn his creative attentions to poetry. His relation to Wordsworth is, however, much more complicated. Although we might expect the Wordsworthian example to loom large in Thomas's poetic heritage, the influence appears at first sight (but *only* at first sight) to be minimal. His treatment of Wordsworth in the posthumously published *Literary Pilgrim in England* is strangely flat and uninteresting, and his other references are less incisive than we might expect of a man with Thomas's critical gifts. His most illuminating comments on Wordsworth are probably those that appear in the reviews of Frost, where he is quick to recognize the connections between their respective principles concerning poetic language.

It may well be that he was acutely conscious of falling into pseudo-Wordsworthian attitudes in his own verse, and so made strong efforts to avoid any comparison. In many respects, however, the two can be regarded as similar. Both continually present themselves in their poems as travellers across country, both offer detailed analyses of the condition of solitude, both are constantly passing from observation of the natural world to examination of their own minds. On the other hand, no one could be further than Thomas from any suggestion of the egotistical sublime, and although both are unquestionably detached from what they observe, the detachment is essentially different. Above all, Wordsworth's habit of deliberately extracting meaning and understanding from his experience in the natural world is absent in Thomas. To take a brief and simple example, 'The New Year' is sufficiently close to the Wordsworthian pattern that one can imagine an incautious critic describing it as Thomas's version of 'Resolution and Independence.' Certainly, the 'old man bent,' with his wheelbarrow 'in profile ... like a pig' and his head 'rolled under his cap like a tortoise's,' recalls the leech-gatherer in his age, his frailty, and the poet's insistence on using natural imagery to describe him, but all he has to offer is a murmured, perfunctory New Year greeting:

> He took an unlit pipe out of his mouth
> Politely ere I wished him 'A Happy New Year',
> And with his head cast upward sideways muttered –
> So far as I could hear through the trees' roar –
> 'Happy New Year, and may it come fastish, too',
> While I strode by and he turned to raking leaves.[2]

There is no stated 'moral,' no revelation; the significance of the incident is contained within itself. Clearly Thomas had no need of the elaborate ways to communicate meaning and interpretation that I stressed in my discussion of Wordsworth.

In 'Over the Hills' Thomas again chooses a Wordsworthian subject but subtly demonstrates his independence of the earlier poet. Thomas begins with more than a suggestion of 'emotion recollected in tranquillity':

> Often and often it came back again
> To mind, the day I passed the horizon ridge
> To a new country, the path I had to find
> By half-gaps that were stiles once in the hedge,
> The pack of scarlet clouds running across
> The harvest evening that seemed endless then
> And after, and the inn where all were kind,
> All were strangers.

Typical of Thomas is the effect that points towards symbolic speech but never quite commits itself to allegory. Wordsworth, by contrast, would have elaborated on the experience and forced a deeper meaning from it ('An emblem here behold of thy own life' [*Prelude*, iv, 61]); Thomas prefers the ambiguous uncertainty of the everyday – unfixed, open-ended, with no preconceived interpretation. Commentators who insist upon elaborating his hints into full-fledged universal statements do his art a disservice. He prefers to attain his effects indirectly, as in the description of clouds at sunset, where the underlying hunting image emphasizes both colour and movement, the 'scarlet' of the huntsmen and the running of the 'pack' fused within a single metaphor.

But this is the mere foundation on which the poem is built. Thomas continues:

> I did not know my loss
> Till one day twelve months later suddenly
> I leaned upon my spade and saw it all,
> Though far beyond the sky-line. It became
> Almost a habit through the year for me
> To lean and see it and think to do the same
> Again for two days and a night.

The analysis of the response is direct, spare, almost prosaically straightforward, but the word 'loss' is deliberately chosen and placed for maximum emphasis. We may well ask: what loss? Recollection, for Thomas, clearly fails to bring either wealth or joy; the inward eye provokes memories that prevent any over-confident identification with 'the bliss of solitude.' Where Wordsworth stresses the satisfactions of recalling past achievements 'in years that bring the philosophic mind,' Thomas is always aware of the pastness of the past.

> Recall
> Was vain: no more could the restless brook
> Ever turn back and climb the waterfall
> To the lake that rests and stirs not in its nook,
> As in the hollow of the collar-bone,
> Under the mountain's head of rush and stone.

Once again there is the hint of possible allegory, but we should be distorting if we simply equated the restless Thomas with the restless brook and saw him yearning back to a condition of unattainable stillness and peace. Thomas's effect is elaborate; he concludes the poem within the analogous image (uncharacteristic of his own countryside but close to Wordsworth's – a sly allusion, perhaps, to his reversal of a Wordsworthian pattern?) and subtly allows the simile to counter the argument of the poem. The logical movement from description to poetic analogy is disciplined and clear-cut; in the pictorial movement of the simile, however, the impossible can be achieved. Here, despite the 'no more,' we imagine the brook returning to its lake-source, which is humanized by the imagery of its setting in 'the hollow of the collar-bone' under the 'head' of the mountain. Wordsworth's 'diurnal round,' then, is suggested only to be denied. Similarly recall, analogous to Wordsworth's recollection in tranquillity, is recognized as 'vain,' possible only in a whimsical and ultimately irresponsible fancy. The poem leaves us within the fancy because Thomas doubts the efficacy of any escape (and only now do we comprehend the irony in the title) 'over the hills.'

As I have indicated, the two poets differ in the kind of countryside about which they write. Thomas is essentially a poet of southern England, of Wiltshire and Hampshire in particular, a countryside of low rolling hills with villages tucked away in sheltered coombes off main roads, of thick hedgerows and overgrown pathways. He is not a poet of wild ranges and rocky crags; his nature is less dramatic and on a smaller scale. Himself a lover of the gentle beauty of the unnoticed (he hated recognized 'beauty-spots'), chronicler of the tall nettles in the corners of neglected farmyards, of sedge-warblers rather than the more publicized skylarks and nightingales, Thomas was closer to Hardy's 'man who used to notice such things' than to the Wordsworth who sought the more sublime scenery of the Alps, Snowdon, or the Lake District, but who, according to his own testimony, took thirty years to notice the beauty of the lesser celandine.

Perhaps because Thomas did not begin to write poetry seriously until he had attained literary maturity, he had no need to go through an apprenticeship of influences. Even the influence of Frost is more apparent than real. The story of Frost's releasing of Thomas's poetic gifts by encouraging him to recast some of his prose-descriptions in the form of verse is well known. Less often noted are various earlier references suggesting that Thomas was himself thinking along these lines. That he had dabbled in verse as an undergraduate may not be particularly significant, but, when writing to Gordon Bottomley in 1906, he referred to much of the contents of *The Heart of England* as 'spurred lyric,'[3] and although this is said in criticism it suggests an awareness of poetic possibilities. Indeed, Thomas is frequently on the brink of verse in this book – even to the extent of producing an iambic-pentameter line, 'The high white halcyons of summer skies,' set off, verbless and unconnected, as a separate paragraph as if it were an imagistic poem.[4] Others, including Bottomley and Walter de la Mare, had advised him to turn his attention to poetry before Frost.[5] Moreover, Thomas seems actually to have initiated the discussion that led to Frost's specific suggestion. 'I wonder whether you can imagine me taking to verse,' he wrote to the American in May 1914.[6] Sufficient evidence exists to indicate that Thomas was impelled towards poetic expression long before the outbreak of the First World War. This in no way lessens the importance of Frost's role in drawing a reluctant poet into being; it merely insists on the fact that Thomas's verse was the last stage in a continuous development, not an unprecedented new start.

Consider, for example, the following lines:

> And much he had to say of that old house
> Shadowed and smothered in leaves, and of himself
> Doing as he liked in it, and in the woods,
> And of the farmers, the labourers, the inn-keeper,
> The squire, and other well-preserved
> Fragments of old England, and in particular
> Of the only man he had ever met
> In those huge woods on the hills above his home.

These words were written by Thomas, but they will not be found in his *Collected Poems*. They occur in an essay entitled *The Country* (1913), where they appear as a complete prose-paragraph.[7] I have reproduced this paragraph word for word without alteration, save for the division into verse-lines and consequent capitalization. It seemed a dramatic way of enforcing the point that most Thomas admirers know as a fact but few, I suspect, have really felt on their poetic pulses: that the poems are a direct, even inevitable product of his prose.[8]

Thomas's verse shares with Frost's many of the characteristics that he identified in his reviews of *A Boy's Will* and *North of Boston*. But the reason for this is not that Thomas deliberately imitated Frost; rather, their artistic principles coincided. As R. George Thomas has pointed out, he had expressed stylistic sentiments remarkably similar to those of the American poet in the essay 'How I Began,' which first appeared before he had either met Frost or read his poetry.[9] And within a few months of their meeting, we find him writing to Frost: 'You really should start doing a book on speech and literature, or you will find me mistaking your ideas for mine and doing it myself ... However, my *Pater* [1913] would show you I had got on to the scent already.'[10] Frost's account of their conversations strengthens the impression that both poets were developing along converging paths. Occasionally, it is true, Thomas may have tried to imitate Frost, but at best the resemblances are superficial. Frost once observed: 'It must be admitted some of [Thomas's poems] *do* sound like some of mine, only he had plenty that didn't sound like mine at all, quite his own. He used to read me one and say, "That's just like Frost." But it wasn't, either in look, tone or manner.'[11] Thomas, then, was indebted to Frost not so much for poetic instruction as for encouragement, good advice, and faith in his poetic powers.

Although Thomas's poetry presents a remarkable evenness of texture, three individual strands can be recognized within it. The first, a concern to present simple rural experience in a direct and unpretentious manner, links him to his contemporary Georgians; the second, an interest in the poetic tensions possible within dialogue poems, can be traced to the friendship with Frost; the third, an impulse to isolate his own individual response to the natural world, produces his most important and characteristic verse, though this is stimulated by his sense of a continuing if threatened rural culture derived from the earlier writers considered in this book. In the ensuing sections I shall explore each of these strands in turn.

THOMAS AMONG THE GEORGIANS

As a prolific, astute, and conscientious reviewer, Thomas brought to the writing of his own poetry an intimate and sensitive knowledge of the verse that was being written in his own time. This verse has come to be labelled 'Georgian' and assigned the doubtful designation of a 'Movement.' Ever since the so-called Georgians (whom I shall be discussing briefly in the next chapter) fell into poetic disrepute, admirers of Thomas have generally insisted that he cannot properly be considered in their company, stressing the fact that his verse was continually rejected by editors during his lifetime and that it never appeared in Edward Marsh's famous *Georgian Poetry* anthologies. That Thomas's verse shares some of the qualities of Georgianism seems to me undeniable; on the other hand, his unique viewpoint and independent practice inevitably set him apart. Anyone who knows his work at all intimately must grant that his interests, circumstances, and (particularly) his temperament all prevented him from becoming closely associated with any tightly knit movement or clique. Like Frost, Joseph Conrad, and W.H. Hudson (all his friends, probably because they were all, at heart, solitaries), Thomas went his own way. In that sense the Georgian label (or any other, for that matter) has no meaning. At the same time, Thomas, however independent, was a man of his age and shared many of the attitudes of his fellow-poets. If we see the essential characteristics of Georgian poetry as a loving concern for the minutiae of rural life, a distrust of the sublime and an avoidance of high-flown 'poetic' rhetoric, then Thomas's poetry becomes not so much an honorable exception as an impressive centre. His work differs from that of the acknowledged Georgians in profundity and quality rather than in any basic response to life and letters. If we define 'Georgian' in purely historical terms as the generation of poets – good, bad, or indifferent – who began to come to prominence at the time of the accession of George v in 1910 (and this seems to me the only practical definition), then Thomas need not be seen in isolation but rather as representative, the hesitant, scrupulous, but none the less individual mouthpiece of a confused and puzzled age.[12]

If we wish to examine the kind of poetry that Thomas shares with his Georgian contemporaries, 'Thaw' is a convenient example. I quote it in full:

> Over the land freckled with snow half-thawed
> The speculating rooks at their nests cawed
> And saw from elm-tops, delicate as flower of grass,
> What we below could not see, Winter pass.

While this is obviously a more modest poem than most that I have been discussing, it would be a mistake to dismiss it as trivial. The thought which the poem embodies is simple and unremarkable, but its expression is sufficiently accomplished to render it of more than passing interest. 'Freckled' and 'speculating' are challenging words within the context; not only are they unexpected so that we are forced to linger over them and thus come to acknowledge their clear-cut appropriateness, but the hint of an internal rhyme between them, repeated in 'cawed' and 'saw' a few words later, indicates that Thomas is a dexterous manipulator of words with noteworthy technical resources at his command. The rhythmical felicity of 'delicate,' startling after the aptly harsh sounds used to imitate the cawing rooks, similarly jolts us into appreciating Thomas's control of perspective. Part of the symmetry of the poem, indeed, lies in the juxtaposition of the rooks' perspective with our own. Whereas we can look up and see the delicacy of the elm-tops which the rooks, perched on them, miss, so they can watch the passing of Winter which eludes us.

I have said enough, perhaps, to show that the poem is considerably more complex than a cursory reading might indicate. It may be, in a limiting sense, 'Georgian' but it exemplifies what a skilled poet can achieve within the Georgian mode. At the same time, though not out of place in his work, 'Thaw' can hardly be considered typical of Thomas at his best. In sheer artistry, in formal conception and poetic control, it is beyond the capacity of many of Thomas's contemporaries (W.H. Davies's name springs to mind), though it could, I think, have been written by Andrew Young, whose exquisite poetic miniatures will be considered in the final chapter. But for Thomas it represents no more than a minor success; the subject gives him no challenge to stretch his poetic abilities to their fullest extent.

The much-anthologized 'Adlestrop' shows Thomas a little further along the road towards his most characteristic and inimitable work. Thomas never allows the poem to degenerate, as it so easily might, into sentimental escapism. The express-train is as central to the subject as the birds of Oxfordshire and Gloucestershire; it links Adlestrop with the great world, yet the point of the poem lies in the fact that no real communication is established. But 'Adlestrop' is of particular interest to the serious critic of Thomas's verse on account of its diction, and I want to focus my discussion upon the crucial subject of Thomas's use of language. The first line,

> Yes, I remember Adlestrop – ,

is admirably colloquial, the abrupt opening suitably imitative of the sudden 'epiphany' that the poem records. The language is natural and restrained through the first two stanzas, but alters (and the modern reader will almost certainly conclude that it deteriorates) during the third. The lines,

> No whit less still and lonely fair
> Than the high cloudlets in the sky,

seem to have been wrenched out of a different, and lesser, poem. They represent 'poetic diction' in the derogatory sense of that term; 'no whit' is a slack archaism, 'lonely fair' sentimental and vague, 'high' seems makeweight, while 'cloudlets' suggests the conventional Georgian obsession with littleness. In these lines Thomas is, I assume, attempting to convey a feeling of heightened awareness by deliberately elevating the tone of his speech, but because this is a style we have encountered too often in the minor Georgians, it fails to convince. One recalls (most commentators quote it) his statement of intention in a letter to Eleanor Farjeon: 'If I am consciously doing anything I am trying to get rid of the last rags of rhetoric and formality which left my prose so often with a dead rhythm only.'[13] Here I am concerned primarily with diction, but diction and rhythm can hardly be separated, and in the lines in question the words seem forced because fitted too smoothly and artificially into the metrical beat. Oddly enough, we now know, thanks to the researches of William Cooke, that 'Adlestrop' was written only two days before the letter to Miss Farjeon.[14] With the exception of these two lines, the poem is an admirable example of what Thomas was trying to do. (The 'mistier/Gloucestershire' rhyme in the last stanza is boldly innovative – it must have offended the purists – and seems to me wholly successful.)

A number of Thomas's poems, including 'The Cherry Trees,' 'April,' 'Snow' and even 'Cock-Crow,' would not have seemed out of place in one of the *Georgian Poetry* volumes. In other poems, such as 'Head and Bottle' and the well-known 'Tall Nettles,' we can see Thomas in the process of transcending the Georgian norm. Here the development of a distinctive individual voice proves a crucial factor, and the simultaneous presence of colloquial rhythms and conventional poeticisms in 'Adlestrop' is indicative of Thomas's uncertain progress towards full artistic mastery. Forms like ''Tis' and ''Twas,' self-conscious inversions of customary word order and elevated words that depend upon a stock response too often suggest a preciosity alien to Thomas's true self. Even some of his most effective poems are marred (though generally the blemish is only slight and temporary) by an awkward unevenness of diction. Frost had already learned to purge his style of archaisms and poetic clichés. He once remarked that he had taken out 'a poetic license' to use the word 'beauty' no more than three times in his verse, and at the time of the conversation claimed not to have used it once;[15] one sometimes wishes that Thomas had done the same. As it is, we can never say with confidence of Thomas, as Thomas himself had said of Frost, that he 'refused the "glory of words" which is the modern poet's embarrassing heritage.'[16] But Frost had taken twenty years to lay the foundations of his art, and to refine his language with the radical but effective assistance of the waste-paper basket. Thomas had neither the time nor the leisure to follow Frost's example; most of his poems were produced under less than ideal conditions – some, indeed, in army camps – and he had no opportunity to collect his work together and either suppress or (in any extended sense) revise in the light of subsequent experience. None the less, his search for 'a language not to be betrayed' ('I Never Saw That Land Before') was constant and unswerving. In his best poems, whether dialogues or interior meditations, this quest was achieved.

THE DIALOGUE POEMS

The quest pattern is central to Thomas's work, and its direction may be either internal or external. His longest poem, 'The Other,' is a central and individual statement of his self-questing and self-questioning.[17] In a number of poems, however, he seeks something 'out there,' which may be identified as the essence of the rural landscape or, to use the phrase Thomas made his own, 'the heart of England.' These poems almost invariably involve dialogue since the sought-for meaning resides in the tension between differing viewpoints. In 'Up in the Wind,' 'Man and Dog,' 'The Chalk Pit,' 'Wind and Mist,' 'As the Team's Head-Brass' and 'Lob,' the recognition emerges in each case through conversation between the poet and a countryman (though often enough – 'Wind and Mist' is the most conspicuous instance – both speakers seem to reflect conflicting aspects of the same basic self). Analogies with some of Frost's poems like 'The Mountain' and 'Mending Wall' are clearly legitimate, but even if Thomas were trying to imitate Frost, his own character inevitably imprinted itself on his work and ensured its distinct individuality. Here I wish to discuss two such poems: 'Up in the Wind,' where the reader comes to an understanding of the locality by mediating between the responses of Thomas himself and the barmaid with whom he converses, and 'Lob,' where Thomas's encounter with the squire's son constitutes his most substantial exploration of 'Englishness.'

'Up in the Wind' is generally acknowledged as, with the exception of the suppressed undergraduate verse, the first of Thomas's poems to be written. As we might expect, it bears some resemblance to the work of Frost, recalling in particular the conversation poems in *North of Boston*. The abrupt, vigorous opening, plunging the reader *in medias res*, and the irregular, staccato iambic pentameter accurately reproducing an individual speech-rhythm, both suggest that Thomas is not only accepting Frost's advice in turning to verse but is even following his example.

> 'I could wring the old thing's neck that put it here!
> A public house! it may be public for birds,
> Squirrels, and suchlike, ghosts of charcoal-burners
> And highwaymen.' The wild girl laughed. 'But I
> Hate it since I came back from Kennington.
> I gave up a good place.'   (ll. 1–6)

The accent is Cockney rather than New England, but the poetic procedure is identical. Yet it would be unwise to expect the poem to continue in transparently imitative fashion, and in the second verse-paragraph we encounter a different note that can be recognized as pure, unadulterated Edward Thomas:

>   While I drank
> I might have mused of coaches and highwaymen,
> Charcoal-burners and life that loves the wild.
> For who now used these roads except myself,
> A market waggon every other Wednesday,
> A solitary tramp, some very fresh one
> Ignorant of these eleven houseless miles ...?
> But the land is wild, and there's a spirit of wildness
> Much older, crying when the stone-curlew yodels
> His sea and mountain cry, high up in Spring.   (ll. 14–20, 28–30)

The verse moves at a different tempo; indeed, the contrast between the barmaid's strident vernacular (her 'shriek') and Thomas's quiet, ruminative meditations creates the all-important tension within the poem. Once we notice the way in which Thomas repeats the girl's references to highwaymen and charcoal-burners, but translates them, as it were, into a different idiom, we shall begin to appreciate the verbal and rhythmical skill that underlies Thomas's art.

We may also note the unostentatious but deliberate repetition of 'wild' and 'wildness' at the opening of the poem. Thomas christens the barmaid 'the wild girl,' and adds:

> Her cockney accent
> Made her and the house seem wilder by calling up –
> Only to be subdued at once by wildness –
> The idea of London.   (ll. 6–9)

There is a sense, indeed, in which the poem is a meditation on the nature of wildness. Once, Thomas deduces from what he sees, the house stood 'on the border of a waste,' in a time 'when all was open and common' (ll. 36, 32). Since then, the countryside has been tamed. The common remains only in a place-name and, for the sharp-eyed, in the surviving traces of bracken and gorse which 'still hold the hedge where plough and scythe have chased them' (l. 34). But wildness has been replaced by lonely, even desolate solitude; what was once a waste is now a backwater 'midway between two railway lines / Far out of sight and sound of them' (ll. 24–5), a countryside through which cars travel without any inducement to stop. The post and empy frame lacking the identifying inn-sign provide the necessary image of desolation, remaining (like similar imagery in Frost) firmly this side of the over-insistently symbolic.[18] Without seeming to do so, Thomas offers here a concise yet profound insight into the state of much of southern England in his own time; his honest, undeceived report on what he observes represents a quality in Thomas which, as we shall see, appeals to later poetic commentators on a diminished rural England.

Thomas and the 'wild girl' offer opposed interpretations of the landscape. Male, female; outsider, native; passive, active; quiet, garrulous; meditative, unintellectual: their respective viewpoints could hardly be more firmly at odds, and as readers we build up our understanding of the house and its setting from an attempted reconciliation of the two responses. Curiously, however, both speakers are linked by a fascination for the place. Technically unstated in the poem, Thomas's love is implicit in every line of tender description, and his fondness is prominent in the prose-draft from which the poem is derived;[19] the girl's reluctant love is revealed when Thomas shrewdly hints at a possible return to Kennington (a London suburb):

> 'Not me:
> Not back to Kennington. Here I was born,
> And I've a notion on these windy nights
> Here I shall die. Perhaps I want to die here.
> I reckon I shall stay.'   (ll. 98–102)

Consequently her final remark that concludes the poem –

'Look at those calves. Hark at the trees again' –

is admirably poised between irritation and affection.

Although Frost praised it highly and John Moore described it as 'probably Edward Thomas's best poem,'[20] 'Lob' is not invariably regarded, especially among literary commentators, as one of his most important and successful works. Such, however, I believe it to be, and it is gratifying to find Edna Longley describing it in her recent edition as 'a main pillar of Thomas's poetic edifice,' 'undoubtedly one of [his] finest achievements.'[21] One reason for the comparative neglect may be that the poem appears, on the surface at least, untypical of Thomas because of the less personal nature of the subject; I hope to demonstrate, however, that it is closer to his central preoccupations than is generally realized. But a more important reason, I suspect, is the sentiment that pervades the poem. It supposedly conjures up the rural clichés (as seen by outsiders) of morris dancing and maypoles, of picturesque thatched cottages and teashops, of ruddy-cheeked yokels in country inns. We have all learned to be wary of such caricatures; unfortunately we have not yet learned to discriminate between the cocknified parody and the genuine rural culture which it vulgarizes. Thomas saw through not merely the caricature but the urban sophistication that chose to see it as an excuse to dismiss all 'country things.' Himself an urban outsider, Thomas knew both the temptation to sentimentalize and the tendency to 'over-react' in the opposite direction.

Before I proceed to examine 'Lob,' it will be as well to consider the case against it. Raymond Williams, in *The Country and the City*, is particularly critical, and his strictures need answering. After a brief précis of the poem's narrative movement Williams writes:

> The varied idioms of specific country communities – the flowers, for example, have many local names – are reduced not only to one 'country' idiom but to a legendary, timeless inventor, who is more readily seen than any actual people. And this is the point at which the Georgian imagination broke down: the respect of authentic observation overcome by a sub-intellectual fantasy: a working man becoming 'my ancient' and then the casual figure of a dream of England, in which rural labour and rural revolt, foreign wars and internal dynastic wars, history, legend and literature, are indiscriminately enfolded into a single emotional gesture. Lob or Lud, immemorial peasant or yeoman or labourer: the figure was now fixed and its name was Old England. The self-regarding patriotism of the high English imperialist period found this sweetest and most insidious of its forms in a version of the rural past.[22]

This commentary is itself insidious. It is possible, I suppose, to get so carried away by the rhetorical sweep of the indictment not to notice the distance Williams has opened up by the end of the paragraph between his argument and Thomas's poem. There is, in fact, no connection whatsoever between 'the self-regarding patriotism of the high English imperialist period' and Thomas. In his long, separately published essay *The Country*, a figure who is clearly a mouthpiece for Thomas himself claims 'that we have been robbed ... of the small intelligible England of Elizabeth and given the word Imperialism instead.'[23] Thomas is consistently critical of the attitudes scarified by Williams in this passage, and R. George Thomas is far more accurate when he calls 'Lob' 'a direct answer to the false sentiment of Georgian pastoralism.'[24]

Williams's earlier argument bears more relation to literature, but cannot be accepted as fair criticism of 'Lob.' There is nothing uniquely Georgian about creating a composite figure to stand for a race or nation or group, and there is no reason why Thomas shouldn't create an archetypal countryman to represent the essence of the England he considered worth fighting for. In any case, Lob is not excessively generalized; the poem is steeped in a specific area of Wiltshire and makes no attempt to reduce the varieties of country life or speech to a common mould. Moreover, as my commentary on the poem will, I hope, show, the phrases 'sub-intellectual fantasy' and 'single emotional gesture' are hopelessly off-target if we are seriously concerned to describe Thomas's creation.

The history of the name 'Lob' has attracted little attention. It appears frequently in earlier literature, especially in Elizabethan and Jacobean drama, where examples may be found in Preston's *Cambyses* and Beaumont and Fletcher's *Knight of the Burning Pestle* as well as *A Midsummer Night's Dream* (II, i, 16). The name is not as idyllic as is sometimes assumed. As most Shakespearean annotators point out, the word derives from the Celtic 'llob' meaning a clown or dolt, with an underlying reference to size and awkwardness. In folklore, Lob-lie-by-the-Fire is virtually identifiable with the Devil. The definition in Joseph Wright's *English Dialect Dictionary* would have appealed to Thomas's wry sense of humour; it reads: 'A clown, a clumsy fellow; an assistant gamekeeper.'

Although the poem begins with Thomas in a characteristic situation, 'in search of something chance would never bring,' the centre of attention soon shifts from the vaguely questing narrator to the old man who becomes the first manifestation of Lob within the poem. His speech is faithfully reproduced by Thomas, and its inflections (though integrated within the iambic pentameter) are totally different from his own. But what is most noticeable about the old man's talk is the thought-process from sentence to sentence – a progression of sorts, but one that does not display any intellectualized logical development. However, it represents an alternative way of thinking and emphasizes the characteristics that are to distinguish Lob throughout the poem: independence, reverence for the past, and an instinctive response to the immeasurable, intangible but distinct essence of rural England. His first remark is a vigorous defiance of any attempt to limit the liberty of the traveller:

'Nobody can't stop 'ee. It's
A footpath, right enough.'   (ll. 7–8)

He is insistent upon age-old rights. (The point is reiterated later in the poem: 'Does he keep up old paths that no one uses / But once a lifetime when he loves or muses?' [ll. 53–4]) He then goes on, by reference to the ancient right of way, to a consideration of the past:

'You see those bits
Of mounds – that's where they opened up the barrows
Sixty years since, while I was scaring sparrows.'   (ll. 8–10)

We are involved here, of course, with two pasts: that of the speaker's own childhood (which, the last clause reminds us, is by no means idealized) and that of prehistoric times, a record of the first peoples to leave a physical mark on the landscape – the beginnings, it is implied, of a long continuity. But the next two lines significantly shift focus:

'They thought as there was something to find there,
But couldn't find it, by digging, anywhere.'   (ll. 11–12)

The archaeologists, then, were like Thomas 'in search of something,' and the old countryman suggests with the emphatic qualification 'by digging' that whatever is to be found does not lie beneath a literal surface. As we experience the poem, we come to realize that he is himself a representative of what is to be sought.

In his immediate, if checked, impulse 'to turn back then and seek him' (l. 13), Thomas testifies to an awareness that the old man possesses something valuable (not in material terms but the 'gold' of 'dandelions' [ll. 29–30]) from which he can learn. That he only realizes this later ('When I had left him many a mile behind' [l. 6]) suggests that the wisdom in question will be as elusive as the old man himself. Yet Thomas is careful, aware perhaps of the dangers of a generalized composite landscape, to specify his search by focusing on a particular stretch of country as a representative microcosm of rural England, one of the 'innumerable holes and corners' that he praises in *The Last Sheaf*.[25] He sets his poem not merely in Wiltshire but in a distinct geographical area within Wiltshire, the Pewsey Vale. Here may be found not only the villages mentioned in the poem (it may be worth noting that a footpath into Alton Priors following the line of the prehistoric Wiltshire Ridgeway is still 'marked on the maps' [l. 42]) but the names applied later to people and places. Thus the name 'Bottlesford' (l. 36) is taken from a community a mile north-west of Manningford Bruce, while the reference to 'Jack Button up at the White Horse' (l. 38) may indicate a public house, but is just as likely to allude to the Alton Barnes white horse cut into the surface of the chalk down. Walker's Hill (l. 40) is on the Ridgeway just north of the Altons, and a long barrow named Adam's Grave (cf. l. 41) lies on its crest. It is clear that Thomas has taken considerable pains to root his Lob-figure in a specific countryside.

Having established the particularity of his initial setting, Thomas has now, I submit, earned the right to extend beyond the boundaries of Pewsey Vale, to show that the qualities manifest in the old man from Alton or Manningford are, despite distinct and essential local variations, present as recognizable traits in the rural English as a whole. The bulk of the poem is spoken by

> a squire's son
> Who loved wild bird and beast, and dog and gun
> For killing them. (ll. 43–5)

He proves himself, in the event, a second manifestation of Lob, and the contradictory nature of his pursuits, as well as his contrast in status with the sparrow-scaring labourer, reveal him as a composite figure, but this in no way detracts from his authority. He belongs in the company of Jefferies' Keeper Haylock and Hodge (in *The Gamekeeper at Home* and *Hodge and His Masters* respectively), of Kipling's Hobden (in *Puck of Pook's Hill* and *A Diversity of Creatures*), of Sturt's Bettesworth, of Doughty's Hobbe (whom Thomas quotes in *The Last Sheaf*), of R.S. Thomas's dour Welsh equivalent, Iago Prytherch. He becomes the mouthpiece, a generalized but by no means abstract 'folk' voice, for the England Thomas is anxious to define.

The heart of the poem is the Wiltshireman's description of Lob's characteristics and metamorphoses. It is an anthology – almost a *collage* – of English folklore, names of places, birds and flowers, country proverbs, rustic humour. Yet it is more than a mere hodge-podge. Thomas once observed of Clare: 'He often wrote long formless pieces full of place-names and of field-lore charmingly expressed' (*CCH*, 317). Characteristically, he responds to Clare's virtues without overlooking his formal weaknesses, but his own poems are *not* formless. The extending references, for instance, to such places as Exeter, Leeds, and Canterbury deliberately include the west, north, and east of England within this southern-based poem. There are, to be sure, aspects of a deliberate *tour de force* about his loading every rift of his poem with rustic ore, and we come to share with him the satisfaction of bringing so many seemingly stray bits of rural Englishness into the poetic orbit. But, over and above all this, there exists a basic seriousness. There is nothing cosy or sentimental or casual about the rural reference. 'He is English as this gate, these flowers, this mire' (l. 55) – specific natural things, and the third receives a deliberate emphasis; Lob is 'of the earth, earthy,' and Thomas is celebrating an earthy, unwritten, oral culture. This concentration upon something outside himself is relatively unusual in Thomas's verse, but provides an important rural base for his other, more personal poems. 'Lob' is, moreover, firmly controlled by the narrative conversation which, as Thomas would be the first to acknowledge, he derives from Frost.

The Wiltshireman ends with a rhetorical flourish in which all the manifestations of Lob in history, folklore, and general living combine to defy the forces of intolerance and injustice.

> 'He never will admit he is dead
> Till millers cease to grind men's bones for bread' ...   (ll. 141–2)

He then disappears into the countryside of which he is both defender and symbol, and Thomas acknowledges him 'of old Jack's blood' (l. 148). It is appropriate that Lob, like the 'heart of England' that he represents, is not recognized until he has (at least temporarily) disappeared. As with the bird-scaring labourer, the narrator (though not, one hopes, the reader) only realizes his identity later, possibly too late. The recognition is strengthening and disturbing at the same time, like the moments of happiness which, in his more personal poems, Thomas grants as happy only when they have become a part of his past.

INTERIOR MEDITATIONS

Although not conspicuously so, Thomas's poems are among the most personal in rural poetry. The reader may have noticed that in this discussion, contrary to my usual practice, I have not hesitated to equate Thomas with the 'I' of the poems. This points to a characteristic that distinguishes Thomas from Frost (and, indeed, from all the poets I have so far discussed, with the partial exception of Clare). If we discount three untypical and not really successful experiments in dramatic monologue ('The Cuckoo,' 'The Child on the Cliffs,' 'The Child in the Orchard'), the first person in Thomas's poetry is always himself, and moreover it is an 'I' who, despite occasional variations of mood, never changes in essentials. It is not the generalized 'I' we often find in Frost, whom the reader can take over and assume as himself, and only rarely the selective 'I' favoured by Wordsworth, in which particular aspects of the self are emphasized or suppressed in the interests of the individual poem. (The exceptions in Thomas are a few of the later poems written in the army, in which the 'I' may be said to represent any thinking soldier.) The speaking voice in the poems, then, is that of a wanderer and outsider, countrylover rather than countryman, hesitant, self-questioning, yet doggedly independent, for whom happiness and melancholy are inseparably connected, a man always in search but not always sure what he is looking for. None the less (and this distinguishes the 'I' of the poetry from the weaker, less attractive first person in the prose) Thomas is not immersed in his own consciousness. In the shorter introspective poems the 'I' can be subjective and personal (though not in the high romantic sense) yet at the same time aloof, capable of seeing himself and the world as related objects. Out of this tension comes a subtle, deceptively straightforward, but inimitable poetry.

John Burrow has pointed out that the phrase which Thomas used to describe Keats's 1817 volume, 'an intimate poetic journal,' is readily applicable to his own verse.[26] This is especially true of the considerable number of quietly introspective poems written in blank verse or rhymed couplets or employing an irregular and inconspicuous rhyme-scheme that are to be found scattered throughout the Collected Poems. These may be regarded as the central core of Thomas's verse. While they can legitimately qualify as nature poetry, since the occasion of the poem is almost invariably a rural experience, the emphasis is firmly on the self, a self that is always alone, brooding on its responses, and continually preoccupied with the condition of being 'born into this solitude' ('Rain'). Thomas rarely offers us descriptive poetry for its own sake, and the effect differs from that of his earlier prose because here he concentrates on understanding the self rather than expressing or even flaunting it.

These poems are about time and change and what does not change, whether in the outer landscape of the natural world or in the inner landscape of Thomas's psyche. Often, indeed, they are carefully isolated 'spots of time,' though they differ from Wordsworth's in The Prelude because, far from demonstrating a progressive stage in the growth of a poet's mind, they bear witness to the painful slowness and uncertainty of comprehending the significance of any experience. Wordsworth's rhythms reflect his attitude by being generally confident and assertive; Thomas's (at least, in these poems) are hesitant, tentative. Wordsworth addresses us; we feel we are overhearing Thomas. What distinguishes his poems more than anything else is a tone in which quiet assertiveness never becomes languid, in which troubled sensitivity, though tremulously poised at times, never falls into weakness or self-pity.

We find this clearly exemplified in 'The Manor Farm,' where the opening

lines demonstrate the individual rhythm that Thomas can impose upon traditional blank verse:

> The rock-like mud unfroze a little and rills
> Ran and sparkled down each side of the road
> Under the catkins wagging in the hedge.

To the undiscriminating classifier of metres, Thomas is writing in the same
form as Wordsworth's 'Tintern Abbey' or 'There Was a Boy' or 'The Ruined
Cottage,' but such is the distinctive treatment of the two poets (and I am here, of
course, ignoring the variety *within* Wordsworth's use of blank verse) that the
effect is totally different. Wordsworth's bedrock assurance, reflected in the
smoothness of his verse, is replaced by a much slower, more deliberate and less
insistent style. Yet, for all the rhythmic angularities, Thomas's control here is
masterly. The solidity of the mud is conveyed by the thick, clotted syllables of
the opening words, and the suggestion of speed in the second line ('Ran and
sparkled') is qualified by the irregular stresses (trochees instead of iambs) even
as their deviation from the metrical norm parallels the lively defiance of winter's
grip; above all, the sense of haphazard movement as the catkins sway in the
breeze is vigorously caught in the unexpectedness of 'wagging.' Even if description were the *raison d'être* of the poem, which it is not, these initial lines would
show Thomas transcending the standards of conventional nature poetry.

This opening description is stiffly formal in its meticulousness. As Thomas
turns from the external scene to his own response, the rhythms become more
relaxed:

> But earth would have her sleep out, spite of the sun;
> Nor did I value that thin gilding beam
> More than a pretty February thing
> Till I came down to the old Manor Farm,
> And church and yew-tree opposite, in age
> Its equals and in size.

As so often elsewhere, Thomas is here direct without being colloquial in any
cajoling way. Because the 'I' straightforwardly represents the poet himself, the
colloquial element in the verse is not the rural colloquial (like the Dorset dialect
in Barnes or the New England intonations of Frost); it is Thomas's own personal
vernacular: that of a reticent but precise and educated man trained to use words
with a subtle discrimination of meanings to be indicated by the slightest gesture
or stress. The lines just quoted establish an individual voice; we are aware of a
recognizable sensibility behind the verse. Thomas thus provides a significant

illustration of the valuable distinction recently made by Michael Kirkham, in a discussion of Hardy's poetry, between 'the *personal* voice' and 'the *human* voice.'[27] He speaks for and to himself, and a crucial difference from Frost is that with Thomas we are never mindful of a performance being put on for our benefit.

The lines immediately following enforce this sense of a personal voice with examples of a uniquely individual poetic language:

> Small church, great yew
> And farmhouse slept in a Sunday silentness.
> The air raised not a straw. The steep farm roof,
> With tiles duskily glowing, entertained
> The midday sun.

Superficially straightforward description,[28] these lines are distinguished by a special quality of insight that can achieve a striking effect by employing 'Sunday' as an adjective and create a complex of meaning with 'entertained.' This personal use of language (who but Thomas uses words in quite this way?) ensures that description and response are ultimately inseparable. In attempting to transfer the essence of the scene into his poem, Thomas is at once probing and analysing his own reaction. This period of the year cannot, he decides, be defined as Winter, but

> Rather a season of bliss unchangeable
> Awakened from farm and church where it had lain
> Safe under tile and thatch for ages since
> This England, Old already, was called Merry.

'Bliss unchangeable' is not a phrase we would normally associate with Thomas, and part of the interest in the poem derives from the tension created between this awareness of 'bliss' (it would be distorting to call it an experience) and the habitual accent of controlled melancholy conveyed by the tone and rhythm. He can find peace, satisfaction, fulfilment, 'bliss' (no comprehensive word exists) only through subsuming his own responses to a greater and less personal entity that Thomas boldly but in some respects rather dangerously associates with 'This England.'

If we are looking for a central, classic expression of Thomas's poetic self, we can do no better than turn to 'October,' which, like 'The Manor Farm,' moves from plain description to a uniquely personal response to both scene and season. The first two lines are so exact and complete in themselves that they might on their own constitute a poem written in the tradition of Imagism:

> The green elm with the one great bough of gold
> Lets leaves into the grass slip, one by one.

There is an exquisite finality about this, the kind of preternaturally clear focus that we associate with Japanese *haiku*. In itself it establishes the 'essence' of October, but for Thomas it is merely the beginning for a searching and admirably honest analysis of his own reactions. The gradual but steady movement from outer to inner landscape is noticeable. The opening lines are unusually detached, but with 'The gossamers wander at their own will' we begin to detect (in addition to the verbal echo of Wordsworth's 'Westminster Bridge' sonnet) the alternative will of an observer, and it is at his 'heavier steps,' we assume, that the squirrels scold. The personal element becomes stronger in the succeeding lines:

> The late year has grown fresh again and new
> As Spring and to the touch is not more cool
> Than it is warm to the gaze.

Thomas's own unmistakable 'way of looking' now comes to the fore; the distinction between kinds of perception conveys a delicate but acute sensitiveness which few but Thomas would distinguish and only Thomas could communicate. It prepares us for the intensely moving, intensely personal insight that concludes the poem:

> and now I might
> As happy be as earth is beautiful,
> Were I some other or with earth could turn
> In alternation of violet and rose,
> Harebell and snowdrop, at their season due,
> And gorse that has no time not to be gay.
> But if this be not happiness, who knows?
> Some day I shall think this a happy day,
> And this mood by the name of melancholy
> Shall no more blackened and obscured be.

Thomas's own distinction between man and the natural world here receives its supreme formulation. While acknowledging his own individual reaction ('Were I some other'), he perceives (and accepts) a non-human order within the universe; violet, rose, harebell, and snowdrop become natural emblems for the ever-succeeding seasons of spring, summer, autumn, and winter. The folklore belief that gorse is the only flower to bloom in every month of the year is

transformed into an observation that recognizes both the attractions and limitations of an emotionless natural world. Because Thomas is human he has time
'not to be gay.' Throughout his poetry, words like 'happy' and 'melancholy'
recur, and Thomas knows that, far from being opposites, the two are closely
enmeshed. At best he must be 'content with discontent,' to use the phrasing of
'The Glory.' 'October' is a definitive presentation of the dilemma (if indeed it is
a dilemma) since the beauty of the landscape and the evidences of the declining
year combine to become a natural, external symbol of Thomas's personal and
inner state.

Finally, 'The Brook' might well be considered Thomas's quintessential
meditative poem. Its basic structure, the incident out of which it is created, is
characteristically Georgian. Thomas is intent upon communicating his complex
feelings while quietly observing the wild life by a stream and a young girl
paddling. The scene itself is commonplace; the quality of the poem depends
upon the quality of the observer, and Thomas succeeds in creating out of these
simple ingredients a 'spot of time' that is gentler and less dramatic than
Wordsworth's but by no means less profound. He begins by setting the scene
clearly and directly:

> Seated once by a brook, watching a child
> Chiefly that paddled, I was thus beguiled.

'Once' suggests yet again the Wordsworthian 'emotion recollected in tranquillity' but, as the rest of the poem bears witness, Thomas is concerned not so
much with emotion as with the analysis of his responses; he is less interested in
expressing his reaction than in understanding what makes the moment
significant. But the crucial word in these opening lines is clearly 'beguiled,'
unexpected in terms of argument and rendered prominent by the crisp rhyme.
We realize at once, however, that the word is not dictated by the rhyme; on the
contrary, it immediately tightens the poem, announcing that this is no casual
reminiscence. The modern reader (encouraged by the reference in the succeeding line) is more likely to think of Eliot's 'the deception of the thrush' (*Burnt
Norton*) than of an equivalent line in Wordsworth; or, if he thinks of
Wordsworth, will recall that the older poet denies that Nature will ever 'betray /
The heart that loved her.' But Thomas, nature-lover as he is, is often skeptical of
nature's effects upon him. In 'Sedge-Warblers,' for example, the beauty of the
natural scene leads him to dream of a higher state which he recognizes is not so
much an inspiration as a temptation:

> And yet rid of this dream, ere I had drained
> Its poison, quieted was my desire.

So 'beguiled' in 'The Brook' indicates from the outset that Thomas is cautious, alert, not easily to be deceived.

The subsequent lines, etching in the details of the scene, prove that Thomas, in his typically quiet way, was a remarkably exact and informed naturalist. Of the poets considered here, only Clare and Andrew Young surpass him in their knowledge of birds and flowers. 'Mellow the blackbird sang and sharp the thrush' is so effortless a line that we can easily miss the precise distinction made between the two songsters and the superb economy with which this distinction is expressed. Similarly, 'a scent like honeycomb / From mugwort dull' shows that his reference is by no means confined to the commoner, well-known wild flowers, and later in the poem he notices and deliberately links himself with the flycatcher, one of England's most inconspicuous and un-noteworthy birds. The references dotted throughout his poems demonstrate that he favours neither the commonplace nor the exotic birds and flowers but those which, though unsung by the popular poets, form an essential part of the undramatic countryside that he loves. Thomas is the poet of the nettle-creeper and the garden-warbler ('Haymaking'), of 'Harebell and scabious and tormentil' ('October'), of 'Jack-in-the-Hedge, or Robin-run-by-the-wall' ('Lob'). As he admits in 'Old Man,' the very names have an attraction for him, but ultimately he loves them for themselves.

Thomas's attention is now caught by a butterfly that has just alighted on a stone in the path.

> From aloft
> He took the heat of the sun, and from below,
> On the hot stone he perched contented so,
> As if never a cart would pass again
> That way; as if I were the last of men
> And he the first of insects ...

His associating of himself with the butterfly is once again characteristic. The idea of himself as 'the last of men' links with his habitual loneliness, an awareness (which took on *fin-de-siècle* overtones in his prose) that his inheritance from the past, whether the more immediate past or that of the prehistoric England evoked later in the poem, is being surely and relentlessly eroded. The controlled but none the less rather helpless melancholy that pervades so much of Thomas's verse is a direct outcome of this realization. One of the reasons why Thomas is interested in the butterfly is that, unlike himself, it appears 'contented.' Those familiar with Thomas's work will immediately recall the following lines from 'The Glory':

> Or must I be content with discontent
> As larks and swallows are perhaps with wings?

(We should notice, if only parenthetically, the exquisitely quiet irony of that 'perhaps.') One may also remember his request in 'For These'

> for what men call content,
> And also that something may be sent
> To be contented with.

In the last half of 'The Brook,' Thomas notes that he is 'divided' between the living butterfly and the patterns of light and movement presented by the stream. Likening himself to the flycatcher, he feels part of a timelessness that links him with the horseman supposed in numerous local legends to be buried astride his horse in a prominent barrow. Although Thomas sometimes took up an anti-historical stance in his prose, there are numerous passages, like this one, that attest to his feeling for the spirit of history – something very different from the dates and statistics he had come to distrust. For Thomas history must be either natural or human, and the historical timespan assists him (as it did Richard Jefferies, whose reference in *The Story of My Heart* to 'the man in the tumulus' [ch. 3] may be alluded to here) to contemplate eternity, to appreciate in the flycatcher's terms 'Whatever is for ever to a bird' ('Fifty Faggots').

The experience seems positive, but Thomas's next remark is as typical as it is, in context, unexpected: 'All that I could lose / I lost.' He has not yet mentioned a loss, though the word takes us back to the warning represented by 'beguiled' in the opening couplet. He made the same abrupt change of mood, we remember, in 'Over the Hills' where, after a loving recollection of a past experience, he observed: 'I did not know my loss / Till one day twelve months later.' In that poem the loss is explained by the realization that 'recall was vain,' that the experience could never be repeated. In 'The Brook' the loss is less obvious; Thomas is referring, I suppose, to what he must give up to partake of the mindless, timeless 'content' of the butterfly and the flycatcher.

But at this point Thomas is brought back, as Keats would say, to his 'sole self.' The agent, in this case, is the paddling girl who has long been forgotten but who asserts herself to round off the poem:

> And then the child's voice raised the dead.
> 'No one's been here before' was what she said
> And what I felt, yet never should have found
> A word for, while I gathered sight and sound.

The phrase 'raised the dead' has the effect of a violent reawakening. The rapport between Thomas and the dead horseman is shattered. The girl's casual, literally inaccurate but accidentally profound remark strikes home. 'No one's been here before.' It helps Thomas to understand that he has been present at a unique intersection of separate lives – those of the girl, the butterfly, the flycatcher, and Thomas himself – that this same intersection will never recur (recall will again be vain), and that history, to quote T.S. Eliot's more abstractly phrased realization in *Little Gidding*, is 'a pattern / Of timeless moments.' Thomas the man has been gathering sight and sound; meanwhile Thomas the poet lies in abeyance, but is now prompted by the girl to find words to express not only the insight but the circumstances that gave rise to it. What for a lesser Georgian would have provided the impulse for a probably charming but even more probably thin nature lyric has been transformed by Thomas into the materials for a richly rewarding, deeply layered poem that deserves classic status.

THE TRIUMPH OF EARTH

Eleanor Farjeon records how in 1916 she asked Thomas what he was fighting for: 'He stopped, and picked up a pinch of earth. "Literally, for this." He crumbled it between finger and thumb, and let it fall.'[29] A representative incident in many respects, this certainly provides a perfect example of the ease with which he can be misread or misinterpreted. Some will, of course, extrapolate from it an earnestly patriotic gesture, but when Thomas said 'literally,' he meant it. He was fighting for the 'mire' emphasized in 'Lob,' for the 'dark earth' crumbled in 'Digging,' for 'the earth which you prove / That we love' in 'Words.'

His contemporaries found difficulty in accepting Thomas's work on its own terms. Paradoxically, in assuming that he meant more than he said, they frequently ended by deriving less. The 'pinch of earth' was precisely what Thomas was fighting for, but few besides Eleanor Farjeon herself were capable of understanding this in his own time. They searched for more elevated, but conventional, meanings when he chose words 'familiar ... / As the dearest faces / That a man knows ... / Worn new / Again and again' ('Words') to express his sense of the mysterious and deceptive simplicities of life. Similarly his rhythmical subtlety passed unrecognized. His poetry was continually rejected because its irregularities and angularities, which we can now recognize as the stylistic reflections of a deeply probing and acutely honest analysis of human experience, were mistaken for slackness and technical deficiency. His tentative rhythms, following but not quite fulfilling the expectations of the metrical norm, were perfectly fitted to the unassertive, questioning independence of his thought.

But the greatest and most unfortunate temptation is to allegorize Thomas. More than anything else, his discreet use of speech that verges on the symbolic but never insists on a universalizing dimension has proved a stumbling-block. Twentieth-century critics, whatever the theorists may say, have shown themselves notoriously heavy-handed when treating symbolic reference, and the delicacy with which Thomas makes possible a more than literal reading without ever losing contact with the specific object, itself and incomparable, is all too often destroyed by extended, abstract interpretation. It is tempting but fundamentally misguided to invoke, for example, Dante's *selva oscura* whenever Thomas alludes to woods or forests, or to turn every road, path, or way into the starting-point for an allegorical journey. While I am by no means denying that possible associations of this kind exist on the periphery of Thomas's meaning, he is not a poet whose work responds to an overlay of erudite and forced exegesis.

Nor is the rural poetry of encounter in general an appropriate area for elaborate symbolic explanation. When Wordsworth began to see individual components of the natural world as emblems rather than objects, he upset the admirable balance manifest in his best work. Clare's specific images communicate a sense of universality when Clare himself is least aware of an ambitious, more-than-local purpose. Barnes often grafts a parabolic interpretation on to a descriptive poem, but never violates the natural terms of the description itself, while Hardy is less concerned with the meaning of the objects he sees around him than with their associations – the human memories that attach to them. Frost is closest to Thomas in consciously skirting the symbolic possibilities ('After Apple-Picking' is a supreme example), but never unequivocally committing either the reader or himself to a meaning that extends beyond the literal. Thomas's phrase 'naturally symbolical' in discussing 'The Road Not Taken' brilliantly epitomizes this process.[30] In Thomas himself, however, the attainment of an effect poised between literalness and metaphor is recurrent and even pervasive. It may well be that twentieth-century experience is particularly fitted for this kind of treatment, that a scrupulous compromise between specificity of facts and openness of interpretation is best conveyed by this method. If so, it is yet another indication that Thomas is closer to the mainstream of modern literature than a judgment based on his relatively narrow subject-matter and quiet, undemonstrative tone would suggest.

Modern or not, he took the path less travelled by. The speaker in Frost's poem may well have been modelled on Thomas (see p. 136 above), but in any case the identification is appropriate. The image is itself comparable to Thomas's literal statements that simultaneously suggest and evade broader connotations. In this way, Thomas is able to mediate the enduring qualities of traditional nature poetry to our own more skeptical age. When he associates himself with natural or rural objects, he does so with a defensive irony acceptable to the modern sensibility. With the aspen in the wind, for instance, he 'ceaselessly, unreasonably grieves, / Or so men think who like a different tree' ('Aspens'). Is Thomas writing personally or presenting himself as emblem of all neglected poets? We cannot be sure. In another poem, an elm overhanging a dilapidated barn is 'old / But good, not like the barn and me' ('The Barn'). The elm is about to be felled; the barn is spared because ''Twould not pay to pull down.' Left 'as I shall be left, maybe,' the barn will soon collapse in decay, but it represents tradition and connection with the past. Again, possible larger meanings are left unstated, but the association of man and barn has been firmly but quietly established. Thomas may write of subjects no longer considered 'modern,' but his personal voice is congenial and we are inclined to trust him, even when he celebrates 'the triumph of earth' ('The Source'). Like all good poets, Thomas eludes the rigid categories. I would submit, however, that he is best considered as an independent associate of those who explore human consciousness as it defines itself against the ever-varying background and challenge of the natural world.

EIGHT

The Georgians and After

WHAT TO MAKE OF A DIMINISHED THING

In a century whose dominant symbol is the waste land, poetry that persists in looking towards a natural world still undeveloped and unpolluted will inevitably, if it wishes to avoid sounding ludicrously irrelevant, adopt the hesitant rhythm and the minor key. The clock (even Grantchester's) cannot be stopped or put back, and if the representative poetic landscape of the nineteenth century was an extension of Wordsworth's Lake District, that of the twentieth is made up of Auden's derelict industries, abandoned branch-lines, and harvests rotting in the valleys, or Philip Larkin's diminished England of raw estates and acres of dismantled cars. In our time the countryside, whether spoilt or unspoilt, is not likely to be approached with buoyant confidence; the tone of the sub-Wordsworthian can now, ironically, be equated with that of the suburban. Instead, the modern countryside will be presented indirectly and tentatively, with the saving sophisticated irony of an Auden or that combination of deadened response and 'awkward reverence' that we find in Larkin's church-going persona ('bored, uninformed').[1]

None the less, as my use of the word 'persona' should indicate, though the mood and attitudes may be the reverse of Wordsworthian, the method – creating an appropriate spokesman to interpet the unique landscape of the poem – is by no means without Wordsworthian precedent. Larkin himself is certainly not uninformed and probably not bored, but he needs that particular kind of speaker for his poem just as Wordsworth required for 'Resolution and Independence' a narrator who was less mature and less stable than himself. But Wordsworth is perhaps the wrong poet to bring forward in this context. Both

Auden and Larkin have independently pointed to Hardy as an important poetic mentor. In 1940 Auden (who at the same time paid a brief but significant tribute to Edward Thomas) acknowledged Hardy as his 'poetical father,' and more recently Larkin has gone so far as to describe Hardy's *Collected Poems* as 'many times over the best body of poetic work this century so far has to show.'[2] A number of reasons can be offered to explain these tributes (Auden declared that Hardy had taught him 'much about the influence of form upon content' and also 'much about direct colloquial diction'),[3] but the most important would seem to be that Hardy provided both poets with a poetic strategy by which to convey a possibly unfashionable attitude in a probably uncaring world.

At the beginning of the century, however, the prospects seemed less bleak. It was the poets of the Georgian movement, the friends of Frost and Edward Thomas, who, with what seems to us a blithely carefree alacrity, took upon themselves the task of restoring to English verse the simpler, more natural virtues that had been submerged by the cosmopolitan aestheticism of the 1890s and the reactionary jingoism of Edwardians like Austin, Newbolt, and Watson. Two of the main qualities of Georgianism were its committed but unchauvinistic Englishness and its concentration on rural themes and rural imagery. As James Reeves has written,

> the celebration of England, whether at peace or at war, became a principal aim of Georgian poetry. The English countryside, English crafts, and English sports offered suitable subject-matter. Poems about country cottages, old furniture, moss-covered barns, rose-scented lanes, apple and cherry orchards, village inns, and village cricket expressed the nostalgia of the soldier on active service and the threat to country life which educated readers feared from the growth of urbanism.[4]

Compared with the poetry of natural encounter with which I have been concerned in earlier chapters, this reads like withdrawal and degeneration, and in many respects it is. But some important discriminations need to be made. When Reeves includes old furniture in his list, one immediately thinks of Hardy, and this leads to two qualifications: first, Hardy's poem of that name cannot adequately be categorized as 'about' old furniture since his subject is his response to old furniture – a very different thing; second, the Georgian movement was a small group within a larger context, this context including not only Hardy but Frost (not to mention Edward Thomas, whose status in relation to the Georgians is, as I have noted, in dispute).

It is customary (and not wholly illegitimate) to see the achievements of the Georgian poets in either negative or diminutive terms. They displayed a *naiveté* inappropriate to the calamitous times in which they lived; they were too easily satisfied with a minor success; their poems lack intellectual rigour; they reveal an obsession with littleness that can be damagingly interpreted; if concerned with rural themes, they serve up what John Wain has called 'Nature from a simple recipe.'[5] But there is another way of approaching this kind of poetry, and it involves not only the poets whom Edward Marsh forced into a loosely organized 'movement' through the influence of his Georgian anthologies, but also a number of more modern writers who would doubtless object violently to any attempt to associate them with the unfashionable Georgians. My point can best be made by juxtaposing two fairly recent critical comments. Here is C.K. Stead on Georgianism:

> The characteristics which mark off the Georgians from their immediate predecessors [i.e., the tub-thumping Edwardians] are shared by Lawrence, Graves, Owen, and Sassoon: a rejection of large themes and of the language of rhetoric that accompanied them in the nineteenth century; and an attempt to come to terms with immediate experience, sensuous or imaginative, in a language close to common speech.[6]

And here is Donald Davie on more contemporary writing:

> Some of the features of later British poetry which have baffled and offended readers, especially in America – I have in mind an apparent meanness of spirit, a painful modesty of intention, extremely limited objectives – fall into place if they are seen as part of an inheritance from Hardy ... And I want to do more than merely excuse these characteristics of writing in the Hardyesque tradition; I want to present them as challenging, and to ask in effect, 'Are not Hardy and his successors right in severely curtailing for themselves the liberties that other poets continue to take?'[7]

When these remarks are linked with Frost's theories of 'the sound of sense,' which I have already compared to Wordsworth's manifesto in the Preface to *Lyrical Ballads*, (see p. 120 above), the terms of my argument will, I hope, become clearer. Just as Wordsworth protested against the elevated rhetoric of the later eighteenth century which had, he believed, lost contact with the realities of ordinary human living, so various poets in the twentieth century, both the Georgians and a number of writers who have come into prominence since the Second World War, have reacted against inflated style and pretentious posturing. The continuity of this process has been obscured until quite recently by the more immediately influential response of 'Modernism,' particularly on the part of Eliot and Pound, who succeeded in forging a new poetic language and rhythm that enabled them to express the sophisticated complexities of urban intellectualism. They were impelled by a similar impulse to renounce a deadened poetic diction but for an opposite purpose: to create a vehicle for an erudite 'minority culture' rather than, like the Georgians, to re-establish connection between poetry and a broader reading public.

But the analogy between Wordsworth's situation and that of the beginning of our century is not, of course, exact. Far from eschewing large themes or seeking limited objectives, Wordsworth saw himself as opening up vast new possibilities for poetry. The Georgians may have considered themselves restorers, but they were in no way pioneers. True, there was a brief, comparable period of buoyant optimism at the opening of the Georgian period; this is reflected in D.H. Lawrence's review of the first *Georgian Poetry*, one of the few Lawrencean statements that already reads like a period piece.[8] But the shadows of 1914 soon overcame it. Yet it could hardly, one feels, have been maintained in any foreseeable circumstances. Not only had Wordsworth's discovery of new poetic lands been consolidated and exploited for over a hundred years, but, more significantly, the twentieth-century poets were born into a very different England. Wordsworth's rustic environment had receded; Hardy, born as far back as 1840, was in terms of his birth a curious survival, even if his self-effacing response to the burden of modern living revealed him as a precursor of the contemporary consciousness. Small wonder that the energy and urgency of Wordsworth's verse gave way in the work of the more responsible later nature poets to a modest tentativeness. Edmund Blunden's revival of the tone of eighteenth-century retirement poetry may be seen as emblematic of a strategic withdrawal. The new literary temper (at least after 1914) could find no justification for any more positive response.

I contend nevertheless that Wordsworth's example still had much to offer the rural poet. Unfortunately, although the Georgians took over his general attitudes to language, too many of them appropriated his subject-matter without coming to any adequate understanding of his poetic method. They wrote, to be sure, 'about' the countryside, recommending its repose and praising its charms, but did not examine their personal reactions to it with any seriousness. Rather, they brought preconceived reactions to bear upon their material. They might imitate Wordsworth, but few could learn from him in any subtler, less parasitic sense. In representative Georgian nature poetry, like that of W.H. Davies, we find a pleasant casualness, a childlike clarity, but no depth, no sense of startled discovery. Above all, the language is notable for simplicity but not for precision. We find ourselves in disappointingly familiar territory, recognizing not tradition but mere derivativeness.

'What to make of a diminished thing.' Frost's oven-bird articulates the problem of that select minority of modern poets who have found themselves closer to the values of a rural society amid a natural environment than to those of the sophisticated, industrialized modern city. How to convey a deliberate choice when the positives have been dulled by repetition or vulgarized by the unskilled or the insincere, when the cult of complexity has rendered the simple verities suspect even when a genuine complexity of response is manifest behind them? 'The temptation is to go back,' to quote R.S. Thomas,[9] to offer nostalgic evocations of *temps perdu*. But the test is to come to terms with the present. In the ensuing sections, I intend to discuss the work of three writers who not only belong within the category of nature poets but have succeeded in conveying a recognizably personal response and an equally individual idiom. In Edmund Blunden, who appeared in the last *Georgian Poetry*, the beguilements of the past are strongest, and his response sometimes leads him into literary pastiche, but his modest achievement in maintaining a continuity with traditionalist verse in an unpropitious age is worthy of attention, and his best, quietly controlled rural poetry has acquired an additional interest in being produced alongside his admirable critical championing of earlier writers with similar inclinations. The work of Andrew Young, whose active poetic career began in 1910 and extended for half a century, is recognizably Georgian, but develops its own inimitable integrity unruffled by violent changes in poetic fashion, and is acquiring a deserved reputation by virtue of its sustained high quality. Last but by no means least, R.S. Thomas emerges just after the Second World War as a new and exciting poetic presence, best known for the staccato beat of his individual rhythm, but equally remarkable for the variety of his poetic perspectives derived, I am convinced, from the tradition that Wordsworth initiated.

EDMUND BLUNDEN

To consider Edmund Blunden (1896–1974) as a rural poet inevitably does him an injustice. His verse as a whole exists within the experienced extremes of the English countryside at its most peaceful and the apocalyptic trenches of the First World War. Any emphasis on his presentation of the former will obviously set his total achievement off balance. Moreover, since Blunden's work can easily be under- (as well, I think, as over-) valued, this caveat should be borne in mind during the discussion to follow.

While examining Blunden's verse in *New Bearings in English Poetry*, F.R. Leavis stressed its 'frank literary quality.'[10] This is indeed a conspicuous element in his work, and it is noteworthy because, although all the poets I have been considering (with the exception of Clare) can reasonably be regarded as 'men of letters,' in no case do they write as men of letters. We accept them as learned but they rarely display their learning.[11] Blunden does – though not, of course, in any ostentatious way; rather, his literariness reveals itself inevitably as he writes. His nature poetry, as a result, often harks back to the descriptive poetry of the eighteenth century and thereby suffers by juxtaposition with those poets who inherited and developed Wordsworth's innovations concerning viewpoint. It is tempting to wrest one of his own phrases out of its context and apply it to his work in general: 'I run a backward race.'[12]

The impression of the poet that we derive from his poems – the persona he communicates, the voice through which he speaks – is of a sensitive, intelligent, well-educated man, quietly introspective, recognizably middle-class in his attitudes. This is, of course, a perfectly acceptable stance for a rural poet; the same description could be applied to Andrew Young and even to Edward Thomas. But in Blunden's case it leads to certain difficulties. His fondness for classical and literary allusions, his tendency towards pastiche ('Old Homes,' for example, which belongs to the tradition of eighteenth- and nineteenth-century 'village poems'), his painstaking descriptions offered as if for their own sake, his leisurely contemplative tone, all these characterize his poetry as belonging, so far as the modern period is concerned, to a minor key. The gentleness in his personality links him with a no-longer-fashionable tradition of 'gentility.' Even his countryside is sheltered: Kent, 'the garden of England.' One poem is challengingly entitled 'Wilderness,' but the landscape it conjures up is revealingly domestic, tame, almost cosy.

But though in themselves accurate enough, these initial impressions are not altogether just. Below the superficially calm surface of his bucolic poetry, there frequently lurks a menacing, even monstrous threat of violence which, though expressing in metaphor the scourge of war, is none the less an actual violence within the natural order. 'The Pike' is a well-known illustration of this, but even in 'Wilderness' the tameness I have just noted is subtly qualified by the account of a spider who 'runs his glittering maze / To *murder* doddering hungry flies' (*BP*, 56 [my italics]). Blunden's nature is less idyllic than appears at first sight, and, as Leavis noted so acutely in 1932, he proves 'significant enough to show up the crowd of Georgian pastoralists.'[13] But it is not invariably the reader's fault if he fails to recognize the subtleties and qualifications. The regularity of Blunden's versification is too often lulling, and although his insight (and, perhaps, his sensibility) is 'modern,' his language and poetic attitudes are not. This becomes especially evident, I think, within the context of other rural poets. To bring his poetic powers to full flower, Blunden needed to control and vary his viewpoint, to stay (like Andrew Young) within the boundaries of his limitations, to sharpen his language and keep his rhythms and vocabulary both challenging and vital.

Valuable as Blunden's quietly impressive poetic voice has been, it can make no claims to greatness, nor indeed to originality. This is well illustrated (and the instance is of particular interest here) by his legacy from Clare. The possibilities for rural poetry that Clare's example opened up were not developed by his immediate successors (there were perhaps social, 'class' reasons for this). Indeed Blunden was a leading figure in drawing attention, both as editor and as literary critic, to Clare's unique qualities. Yet we can now see that his own view of Clare was partial. As his poems on the earlier poet reveal, it was decidedly 'romantic': in 'Clare's Ghost,' for example, with its description of his eyes

> Piercing beyond our human firmament
> Lit with a burning deathless discontent. (*BP*, 47)

As an anonymous reviewer in *The Times Literary Supplement* remarked astutely, 'Mr Edmund Blunden ... fused or confused Clare with his own poetic circumference' (*CCH*, 417). When Blunden 'imitates' Clare, the effect is inevitably diluted since he cannot bring to his subject the labourer's-eye-view which for Clare was habitual and unquestioned. Language is involved as well as viewpoint. When, for example, Blunden writes in 'A Country God' of 'stolchy ploughlands' (*BP*, 49), he deliberately reproduces as a scholar the rustic dialect which for Clare came, in Keats's phrase, as naturally as leaves on a tree.

For illustration it is worthwhile to turn to one of Blunden's early and effective descriptive sonnets, 'The Sunken Lane' (*BP*, 4). It opens with a successful evocation of his favourite landscape of waste places and decaying vegetation:

> Behind the meadow where the windmill stood
> There lies a swampy, unfrequented lane.
> There lodges all the high ground's winter rain,
> And stores sharp scent of sodden underwood.

This leads, equally typically, to a vision of possible violence or even terror beneath the calm surface of the description. The lane is sunken temporally as well as geologically (a convenient instance of Blunden's inconspicuous subtlety) and the plants presented objectively in the opening lines become to the now-personalized observer suggestive of 'primeval scenes':

> So in this lane to-day my half-shut eyes
> Saw monstrous waterwoods and weeds coiled high,
> Whose heavy heat and shadow seemed to stun,
> And saurians horrible of form and size.

But, as we might have predicted, the peaceful world of normality returns in the last two lines:

> Softly the twinkling water travelled by,
> The jutting stones stood whitened with the sun.

In both cadence and imagery this inevitably recalls, in a gentler key, the close of Clare's 'Mouse's Nest' examined earlier:

> The water o'er the pebbles scarce could run
> And broad old cesspools glittered in the sun.

As so often with Blunden's apparent borrowings from Clare, it would be difficult to establish a direct connection. 'Mouse's Nest' was not published until 1935, and Blunden may not have seen it in manuscript at the time that 'The Sunken Lane' was written. But my argument concerns similarities of effect rather than direct influence. Though Clare-like, Blunden's poem could hardly be mistaken for one of Clare's. The observer who muses with 'half-shut eyes' is an educated man of leisure to whom the vocabulary of prehistory comes easily. The resemblance between the 'sodden underwood' and primeval forests is willed within the mind of this observer; the two are connected, in Coleridge's terminology, through Fancy rather than Imagination. And in consequence the last two lines provide a facile comfort totally distinct from the sense of new discovery revealed in context by Clare's final couplet.

'The Sunken Lane' is in many respects representative of Blunden's best rural poetry. It is accomplished and controlled, but the basic ingredients are simple, and if repeated too often can become dissipated. The 'I' in Blunden's work is too often this same introspective outsider, and the language, though pure, is not sufficiently arresting to retain our interest. The poetic voice implies personality but generally lacks it. Sometimes, indeed, the 'I' becomes irritating: in 'Country Sale' (*BP*, 98–9), for instance, where the pity shown for the countryman whose home is being sold up reveals itself as a weak helplessness. The old man who 'cries how this belonged here sixty years' is seen with a sensitivity to the picturesque rather than with a genuine anguish. All the speaker can offer by way of commentary is a literary echo: 'So runs the world away.' And the tone of 'Old Homes' (*BP*, 94–8) is set by the opening lines:

> O happiest village! how I turned to you
> Beyond estranging years that cloaked my view
> With all their wintriness of fear and strain.

We may find this charming or exasperating according to taste, but, however we react, it is hardly a compelling piece of twentieth-century verse. Blunden's habitual poetic voice is sympathetic, sensitive, sincere. It possesses all the gentler virtues, but lacks breadth of vision and above all the linguistic vitality that we have a right to expect in major poetry.

I confine myself here to a consideration of some of Blunden's rural poems that transcend the limitations of his characteristic mode. One of the best is 'Forefathers' (*BP*, 67–8) which in subject recalls certain communal poems of Barnes, such as 'Lydlinch Bells' and 'Our Father's Works' (see pp. 73–4 above), but ultimately proves very different in approach and effect. It begins as a straightforward celebration of village predecessors:

> Here they went with smock and crook,
> Toiled in the sun, lolled in the shade.

It records the moulding of their lives according to the pattern of the seasons –

> Harvest supper woke their wit,
> Huntsman's moon their wooings lit –

and the recurrent rituals of the Christian cycle:

> From this church they led their brides,
> From this church themselves were led
> Shoulder-high.

Paying tribute to a rural culture which, though unlettered, expressed itself in practical achievements, it rejoices in the fact that men who

> Scarce could read or hold a quill,
> Built the barn, the forge, the mill.

So far, the poem may seem pleasant but conventional, a representative example of charming but essentially 'minor' Georgian verse. Yet the assurance and careful modulation of the rhythms should be sufficient to prepare us for the deeper notes sounded in the second half of the poem. The first three stanzas have implied an observer, but he remained unindividualized, and Blunden offers no clue (save, possibly, in the title) to any connection between villagers and speaker. Now he reveals the closeness of the relationship:

> On the green they watched their sons
> Playing till too dark to see,
> As their fathers watched them once,
> As my father once watched me.

The centre of interest has shifted from the forefathers themselves to the speaker's relation to them, but the poem does not end in any facile sense of association. On the contrary, the 'I' of the poem faces up not only to the unbridgeable gulf that has opened between himself and his ancestors but also to the poignant anonymity of those who created what he enjoys:

> Unrecorded, unrenowned,
>   Men from whom my ways begin,
> Here I know you by your ground
>   But I know you not within –
> There is silence, there survives
> Not a moment of your lives.

Because of its contrast with the restrained objectivity of the opening lines, the intimate note sounded at the conclusion (not only 'I' but 'you') becomes doubly moving. And the ease with which the effect is achieved should not blind us to the mastery of Blunden's poetic control. Superficially the 'I' is doubtless the poet himself, but he has rigorously pared down his character to suit the requirements of the poem. Here is no languid literary sentiment, no escapism. The punning conclusion (the materially successful speaker likens his situation to that of a bee that has just brushed his hand:

> I'm in clover now, nor know
> Who made honey long ago)

exemplifies the gulf between the articulate, sophisticated present and the silent, more rugged past about which the present is becoming increasingly ignorant. Paradoxically, Blunden succeeds in conveying a sense of immediacy and deep sincerity by means of an 'I' who is adroitly impersonalized, a separate and carefully moulded persona.

'Mole Catcher' (*BP*, 82–3), a radically different poem, is particularly interesting for our purposes since it shows Blunden both learning from Clare and creating his own poem out of Clare's materials. It is, indeed, a profitable exercise in literary discrimination to compare the poem with two of Clare's, both entitled 'The Mole-Catcher' (*Poems*, ii. 57–9, 351). There can be no doubt that Blunden has borrowed a number of specific details, notably the technical means by which the trapper sets up his snares, from Clare's versions.[14] In addition, especially in the opening verse-paragraph, he is at pains to take over Clare's tough, unsentimental neutrality. But whereas Clare reproduces what he sees bluntly, almost carelessly, without any obvious sense of formal requirements, the process in Blunden demands a deliberate artistic stance, a conscious refusal to do more than report. Blunden not only has to make an effort to put himself into a position resembling Clare's, but must even suppress any hint of an individual, observing presence.

Certain differences emerge at once. Here, for example, is Blunden:

> And where the lob-worms writhe up in alarm
> And easy sinks the spade, he takes his stand
> Knowing the moles' dark highroad runs below:
> Then sharp and square he chops the turf, and day
> Gloats on the opened turnpike through the clay.

And here is the equivalent in Clare:

> Pricking the greensward where they love to hide,
> He sets his treacherous snares, resolved to kill.   (ii. 57)

We would not expect in Clare the deliberately constructed imagery of 'the moles' dark highroad' followed by 'the opened turnpike,' nor the non-visual effect of the day gloating (which is closer to Hardy). By the same token, the violence of Clare's 'treacherous snares, resolved to kill,' though present in Blunden's poem, is not rendered so directly; rather, it is a realization that emerges gradually as we absorb the whole poem. Blunden's 'Mole Catcher,' then, though dependent on Clare, is certainly no plagiarism.

And in the second half of the poem Blunden comes into his own. Here he provides a context for the mole-catcher that is absent (and unwanted) in Clare. Without dominating the poem in any conspicuous way, Blunden none the less develops and controls it, first by noting the fact that the trapper is loving to all creatures except moles, then by presenting him as a model villager, devout in his faith and a regular church-goer. Yet the result is not (as we might at first expect) ironic. The points are made gently, without extraneous comment:

> What his old vicar says is his belief,
> In the side pew he sits, and hears the truth.

Blunden does not paint him as a hypocrite who fails to practise what is preached to him; on the contrary, the old man emerges as an authentic countryman who accepts life as it is and is undisturbed by anomalies which the urban mind recognizes as inconsistency. It is a remarkable tribute to Blunden's artistry that he can convey all this by means of juxtaposition and subtle suggestion without entering (and so weakening) his poem in order to state it directly. 'Mole Catcher' is an apparently artless poem that is in fact rigorously controlled by art.

Finally, we recognize in the well-known poem 'The Midnight Skaters' (BP, 104) a remarkable (I believe, unique) effort on Blunden's part to express his darker vision of nature within a concentrated image, to present his poetic world *sub specie aeternitatis*. The Kentish hopfields and the village millpond, recurrent and characteristic Blunden locales, are invoked once again, but they are now stripped of the equally recurrent and characteristic minute detail. Instead 'The pole-tops steeple to the thrones / Of stars,' and we respond with a delighted sense of shock to the unexpected vigour of the boldly original verb. Here his imaginative scope seems boundless; effortlessly this first stanza encompasses the heights of the sky and the unplumbable depths of 'the pond's black bed.' In the second stanza, the anti-human hostility of nature is directly conveyed as death lying in wait 'within those secret waters.' Whereas in 'The Pike' the miller 'stands amazed at the whirl in the water' (*BP*, 63) as the rapacious marauder lances the unfortunate chub, here the violence in nature is extended to include man as a potential victim instead of superior observer; here the recording poet, while sharing the miller's viewpoint, knows himself in the same dilemma as those he observes. 'Earth's heedless sons and daughters' are all not only vulnerable but doomed.

Yet the poet here responds to the menacing challenge with a magnificent exhortation of defiance:

> Then on, blood shouts, on, on,
> Twirl, wheel and whip above him,
> Dance on this ball-floor thin and wan,
> Use him as though you love him;
> Court him, elude him, reel and pass,
> And let him hate you through the glass.

The image of mankind as midnight skaters risking destruction at every twist and turn of the dangerous game of life is as daunting as it is vivid, but this sombre, surrealist picture is transfused with an almost Yeatsian sense of vitality and daring; Blunden's skaters are prepared to go 'Proud, open-eyed and laughing to the tomb.'[15] Inappropriate as it may at first seem to consider this poem in a study of rural poetry, and however much its ending may transcend its beginning, 'The Midnight Skaters' takes its origin from Blunden's rural heritage. Here is a prime instance of the evolution of a profound modernity out of a natural matrix.

Michael Thorpe well characterized Blunden's situation when he observed that 'in Blunden, as in another loosely labelled "Georgian," Edward Thomas, there is a tension between the old romantic "cosmic consciousness" – sometimes really felt but often only willed or desired – and the disenchanted, modern world.'[16] This is well said; unfortunately, however, Blunden was not able to maintain the necessary balance between these opposing world-views. More often than not he indulged in too facile an evocation of the Romantic sensibility, and for this reason we tend to think in terms of derivatives. A poem like 'The

Silver Bird of Herndyke Mill' would have proved startlingly original if it had first appeared in *Lyrical Ballads*; it can only seem quaintly old-fashioned as a product of 'the years of *l'entre deux guerres*.' Blunden was an accomplished practitioner, but he worked a poetic vein that was growing thin; and he made only isolated and unsustained attempts to employ new methods or explore new seams. While he helped to keep alive the traditions of nature poetry, he contributed little to its development.

ANDREW YOUNG

In theory Andrew Young (1885–1971) ought to be a very minor poet indeed. A country clergyman with a passion for botany and topography, he wrote simple, direct, unpretentious poems, reflecting his interest in the natural world, poems that conform – at least at first sight – to the standard Georgian pattern of versified thoughts. He adopts a personal, intimate manner, and many of his poems close, in seemingly perfunctory fashion, with a formula such as 'I wonder ...' or 'I almost feel ...' Superficially, he appears to have little to offer; in fact, his work has a freshness and originality that bespeak a highly individual response. Through precision of language and a firm control of perspective, Young provides a distillation of experience unique in nature poetry. Indeed, perspective becomes not merely the means by which his effects are attained but part of his subject-matter, part of the effects themselves.

When discussing the poetry of Edward Thomas, I suggested that 'Thaw' was a poem that Young might have written (see p. 147 above). The contrast between the observer looking up at the rooks and the rooks looking down at the world below them is one that would have appealed to Young, and the ability to shift into the perspective of what is being observed is one of his characteristic qualities. It is not surprising to find him referring to Thomas as the Georgian poet whom he most admired.[17] A number of his own poems are based on a similar effect. 'A Dead Mole,' quoted here in full, is a good example:

> Strong-shouldered mole,
> That so much lived below the ground,
> Dug, fought and loved, hunted and fed,
> For you to raise a mound
> Was as for us to make a hole; ·
> What wonder now that being dead
> Your body lies here stout and square
> Buried within the blue vault of the air?[18]

At first sight this may seem no more than a conceit, and it is true that from a technical standpoint Young's poetic predecessors are to be found not in the traditional nature poets but in some of the Metaphysical writers of the seventeenth century. Yet further consideration should convince us that Young is being more than merely clever. Ultimately, this is a poem about death (a theme which recurs in his verse). It is typical of Young that he should approach a large subject through a small, seemingly unimportant incident. We soon discover, however, that the real subject is not the dead mole but the relation, in both life and death, between human beings and the animal world which they like to believe they have transcended. By overturning our normal perspective, by picturing a dead mole on the ground as equivalent to a dead man in the earth, Young is able to challenge our complacent assumptions.

The success of the poem is not, however, to be explained by control of perspective alone; the purity and precision of the language is also a major factor. I refer not only to the balanced syntax that enforces the similarities between mole and man ('For you to raise a mound / Was as for us to make a hole') but to the effortless revivification of the hackneyed image of the sky as an airy 'vault' by juxtaposing the phrase with 'buried.' While Young invites us to examine the small, seemingly trivial incidents that happen to us every day, he impels us at the same time to notice the subtleties in apparently simple and straightforward vocabulary. Young was a shy and modest man, and as poet he does not flaunt his effects. But if we underestimate the extent of his artistry, our loss will be considerable.

Young is essentially a miniaturist, but although he may be called, to borrow W.H. Hudson's phrase, a rural 'traveller in little things,' his practice must not be confused with the obsession with smallness so characteristic of many of the Georgians. Young's habit of looking through binoculars (whether literal or metaphorical) is derived, not from any cult of the tiny, but from his experience as a field-naturalist. This too is part of his emphasis on perspective, as the poem entitled 'Field-Glasses' (*YCP*, 162) demonstrates. Here Young writes about his own poetic method. Just as the binoculars bring the natural world closer to Young, so his poetry brings it closer to us. It allows us (and the point is vital to a poet for whom religion was even more important than poetry) a God's-eye-view:

> Why I borrow their sight
> Is not to give small birds a fright
> Creeping up close by inches;
> I make the trees come, bringing tits and finches.
>
> I lift a field itself
> As lightly as I might a shelf,
> And the rooks do not rage
> Caught for a moment in my crystal cage.

> And while I stand and look,
> Their private lives an open book,
> I feel so privileged
> My shoulders prick, as though they were half-fledged.

This poem is, I think, central to his whole work. The poet as exact observer is a constant throughout Young's verse, and the effect we derive from his poems is like looking through a fine lens where natural objects are caught (but only for a moment) in a 'crystal cage.' Once again the final line is more complex than it seems. The process enables Young to become, as it were, a bird, yet by the same token he is privileged to observe the natural world from an angelic perspective; the image of budding wings extends in both directions.

A similar extension both downwards and upwards is to be found in a number of Young's poems. In 'A Prehistoric Camp' (*YCP*, 139–40), the poet notices on his walk up Eggardon Hill in an excessively late spring that the birds are building their nests in the still-bare hedgerows. The observation develops into his characteristic response to the always-bare encampment on the summit:

> But there on the hill-crest,
>   Where only larks or stars look down,
> Earthworks exposed a vaster nest,
>   Its race of men long flown.

The ease and exactitude with which the connection is made renders commentary unnecessary. In another poem primarily concerned with perspective, 'Mole-Hills on the Downs' (*YCP*, 75–6), the mole-hills are compared with the God-created downland on which they exist. Young the observer can look at the little mounds as if from a divine viewpoint:

> I can watch the earth
> Like a volcano at its birth
> Still rise by falling down.

Yet the possible hubris of this position is soon shattered:

> And as by these small hills I pass
> And take them in my stride
> I swell with pride,
> Till the great hills to which I lift my eyes
> Restore my size.

The religious dimensions of this poem are, characteristically, hinted at indirectly; the paradox of rising by falling (*O felix culpa!*) is at the heart of the

Christian mystery, and the echo of Psalm 121 in the penultimate line is (or should be) sufficient to alert the reader to the larger frame of reference. Young is not the kind of clergyman who preaches in his verse, but his religious orthodoxy is central to his way of looking. As a human being, he partakes not only of the animal world (which he observes with enthusiasm since it is a part of the divine creation) but also of the spiritual world (which he celebrates by employing his creative faculty as observer and interpreter of God's earth). Although he clearly qualifies as a rural poet, and although one can think of few poets less alike than Young and Dylan Thomas, Young could say of his poetry as Thomas did in his well-known prefatory note to his *Collected Poems* that it was written 'for the love of Man and in praise of God.'

Young was as familiar as Blunden with the earlier nature poets; this can be seen at a glance in his prose-books on flowers and topography, which are generously spiced with appropriate poetic quotation. Unlike Blunden, however, Young hardly ever reminds us of other rural poets in his verse. His religious attitude may recall that of Barnes, and his poems often display a visionary quality comparable to Clare's, but such resemblances are evidence only of an overlapping response. Poetically, he is never directly imitative. Inconspicuously, unostentatiously, he develops his own poetic method; as a result his *Complete Poems* hang together as, quite unmistakably, the work of one man. The 'I' is constant throughout, a figure carefully moulded out of certain selected aspects of the real Andrew Young, though it is interesting to note that the poetic persona is similar to but not identical with the narrator in such prose-works as *A Prospect of Flowers* and *The New Poly-Olbion*. In the prose his quests often bring him into the company of others; in the poems he is almost invariably alone but (and this distinguishes him from Hardy, Frost, and especially Edward Thomas) he never appears lonely. In the prose he is very much the literary pilgrim, either visiting places associated with the literary or rural dead or bringing the dead to life by quoting them in his work; in the poems, the literary references are suppressed – he is, we might say, himself the poet.

But he is not 'the poet' in any over-conscious way. Rather, he presents himself as an inquisitive field-observer, precise in his identifications, naturally meditative, quietly and genuinely religious. He watches, sits, listens, thinks; such verbs recur. Yet there is a variety of stance within the basic similitude. In some instances, the role of neutral observer is carried to an extreme – in 'March Hares' (*YCP*, 44–5), for example, where, as he says, 'I made myself as a tree,' and the tension in the poem derives from the stiff lifelessness of the observer and the quick, spurting movements of the subjects. In 'The Men' (*YCP*, 58–9), by contrast, his act of watching links him with the animal world against his own kind. While listening to the inconsequential sounds of the wild creatures around him, he is disturbed by a group of men 'crashing through the wood.' Immediately, he puts himself in the position of the wild life thereby endangered:

> And knowing that it meant small good
> To some of us who owned that wood,
> Badger, stoat, rabbit, rook and jay
> And smoky dove that clattered away,
> Although no ill to me at least,
> I too crept off like any stealthy beast.

Once again, the strategic shift in perspective is both central and masterly.

Indeed, so characteristic and controlled is his approach that he does not need the first person to establish his individualized viewpoint – it is there, unmistakably, in his imagery and tone. 'Hard Frost' (YCP, 165–6), for instance, though straightforwardly descriptive, is clearly stamped with Young's poetic signature. Each poetic unit is distinguished by his own 'way of looking' which is strikingly individual without ever seeming idiosyncratic. So, with the freezing of the water,

> Brooks, their own bridges, stop,
> And icicles in long stalactites drop.

Similarly, the 'tinkling trees' are 'changed into weeping willows' while dead boughs, in an audacious and ambivalent image, 'take root in ponds.' Moreover, the first line of the poem, 'Frost called to water "Halt!",' prepares us for the extended metaphor that runs through the final stanza:

> But vainly the fierce frost
> Interns poor fish, ranks trees in an armed host,
> Hangs daggers from house-eaves
> And on the windows ferny ambush weaves;
> In the long war grown warmer
> The sun will strike him dead and strip his armour.

The military image as applied to the seasons is conventional enough, but it is more usually employed to describe the onslaught of winter upon the dying year. Young not only uses it with remarkable precision ('interns' for fish trapped in the frozen stream is beautifully exact, and the idea of ice covering the earth like armour strikingly appropriate), but reverses it in this last stanza so that the offensive is initiated by the spring sun. This, of course, is in line with Young's religious position, and biblical analogues (Christ defeating death, David defeating Goliath, etc.) are available so close beneath the surface of the poem that, if his work is viewed as a whole, they might even be considered part of its content. But Young's originality lies, ultimately, in the tact with which he makes his effect, a point that can be enforced perhaps by noting that we experience the impact of the poem without recalling Shelley's seemingly inevitable 'If Winter comes ...'

This same concentration of detail is manifest in 'Cuckoos' (*YCP*, 142), a superficially playful poem that none the less reveals a serious purpose:

> When coltsfoot withers and begins to wear
> Long silver locks instead of golden hair,
> And fat red catkins from black poplars fall
> And on the ground like caterpillars crawl,
> And bracken lifts up slender arms and wrists
> And stretches them, unfolding sleepy fists,
> The cuckoos in a few well-chosen words
> Tell they give Easter eggs to the small birds.

There is a freshness and clarity about this that recall the poets of an earlier age (the opening lines recapture the rhythmical lilt of the introductory couplets to Chaucer's Prologue to *The Canterbury Tales*), but only Young could have combined the particular kind of observation with the particular form of expression to achieve the tone that is so characteristic of him. There is nothing very original about presenting the change from yellow flowers to downy seeds in terms of whitening hair in old age – quite the reverse, in fact – but Young brings a revivifying piquancy to the image by applying it in the spring season to the coltsfoot, one of the earliest-blooming of English wild flowers. [19] The likening of fallen catkins to caterpillars and bracken fronds to 'sleepy fists' is visually apt and, when pointed out, obvious, though I doubt if the average reader would ever make the connections unassisted. Finally, the conceit of the cuckoos giving 'Easter eggs to the small birds' seems a little 'cute' and facile until we become aware of the full force of the 'few well-chosen words' and recognize the suggestion of Judas-like betrayal. Young is invariably more subtle than the initial impact of his verse might suggest. His poems grow upon us; their associations extend within the mind as we learn to respond to the palpable but unforced allusiveness that is a central part of his design.

His linguistic compression is one of the most remarkable aspects of his poetry, his ability to condense what in most poets would be an extended simile into no more than a line or two. Some scattered examples, compiled as a virtually random sampling, must suffice here:

> Stunt willow-trunks that line the edge,
> Whose roots like buried eels are sunk.   (*YCP*, 64)

> ... one tree-crowned long barrow
> Stretched like a sow that has brought forth her farrow.   (*YCP*, 134)

> ... ivy trickling in green waterfalls ... (YCP, 156)

> Rocks, rising, showed that they were sheep. (YCP, 165)

> ... that slant-legged robin
> With autumn on his chest. (YCP, 34)

Who but Young could so economically describe a fairy ring of mushrooms as 'a small Stonehenge' (YCP, 71)? How better could the gambolling of spring lambs be characterized than in the lines:

> Pale lambs leap with thick leggings on
> Over small hills that are not there ? (YCP, 139)

I called this a *virtually* random sampling because I have chosen out of a multitude of possible examples lines in which one natural (or at least rural) image is seen in terms of another: willow-trunks are compared to eels, the barrow to a sow, and so on. Not all his imagery works in this way, but such effects are sufficiently common to indicate that this is a deliberate strategy on Young's part. It is a way of sustaining his vision of the essential unity of the natural world. Such observations may be minute in scale, but the poetic talent that offers them is not to be belittled.

Andrew Young is an elusive poet because he cuts across the literary-historical boundaries which are convenient enough for the critical discussion of most other poets. Although he was throughout his life independent of literary movements, he is traditional in attitude and belief and (it would be fair to state) Georgian in sensibility. The poet who can express 'some gossamery thought / Of thankfulness' (YCP, 37) – moreover, a poet whose work could be adequately summed up by that phrase – may well seem remote from the poetic trends of the mid-to-late twentieth century. At the same time, Norman Nicholson, in a tribute published in 1957, could justly observe: 'I have not the slightest doubt that Canon Young belongs essentially to my own time. As the years go on, [his] work is seen to be far closer to the central line of the modern movement than either he or anyone else could once have realised.'[20] This comment connects, of course, with our gradually evolving sense, touched upon earlier in this chapter, of the continuity of our verse traditions that were only interrupted and qualified rather than defeated and replaced by the modernist movement of Pound and Eliot. Nicholson rightly identifies Young's immediate poetic predecessors as 'Edward Thomas, Robert Frost, and, to a lesser extent, Thomas Hardy' – though personally I would question the sense in which they can confidently be said to have had 'most influence upon him.' But Nicholson, with the insight of a practising poet, was one of the first to recognize the precise significance of their contribution: 'All three wrote of the landscape of the pre-urban world, then in the glow of its last sunset. In this they might rightly be classed with the other Georgian poets of that time, but unlike the latter, these three were all aware of the crisis of language through which poetry would have to pass if it were to survive.'[21]

Young too, in his own way, was conscious of that 'crisis of language,' which required a number of varying responses. It would be both foolish and futile to deny or underestimate the contribution of the champions of modernism in their linguistically radical reactions to the challenge. But it would be equally foolish (and, in the modern climate, more tempting) to ignore the writers who chose the road less travelled by and, instead of seeking out new methods, preferred to refine and revivify the traditional modes. Young was indisputably one of these. His intense self-discipline, which insisted upon both precision of language to match his precision of observation and a controlled perspective that, however gentle in its effects, contributes to what can legitimately be termed a poetry of encounter, ensures him a place among the select few able to produce a viable nature poetry in our time.[22]

R.S. THOMAS

A wild, harsh landscape; a spare directness of statement; a resonant accentual rhythm; richness of metaphorical identification; scrupulous manipulation of viewpoint: all these seemingly disparate qualities unite with astonishing ease in the poetry of R.S. Thomas.[23] The unique tension achieved in his verse can be explained in part by the fact that Thomas is a recognizably modern, intellectually sophisticated poet plunged by unusual circumstances into a primitive rural society that is most often looked upon as belonging to the past rather than the present, a country of 'starved pastures' (SYT, 17) where 'the slow poison / And treachery of the seasons' (T, 35) are still factors to be reckoned with. Thomas may well find the dramatic clash between his own temperament and his subject-matter personally troubling, but there can be no doubt that it proves poetically stimulating. He is uncomfortably aware that 'nature's simple equations / In the mind's precincts do not apply' (SYT, 115), and thus seems to have reached the opposite extreme from Wordsworth's confident statement of the exquisite way in which 'The external World is fitted to the Mind' (PW v. 5). Yet Thomas's situation in the remote Montgomery village of Manafon (where he was rector from 1942 until 1954) is subtly similar to Wordsworth's in Grasmere a hundred and fifty years earlier. Both are concerned with the manner in which nature, in Thomas's words, 'manifests itself as the background to a way of life.'[24] And Thomas works out his own response to the terms of this relation, like his predecessor, in a series of tentative, varied, and (in the Wordsworthian sense) experimental poems.

Although we are not likely to think of the twentieth century as an age congenial to nature poetry, there can be few better illustrations of the richness of response that it can still command than the contrast involved in turning from the Georgian milieu out of which both Blunden and Young developed to the totally different world of R.S. Thomas. Part at least of this contrast derives from the clear-cut Englishness of the first two (despite Young's Scottish origins) set against Thomas's palpable Welshness. Indeed, there is a sense in which Thomas represents an association with the English tradition of nature poetry not dis-similar to that of Robert Frost: though related to it, he remains subtly independent. It is easy enough, however, to detect resemblances to most of the earlier poets I have discussed. Wordsworth's name continually recurs when Thomas's poetry is being considered, though commentators are often uncertain whether he belongs in the Wordsworthian or anti-Wordsworthian camp. His admonition to his readers,

> You must revise
> Your bland philosophy of nature, earth
> Has of itself no power to make men wise,   (*SYT*, 106)

looks like yet another instance of a poetic successor alluding to Wordsworthian sentiment in order to deny it. But Thomas has himself edited a selection of Wordsworth,[25] and written of him with respect and admiration. Similarities of technique between the two poets will manifest themselves in due course.

Other connections are evident, but less readily demonstrable. If his use of Welsh metrical and rhythmical devices sometimes suggests Barnes (whom he mentions in *Words and the Poet* [p. 12]), this can be explained in terms of common interests rather than direct influence, while Donald Davie has noted that Thomas is one of the comparatively few modern British poets to claim (legitimately or not) to have learned nothing from Hardy.[26] I strongly suspect, too, that in such lines as

> and there's a spirit of wildness
> Much older, crying when the stone-curlew yodels
> His sea and mountain cry,

Edward Thomas gave the younger poet a clue towards the evolution of his own inimitable and wholly characteristic poetic style. But, as their common surname indicates, this could also be interpreted as an independent response to their Welsh heritage.[27] The analogues with unequivocally English writers for the most part remain, obstinately, no more than analogues.

Although R.S. Thomas has acknowledged that 'it was by way of nature that I myself came to poetry,'[28] he has written few direct nature poems. 'A Blackbird

Singing' (*PS*, 33), however, demonstrates the assurance and skill that he can bring to this kind of verse:

> It seems wrong that out of this bird,
> Black, bold, a suggestion of dark
> Places about it, there yet should come
> Such rich music, as though the notes'
> Ore were changed to a rare metal
> At one touch of that bright bill.

But his usual method is not to present his own reaction but rather to show the responses of other men, generally farmers and peasants, who depend on the natural world for their survival. These responses are rarely aesthetic, since his protagonists do not think in such terms, though the contrast between their attitudes and his own (and, by extension, his readers') often contributes to the creative tension within an individual poem. None the less, there are traditional aspects of his verse which strike a familiar chord, especially the way in which he heightens an effect by presenting man in terms of nature and vice versa. In 'A Labourer' (*SYT*, 18), for instance, the old man's face is 'inscrutable as stone' (Wordsworth's leech-gatherer springs to mind) and 'his back comes straight / Like an old tree lightened of the snow's weight.' In a similarly titled poem, 'The Labourer' (*SYT*, 70), he asks us to

> notice the twitching hands,
> Veined like a leaf, and tough bark of the limbs,
> Wrinkled and gnarled.

Other examples could be assembled readily enough, and as for the vice versa I am thinking of such lines as 'The land's patience and a tree's / Knotted endurance' (*SYT*, 28).

Thomas's originality lies more in his manner than in his material. I have stressed the way in which the best rural poets are careful to create the perspectives from which to write their poems. Here Thomas shows himself particularly skilled. At first sight we may be inclined to the view that for Thomas (as, in very different circumstances, for Clare) the appropriate perspective was ready to hand, part of the biographical situation out of which the poems sprang. Certainly his appointment to the living at Manafon proved poetically enriching. As R. George Thomas has noted, 'all [the] poems from the poet's first decade – in *The Stones of the Field* [1946] and *An Acre of Land* [1952] – derive their strength and power from the cross-tension that exists between the peasant, tied to his soil, and the priest, tied to his people.'[29] But his poems do not rise effortlessly out of this cross-tension; Thomas exploits his own situation for poetic purposes, adapting his standpoint to the intrinsic needs of each poem.

The basic conflict is expressed in 'A Priest to his People' (*SYT*, 29), a poem in which Thomas manages to combine testament and confession. Given the bitter indignation that makes up much of the poem, the very title implies irony, and a conflict within the poet's mind is mirrored by the evident vacillation between contempt for his people's lack of response and admiration of their sheer capacity for endurance:

> How I have hated you for your irreverence, your scorn even
> Of the refinements of art and the mysteries of the Church.

The priest is continually aware of the intellectual gap between himself and his flock. The poet who can write non-rural poems with such titles as 'A Thought from Nietzsche,' 'Coleridge,' 'On a Line in Sandburg,' 'Dialectic,' 'Wallace Stevens,' 'Ivan Karamazov,' finds it difficult either to comprehend or to forgive the 'vacancy' (*SYT*, 21) in the minds of his parishioners. Yet at the same time he can understand, even if he cannot share, the channels into which their artistic instincts have been forced. He admits:

> Your speech has in it
> The source of all poetry, clear as a rill
> Bubbling from your lips; and what brushwork could equal
> The artistry of your living on the bare hill?

Thomas learns what George Sturt had learned earlier in his inquiries into the unlettered culture of his Surrey village, that the so-called 'fine arts' (poetry, brushwork) are by no means the only arts.[30] In other poems he comes to recognize his congregation's 'secret learning, innocent of books' (*SYT*, 45), 'the terrible poetry of [Prytherch's] kind' (*T*, 9), the 'rhythm of the long scythe' (*T*, 35), and even questions 'art's neurosis' as manifested in the self-styled civilized world (*T*, 19). In the present poem, Thomas continues:

> You will forgive, then, my initial hatred,
> My first intolerance of your uncouth ways.

We realize, with something of a shock, that the poem turns on an ironic reversal of roles: the priest ends by confessing to his people.

Although the respective loyalties of priest and poet themselves produce some tensions within his verse, Thomas's position as priest is integral to his poetry, and he is able to turn the possible disadvantages of separation from the people about whom he writes (as clergyman, as intellectual, and – from the villagers' viewpoint – as outsider) into a poetic virtue. Himself detached, he can mediate between the peasant community and the reader. So often in his poems he addresses the reader directly, talking to him about the villagers: 'Shall we follow him down? ... No, wait for him here' (*SYT*, 17); 'Consider this man in the field beneath' (*SYT*, 25). Separation is essential to his poetic purpose. At the same time, he is aware of the 'Affinity' (*SYT*, 25) of all men. Like Wordsworth, he can employ dramatic methods so that the imperatives sometimes come from the villagers themselves; thus a hill-farmer can assert: 'Listen, listen, I am a man like you' (*SYT*, 55). However critical he may be of his congregation, Thomas can always see 'the angel peeping from the latticed eye' (*SYT*, 33).

His priestly function clearly accounts for the openly didactic quality of so much of his verse. As he admits himself, 'there is always lurking at the back of my poetry a kind of moralistic or propagandist intention' (*WP*, 21). The effort of understanding, itself part of the experience to be conveyed, is assisted by Thomas's practice of casting himself (as Wordsworth so often does) in the role of intermediary. 'The Airy Tomb' (*SYT*, 37–41), one of Thomas's longer poems, provides an example, and is worth considering in some detail. Here Thomas presents the harsh, graceless life of a boy born and bred in the wildest recesses of the hill-country, and he succeeds in conveying this through the appropriate vigour and violence of his language. The poem is set in a

> gaunt wilderness, where snow is laid
> Deadly as leprosy till the first of May   (ll. 31–2)

and we are invited to experience with the boy Tomos 'the grey rain's claws / Sharp in the thatch' (ll. 145–6). Once again there is little direct description in the poem, though we obtain a vivid and distinct impression of Tomos's life on the hills that is as fully realized as that of Wordsworth's Margaret or Michael but is communicated to us in a different way. Man and nature are so fused for Tomos that he invariably sees one in terms of the other. The death of his father is comprehended by reference to deaths he has known in the natural world:

> He had seen sheep rotting in the wind and sun,
> And a hawk floating in a bubbling pool,
> Its weedy entrails mocking the breast
> Laced with bright water.   (ll. 52–5)

Later, he equates human love with 'the itch of cattle / At set times and seasons' (ll. 111–12).

Thomas successfully reproduces the boy's responses, and he does so, of course, with an eloquence beyond the capacity of his subject. But he is interpreter as well as mouthpiece, and he never forgets that the reader, for whom a Tomos is probably as alien as a bushman or a desert nomad, needs help in understanding and acknowledging Tomos as 'a man like you.' Remembering his own initial attitude, he begins with his accustomed reference to the boy's lack of learning ('books and sums were poison to Tomos, he was stone blind / To the printer's magic' [ll. 5–6]), and again this is followed by a realization that he had his own culture, that he could read 'the poems, which the rooks wrote in the sky' (l. 39). But he is not content with merely recreating the boy's viewpoint with sympathy and a tough compassion that is the reverse of sentimental; he bullies the reader into making the effort to experience the harsh reality of Tomos's situation:

> Can you picture Tomos now in the house alone,
> The room silent, and the last mourner gone
> Down the hill pathway?   (ll. 82–4)

One notes here the poet's earnest desire to become for Tomos something comparable to what Wordsworth (or, perhaps, the Wanderer) had been for Margaret. 'The Airy Tomb' is a poem about human understanding – or, too often, the lack of it,

>   for folk cannot abide
> The inscrutable riddle, posed by their own kin.   (ll. 131–2)

And the poet is prepared to bludgeon the reader into a reluctant comprehension by exposing his passive complacency:

> And you, hypocrite reader, at ease in your chair,
> Do not mock their conduct, for are you not also weary
> Of this odd tale, preferring the usual climax?   (ll. 133–5)

'You! hypocrite lecteur! – mon semblable, – mon frère!' Thomas's effect here is violent – too violent, I believe, since it betrays a calculated self-consciousness which in the result draws more attention to the poet than to the protagonist of his 'odd tale.' But the point to be stressed is that Thomas's erudite allusion subtly reinforces his own attitude. The suggestion of Baudelaire, via Eliot's *Waste Land*, jolts us into recalling that the world of urban sophistication is contained within another world in which flowers may be scrawny but not evil, where waste lands, though existent, are not composed of bricks and concrete. His protest acts as a kind of indignant challenge to us to follow his own example and recognize Tomos as 'semblable' and 'frère.' I admit that I somewhat exaggerate the effect in the act of drawing attention to it, but it is important to realize what the poet is doing: taking up a narrative stance that can meet the educated reader on his own ground yet remaining close enough to Tomos to act as an understanding spokesman.

But the best place to examine Thomas's poetic perspectives is the series of poems, scattered through the early volumes, that are written around the peasant-figure of Iago Prytherch. Previous commentators have noted the way in which Thomas's attitude to Prytherch develops in the course of the series;[31] here I wish to examine the technical means by which this change is accomplished, to draw attention to the varying angles from which Thomas presents him. We first encounter Prytherch in 'A Peasant' (*SYT*, 21), and Thomas purposefully keeps him at a distance, inviting us to consider him, dispassionately, as a specimen: 'Just an ordinary man of the bald Welsh hills.' His 'half-witted grin' and 'spittled mirth' are pointed out with an almost clinical objectivity, and we are told bluntly: 'There is something frightening in the vacancy of his mind.' The narrator's imperatives ('see him,' 'remember him') control our response. There is certainly no idealization of the countryman here, but Thomas is at the same time anxious to prevent too negative a reaction – the reaction that, we have reason to suspect, may once have been his own. 'This is your prototype,' we are reminded; 'he, too, is a winner of wars.' None the less, Prytherch is to be considered, measured, classified. In controlling the response, the narrator stands, as in 'The Airy Tomb,' between reader and subject.

This is one way of presenting Prytherch – coldly, objectively, weighing the pros and cons. In 'Memories' (*SYT*, 45) Thomas deliberately varies his approach. This is a monologue spoken to Prytherch, not about him, and the first line,

> Come, Iago, my friend, and let us stand together,

is indicative of a corresponding change of attitude. The poet, in a sentiment that comes close to suggesting pastoral, pledges:

> I will sing
> The land's praises, making articulate
> Your strong feelings.

Later, he suggests to Prytherch that his 'lips are sealed / By a natural reticence.' This implies that Prytherch's mind is by no means vacant; it is, moreover, a far cry from other accounts of the reaction of the peasantry to the world about them. In 'Enigma' (*SYT*, 68), for instance (not technically a Prytherch poem), a man in the fields displays no such feelings:

> The earth is beautiful, and he is blind
> To it all. ...
> He cannot read the flower-printed book
> Of nature, nor distinguish the small songs
> The birds bring him. ...

The man in 'Enigma' is a Peter Bell; Iago Prytherch, at least in 'Memories,' is not. (It is worth recalling that we have encountered the same situation in Clare's poetry [see p. 47 above].) Thomas's poems do not complement each other, nor, however, do they cancel each other out. Both present different aspects of the countryman in general. Similarly, the varying technical perspectives taken up in 'A Peasant' and 'Memories' present different aspects of Iago Prytherch in particular. Both have a partial validity; neither presumes to offer the whole truth.

Two other poems in *Song at the Year's Turning* employ the perspectives already discussed; 'The Gap in the Hedge' (*SYT*, 53) is about Prytherch, 'Lament for Prytherch' (*SYT*, 99) an address to him. But 'Invasion on the Farm' (*SYT*, 102) takes the form of a dramatic monologue in which for the first time Prytherch is allowed to speak for himself. Thomas as narrator has withdrawn completely, but he has kept his promise in articulating the 'strong feelings' of his subject: we are confronted with the peasant's direct response to ourselves as interlopers in his territory. Significantly he insists: 'I don't know / What you are talking about.' No effective communication can be established, but Prytherch is instinctively aware of the threat to his way of life that outsiders represent:

> [I] feel the cold
> Winds of the world blowing. The patched gate
> You left open will never be shut again.

Prytherch's wisdom is not to be measured in intellectual terms; his is the response of a wild creature who knows an enemy when he sees one. The poem is complete in itself, but the light it sheds on Prytherch's inner consciousness affects our response to the whole series.

Now that the principle of varied and controlled perspective has.been established, the Prytherch poems in later volumes can be considered more briefly. All four in *Poetry for Supper* are addressed to Prytherch himself; the most remarkable of them is, perhaps, 'Absolution' (*PS*, 44) in which the poet-priest makes another personal confession:

> Prytherch, man, can you forgive ...
> One who strafed you with his scorn
> From the cheap gallery of his mind?
> It was you who were right the whole time.

Even more interesting, however, is the first poem in *Tares*, 'The Dark Well,' where we detect a complete *volte-face* from the opening poems in the series. This time the poet is speaking to Prytherch about the group of anonymous outsiders ('They') of which the reader is representative:

> They see you as they see you,
> A poor farmer with no name. ...
> To me you are Prytherch, the man
> Who more than all directed my slow
> Charity where there was need.

'The Dark Well' is in many respects the high point of the series. Other Prytherch poems follow, but they do not extend the terms already established. Rather, they go on to show Prytherch's pathetic rightness by chronicling the process of decline which he had sensed in 'Invasion on the Farm.' In 'Too Late' (*T*, 25), for example, Thomas looks into Prytherch's future and sees

> The cold breath of the machine
> That will destroy you and your race.

Prytherch has been freed from servitude to the earth only to become slave 'to the pound's whistle.' The poem looks ahead to Thomas's later, increasingly embittered vision of a world in which Prytherch has no place. Appropriately enough, the last of the Prytherch poems, published in the *Anglo-Welsh Review* (Summer, 1969) but not yet included in a collection, is entitled 'The Grave.' The 'machine' has triumphed; Prytherch is dead. More recently, in 'Gone?' even 'Prytherch country' has been destroyed ('Nothing to show for it now').[32]

Most of the poems in Thomas's subsequent volumes fall outside the boundaries of this study. In 'Groping' he notes how

> Wordsworth turned from the great hills
> of the north to the precipice
> of his own mind,[33]

and Thomas may be said to have moved in the same direction. None the less, it is legitimate to note that they explore larger topics by means of the same poetic method. In three recent volumes – *H'm* (1972), *Laboratories of the Spirit* (1975), and *Frequencies* (1978) – sequences of poems on the nature of God are developed, like the Prytherch series, by variations on the angle of presentation. There are poems about God, poems addressed to God, poems in which God himself speaks. And at this point we may agree with Donald Davie that, whatever Thomas may say in a rather irascible poem entitled 'Taste' about Hardy as

> an old stager
> Shuffling about a bogus heath,
> Cobwebbed with his Victorian breath,[34]

the older poet occupies a significant place in Thomas's poetic inheritance. These recent volumes inevitably recall such poems by Hardy as 'New Year's Eve,' 'A Plaint to Man' and 'God's Funeral.' Needless to say, Thomas's poems are in no way derivative (there is no trace of the 'Victorian breath'), but he is exploring in the twentieth century the same ultimate questions that troubled Hardy in the nineteenth. Thomas's religious attitudes are, of course, different, but as poet he imprints his own stamp on a basic continuity.

Thomas is important here not merely as a poet but as living testimony to an essential but unfashionable truth. Nature poetry and the life and attitudes it reflects need not be merely escapist in the modern period; he is insistent on this point, and his poetic practice underlines it. He is, of course, only too aware of the tentacles of the city stretching towards the countryside, enveloping it, destroying it, but he refuses to accept alien urban standards. 'I live in the country by choice,' he insists in *Words and the Poet*; '... I don't allow for a moment the superiority of urban to country life. I don't believe that a poet who chooses to write about an agricultural environment is necessarily insular, escapist, or even provincial' (*WP*, 23, 24). He totally rejects the cult of progress and the assumptions upon which so much of contemporary life is based. More recently he has expressed related sentiments in an interview: 'The quality of life is deteriorating everywhere ... I say to my wife, "All the places we've known, have any of the changes been for the better?"'[35] He is unyielding but (and this is essential) he is not reactionary. His position is summed up supremely in a late Prytherch poem appropriately entitled 'Aside':

> Turn aside, I said; do not turn back.
> There is no forward and no back
> In the fields, only the year's two
> Solstices, and patience between.[36]

CONCLUSION

R.S. Thomas is one of the most distinguished of modern British poets, but he is by no means representative. His solitariness, his religious beliefs and, above all, his residence in remote rural parishes have set him noticeably apart. When we turn to more typical contemporary writing, the poetry of a generation no longer dazzled by the innovations of Pound and Eliot and the poets of the 1930s but reacting at the same time against the undisciplined romanticism of Dylan Thomas and the Apocalyptics, we find an understandable suspicion of extremes. Obscurity and artlessness are both to be avoided. True, there can be no return to the rustic simplicities of a vanished past, but for those who concern themselves with rural subjects continuity with the native tradition is still seen as possible and valuable.

Thomas Hardy is generally recognized as the most important link with the tradition, though the work of Edward Thomas has also proved quietly influential. Through them the more enduring qualities fostered by Georgianism have been filtered down to the modern period. The resemblances, it is true, are often passive rather than active. Robert Conquest's characterization in 1956 of the aims of his *New Lines* group, 'a negative determination to avoid bad principles,'[37] would not have seemed out of place in 1912, the only difference being that his bad principles would include all the faults of the run-of-the-mill Georgians. The work of Philip Larkin and Elizabeth Jennings could legitimately be discussed in this context, but for my present purpose the most significant poem in Conquest's anthology is by John Wain, who was shortly to edit a useful selection of Hardy's verse. His 'Reason for Not Writing Orthodox Nature Poetry'[38] is an impressive statement which conveniently sums up his distance from the Georgians while at the same time manifesting a number of the better Georgian qualities.

The poem's simplicity of diction and directness of statement would have pleased Edward Marsh, but Wain is doubtless thinking of the Georgians when he writes how

> later poets found it easy going
> To give the public what they bargained for,

and in so doing impoverished both nature and poetry. Wain has no patience with 'moderns who devoutly hymn the land,' who merely appropriate the traditional attitudes unthinkingly and uncreatively. His own 'sterner choice' is to note

> How little beauty bids the heart rejoice,
> How little beauty catches at the throat.

His appreciation of the natural world is sincere and genuine ('Simply, I love this mountain and this bay'), but he establishes his own individual reaction. Ironically, in recording a personal response and moulding a language and viewpoint in which to express it, Wain is, I believe, closer to the nature poets who are the subject of this book than are the conventionally minded who would doubtless be shocked at his lack of enthusiasm. The 'orthodox nature poetry' of his title is a degenerate form, properly rejected; Wain himself is more faithful to the continuing example of Wordsworth and Hardy.

The phrase 'orthodox nature poetry,' however interpreted, implies the existence of an unorthodox variety. Robert Langbaum has argued that, since the decline of 'the philosophical and protoreligious concept of nature' in the latter part of the nineteenth century, a new nature poetry has arisen that presents 'the mindlessness of nature, its nonhuman otherness.'[39] He offers examples from D.H. Lawrence, Ted Hughes, Wallace Stevens, Marianne Moore, W.S. Merwin, and others. Langbaum stresses the difference between the two kinds because he is primarily concerned with the philosophical backgrounds to the poetry. My own approach lays greater emphasis on a balancing continuity. The 'nonhuman otherness' can only be identified by a human perceiver, and the human presence in the poem, whether conspicuously assertive in Lawrence or unobtrusive in most of the others, remains central. Langbaum's 'new nature poetry,' then, is a development from, rather than a repudiation of, the old. It exemplifies an appropriately natural process.

'Where man is not, nature is barren.'[40] Blake's apothegm is not as hostile to nature as one might assume; indeed, it would serve as a suitable motto for the present study. R.S. Thomas makes a comparable point in his introduction to *A Choice of Wordsworth's Verse*: 'The inadequacy of the description of him as a nature poet is obvious. Through nature he became aware of the joys and sorrows of the human condition.'[41] Similar accounts have been made about all the rural poets I have been discussing, and the remark usefully brings this book full circle. I have argued that 'nature poetry' should not be regarded as either a trivial or an outmoded form of verse. On the contrary, its capacity to make us aware 'through nature ... of the joys and sorrows of the human condition' is an index to its importance. A world gradually awakening (not, one hopes, in the words of one of R.S. Thomas's poem-titles, 'Too Late') to the necessity of conserving natural resources will find that the relation between the human and the natural worlds becomes more rather than less urgent. As that happens, the reputations of the more talented nature poets may be expected to increase. Thomas makes a related point in the same introduction that pays indirect tribute to the importance of all the serious rural poets from Wordsworth to his own time. Alluding to Wordsworth's fears in 'Lines Written in Early Spring,' he comments: 'To many in these islands two hundred years later, it may be grievous to think what man has made of nature.'[42] The crisis is great, but the testament of the nature poets remains as an example, an inspiration, and a guide.

NOTES

1 / INTRODUCTION

1 Charles G.D. Roberts, *Selected Poetry and Critical Prose*, ed. W.J. Keith (Toronto: University of Toronto Press, 1974), pp. 276, 277, 281.

2 John More, *Strictures, Critical and Sentimental, on Thomson's 'Seasons'* [1777] (New York: Garland Publishing, 1970), p. 33.

3 W.J.B. Owen and Jane Worthington Smyser, eds., *The Prose Works of William Wordsworth* (3 vols. Oxford: Clarendon Press, 1974), I, 140.

4 R.S. Thomas, *Song at the Year's Turning* (London: Hart-Davis, 1955), p. 46.

2 / WILLIAM WORDSWORTH

1 For Wordsworth's poetry, the following texts have been used: *The Poetical Works of William Wordsworth*, ed. Ernest de Selincourt and Helen Darbishire (5 vols. Oxford: Clarendon Press, 1940–9), and *The Prelude, or Growth of a Poet's Mind*, ed. Ernest de Selincourt, rev. Helen Darbishire (2nd ed. Oxford: Clarendon Press, 1959). Quotations from *The Prelude* are from the 1850 text throughout. Because so many editions of Wordsworth are available, page references are not given for easily accessible poems, but line- or stanza-numbers are inserted for longer poems. The above-mentioned editions are cited in the text as *PW* and *Prelude* respectively.

2 Quotations from Dorothy Wordsworth's *Journals* are from Helen Darbishire's edition (World's Classics. London: Oxford University Press, 1970). Hereafter cited in text by date of entry.

3 T.W. Thompson, *Wordsworth's Hawkshead*, ed. Robert Woof (London: Oxford University Press, 1970), p. 56. Note that Tyson was exactly the same age as Wordsworth himself.

4 A similar separation of 'he' and 'I' in Wordsworth may be found in 'Home at Grasmere':

> Since that day forth the place to him – *to me*
> (For I who live to register the truth
> Was that same young and happy Being) becomes
> As beautiful to thought, as it had been,
> When present, to the bodily sense.
>
> (*PW* v. 314)

5 See Geoffrey Hartman, 'Wordsworth, Inscriptions, and Romantic Nature Poetry,' in Frederick W. Hilles and Harold Bloom, eds. *From Sensibility to Romanticism: Essays Presented to Frederick A. Pottle* (New York: Oxford University Press, 1965), pp. 389–413.

6 *Ibid.*, p. 393.

7 *Ibid.*, p. 400.

8 The last phrase does not occur in the 1798 text; the previous quotation appeared in a slightly different form, but the sense is not affected.

9 The similarity between this phrase and 'inly disturbed,' applied to the recluse in the 'Yew-Tree' poem, is worth noting.

10 W.J.B. Owen and Jane Worthington Smyser, eds., *The Prose Works of William Wordsworth* (3 vols. Oxford: Clarendon Press, 1974), I, 148. Hereafter cited in text as *Prose*.

11 The de Selincourt edition reads 'permanently,' a decidedly Wordsworthian but in fact incorrect reading. For the correction, see Mary Jacobus, *Tradition and Experiment in Wordsworth's 'Lyrical Ballads' (1798)* (Oxford: Clarendon Press, 1976), p. 241n.

12 See S.M. Parrish, '"The Thorn": Wordsworth's Dramatic Monologue,' *English Literary History*, 24 (1957), 153–63, later incorporated into *The Art of the Lyrical Ballads* (Cambridge, Mass.: Harvard University Press, 1973).

13 Ernest de Selincourt, ed., *The Letters of William and Dorothy Wordsworth*, second edition, *I: The Early Years*, rev. Chester L. Shaver (Oxford: Clarendon Press, 1967), p. 366.

14 F.R. Leavis, *Revaluation* [1947] (New York: Norton, 1963), p. 179 and 'Wordsworth: The Creative Conditions,' in Reuben A. Brower, ed., *Twentieth-Century Literature in Retrospect* (Cambridge, Mass.: Harvard University Press, 1971), p. 338.

15 Leavis, 'Wordsworth: The Creative Conditions,' p. 335.

16 Quoted in David Perkins, *Wordsworth and the Poetry of Sincerity* (Cambridge, Mass.: Harvard University Press, 1964), p. 149.

3 / JOHN CLARE

1 Geoffrey Grigson, ed., *Poems of John Clare's Madness* (London: Routledge & Kegan Paul, 1949), p. 60.

2 Reprinted in Mark Storey, ed., *Clare: The Critical Heritage* (London: Routledge & Kegan Paul, 1976), p. 246. Hereafter cited in text as *CCH*. To avoid excessive footnoting, I quote earlier Clare criticism wherever possible from this collection.

3 J.W. and Anne Tibble, eds., *The Prose of John Clare* (London: Routledge & Kegan Paul, 1951), p. 118. Hereafter cited in text as *JCP*. I have corrected

spelling and added light punctuation in accordance with the principles described in the following note.

4 J.W. Tibble, ed., *The Poems of John Clare* (2 vols. London: Dent, 1935), I, 60–1. Unless otherwise indicated, quotations from Clare's poetry will be from this edition, identified in the text by volume and page number. This is the most complete edition of Clare's poetry to date. Later editions by Eric Robinson and Geoffrey Summerfield, *The Shepherd's Calendar* (London: Oxford University Press, 1964) and *Selected Poems and Prose of John Clare* (London: Oxford University Press, 1967), offer more reliable textual readings than Tibble, but reproduce all Clare's misspellings, grammatical errors, and lack of punctuation. Such procedure may well reflect a superior, more objective textual principle, but it can also result in a complacent response to Clare's untutored rusticity (how charming! how quaint!). It has the effect of making Clare appear less knowledgeable than he actually is. More significant differences between Clare's poetry and that of other nature poets can best be discussed, I believe, without the distractions of an unpunctuated and uncorrected text.

5 See John Barrell, *The Idea of Landscape and the Sense of Place, 1730–1840: An Approach to the Poetry of John Clare* (Cambridge: Cambridge University Press, 1972), pp. 177–8.

6 Clare's prospectus, quoted in J.W. and Anne Tibble, *John Clare: A Life* (London: Michael Joseph, 1972), p. 314.

7 *Specimens of the Table-Talk of the Late S.T. Coleridge* (2 vols. London: Murray, 1855), II, 72.

8 Barrell, p. 175.

9 J.W. and Anne Tibble, *John Clare: A Life*, p. 406.

10 J.W. and Anne Tibble, eds., *The Letters of John Clare* (London: Routledge & Kegan Paul, 1951), p. 257. Hereafter cited in text as *LJC*.

11 Barrell, p. 176.

12 W.H. Hudson, *British Birds* [1895] (London: Longmans, 1911), p. 44.

13 Ibid., p. 187.

14 Ibid., pp. 97–8.

15 J.W. and Anne Tibble, *John Clare: A Life*, p. 313.

16 Richard Jefferies, *The Story of My Heart* [1883] (London: Constable, 1947), p. 41.

17 There is some doubt on this point since the final stanza occurs on its own in another manuscript. But the stanza-form is not one that Clare uses elsewhere and the subject-matter suggests that this is offered as perhaps a first draft of the conclusion to the poem.

18 I have derived the text of this poem from the Tibbles' Everyman edition, *Selected Poems* (London: Dent, 1965), which prints readings corrected from their 1935 edition. I have, however, substituted more suitable lighter punctuation and rendered the spelling consistent.

4 / WILLIAM BARNES

1 H.J. Massingham, *The Southern Marches* (London: Hale, 1952), p. 80.

2 Bernard Jones, ed., *The Poems of William Barnes* (2 vols. [continuing pagination] London: Centaur Press, 1962), p. 196. All quotations from Barnes's poetry, unless otherwise noted, are taken from this edition, hereafter cited in text as *PWB*. I have, however, replaced the accent on the '-èn' endings of the Dorset present participle which Barnes used consistently but which Jones omits.

3 See William Turner Levy, *William Barnes: The Man and His Poems* (Dorchester: Longmans, 1960), p. 37.

4 William Barnes, *Poems of Rural Life in the Dorset Dialect* (London: Russell Smith, 1844), pp. 36–7.

5 Ibid., p. 37.

6 Lucy Baxter ['Leader Scott'], *The Life of William Barnes* (London: Macmillan, 1887), p. 277.

7 Rolf Gardiner, *England Herself: ventures in rural restoration* (London: Faber, 1943), p. 60.

8 H.J. Massingham, *The English Countryman* (London: Batsford, 1942), pp. 73, 126.

9 Quoted in Giles Dugdale, *William Barnes of Dorset* (London: Cassell, 1953), p. 297.

10 Since it offers a more reliable text than *PWB*, 303, I have quoted here from Thomas Hardy, ed., *Select Poems of William Barnes* (London: Henry Froude and Oxford University Press, 1908), p. 60. Hereafter cited in text as *SPB*.

11 Thomas Hardy, 'Enter a Dragoon,' in *A Changed Man* [1913] (Library edition. London: Macmillan, 1951), p. 158.

12 Geoffrey Grigson, ed., *Selected Poems of William Barnes* (Muses' Library. London: Routledge & Kegan Paul, 1950), p. 12. Hereafter cited in text as *MLB*.

13 *Poems of Rural Life in the Dorset Dialect* (1844), pp. 11–12.

14 A.S.F. Gow, introduction to *The Greek Bucolic Poets* (Cambridge: Cambridge University Press, 1953), pp. xxii–xxiii. For a rather different approach to Theocritus' language, laying greater emphasis on its elegance and stylization – 'the "ordinary" language of cultured conversation' – see Thomas G. Rosenmeyer, *The Green Cabinet: Theocritus and the European Pastoral Lyric* (Berkeley and Los Angeles: University of California Press, 1969), pp. 50–1.

15 William Barnes, *A Glossary of the Dorset Dialect, with a Grammar* [1886] (Guernsey: Toucan Press, 1970), p. 22.

16 Samuel Hynes, *The Pattern of Hardy's Poetry* (Chapel Hill: University of North Carolina Press, 1961), p. 27.

17 Dugdale, p. 151.

18 Lucy Baxter ['Leader Scott'], p. 167.

19 Levy, p. 153.

20 Reprinted in Dwight Macdonald, ed., *Parodies: An Anthology from Chaucer to Beerbohm and After* (London: Faber, 1960), p. 75.

21 H.J. Massingham, *The English Countryman*, p. 125. See also F.T. Palgrave in Dugdale, p. 251.

22 E.H. Mackerness, ed., *The Journals of George Sturt (1890–1927)* (Cambridge: Cambridge University Press, 1967), p. 551.

23 Levy, p. 22.

5 / THOMAS HARDY

1 Donald Davie, *Thomas Hardy and British Poetry* (New York: Oxford University Press, 1972), p. 74.

2 See Florence Emily Hardy, *The Life of Thomas Hardy* (London: Macmillan, 1962), pp. 58, 93, 355. Hereafter cited in text as *LTH*.

3 For a detailed discussion of this point, see J. Hillis Miller, *Thomas Hardy: Distance and Desire* (Cambridge, Mass.: Harvard University Press, 1970). Cf. also the following: 'there is always that slight, but significant split between his self and the voice of the poem.' Tom Paulin, *Thomas Hardy: The Poetry of Perception* (London: Macmillan, 1975), p. 130.

4 Quoted in J.O. Bailey, *The Poetry of Thomas Hardy: A Handbook and Commentary* (Chapel Hill: University of North Carolina Press, 1970), p. 379.

5 See, for example, *The Complete Poems of Thomas Hardy*, ed. James Gibson (London: Macmillan, 1976), p. 556. I have followed this text throughout when quoting from Hardy's poetry, hereafter cited as *CPH*. Because numerous other editions exist, I have not given page reference to the poems. For Hardy's references to Wordsworth and the *Lyrical Ballads*, see also *LTH*, 147, 306, and Bailey, pp. 159–60.

6 J.I.M. Stewart, *Eight Modern Writers* (Oxford: Clarendon Press, 1963), p. 48.

7 R.P. Blackmur, *Form and Value in Modern Poetry* (New York: Doubleday, 1957), p. 22.

8 John Peck, 'Hardy and the Figure in the Scene,' *Agenda*, x (Spring-Summer 1972), 121.

9 Robert Gittings, *Young Thomas Hardy* (London: Heinemann, 1975), p. 219.

10 Introduction to Barnes in Ward's *English Poets*, reprinted in Harold Orel, ed., *Thomas Hardy's Personal Writings* (London: Macmillan, 1967), p. 84.

11 For a detailed account of Hardy's editorial procedures, see my 'Thomas Hardy's Edition of William Barnes,' *Victorian Poetry*, 15 (Summer 1977), 121–31.

12 The analogies with 'The Milkmaïd o' the Farm' and 'Went Hwome' are discussed by Paul Zietlow, 'Thomas Hardy and William Barnes: Two Dorset Poets,' *PMLA*, 84 (March 1969), 293–4, those with 'Vellèn the Tree' by Kenneth Marsden, *The Poems of Thomas Hardy: A Critical Introduction* (London: Athlone Press, 1969), p. 228 and Bailey, p. 585.

13 'The Rev. William Barnes, B.D.,' reprinted in Orel, p. 101.

14 Bailey, p. 548.

15 A good description of the phenomenon may be found in George Ewart Evans, *The Pattern Under the Plough* (London: Faber, 1966), p. 99. For another Hardy reference to the bee-line, see his poem 'The Later Autumn.'

16 This point has been made by Jean Brooks, *Thomas Hardy: The Poetic Structure* (London: Elek, 1971), p. 66.

17 See Douglas Brown, *Thomas Hardy* (London: Longmans, 1954), pp. 147–52; Samuel Hynes, *The Pattern of Hardy's Poetry* (Chapel Hill: University of North Carolina Press, 1961),

pp. 121–3; Thom Gunn, 'Hardy and the Ballads,' *Agenda*, x (Spring-Summer 1972), 28–32; and Paulin, pp. 205–10.

18 Gunn, 31.

19 J. Hillis Miller, '"Wessex Heights": The Persistence of the Past in Hardy's Poetry,' *Critical Quarterly*, 10 (Winter 1968), 339–59.

20 The perspective of this poem has been variously interpreted. Paulin lists the different versions: 'For Bailey the speaker in the first two stanzas is "an observant gossip", for Hillis Miller Hardy is the speaker and is characteristically detached and self-absorbent; and for me the poem is a dialogue between Hardy and Emma' (p. 133). I find Paulin's interpretation rather forced; those of Bailey and Hillis Miller, though apparently conflicting, are in fact not dissimilar to each other or to mine. Irrespective of whether one sees the observer as a stranger or a detached Hardy, his viewpoint from side-stage, like the narrator's in 'A Night Piece,' is disturbingly effective.

21 See J. Hillis Miller, *Thomas Hardy: Distance and Desire*, p. 251, and the forceful rejoinder by Donald Davie in 'Hardy's Virgilian Purples,' *Agenda*, x (Spring-Summer 1972), 154–5.

22 Edward Thomas, 'Haymaking,' *Collected Poems*, ed. R. George Thomas (Oxford: Clarendon Press, 1978), p. 227. Earlier printings of Thomas's poetry read 'Cobbett' for 'Cowper.' The change will be regretted by many readers.

23 James G. Southworth, *The Poetry of Thomas Hardy* [1947] (New York: Russell & Russell, 1966), p. 199.

24 See Bailey, p. 591.

25 Ibid., p. 427.

26 Joseph Warren Beach, *The Concept of Nature in Nineteenth-Century English Poetry* [1936] (New York: Pageant Press, 1956), p. 503.

4 / ROBERT FROST

1 Quoted in Louis Mertins, *Robert Frost: Life and Talks-Walking* (Norman: University of Oklahoma Press, 1965), p. 120.

2 Richard Thornton, ed., *Recognition of Robert Frost* (New York: Holt, 1937), p. 31. Hereafter cited in text as *RRF*.

3 Lawrance Thompson, ed., *Selected Letters of Robert Frost* (New York: Holt, Rinehart & Winston, 1964), p. 160. Hereafter cited in text as *FSL*.

4 Edward Connery Lathem, ed., *Interviews with Robert Frost* (New York: Holt, Rinehart & Winston, 1966), p. 172. Hereafter cited in text as *IRF*.

5 See Reginald Cook, *The Dimensions of Robert Frost* (New York: Rinehart, 1958), p. 65.

6 Hyde Cox and Edward Connery Lathem, eds., *Selected Prose of Robert Frost* (New York: Holt, Rinehart & Winston, 1966), p. 60. Hereafter cited in text as *FSP*.

7 'A Tribute to Wordsworth,' *Cornell Library Journal*, 11 (Spring 1970), 77–99.

8 George W. Nitchie, *Human Values in the Poetry of Frost* (Durham, NC: Duke University Press, 1960), p. 31.

9 'Hyla Brook.' *The Poetry of Robert Frost*, ed. Edward Connery Lathem (New York: Holt, Rinehart & Winston, n.d. [1968?]) has been used throughout when quoting from Frost's poems. Because numerous editions are available, page references have not been given in the text, but line numbers are inserted for longer poems.

10 John F. Lynen, *The Pastoral Art of Robert Frost* [1960] (New Haven and London: Yale University Press, 1967), p. 144.

11 Sidney Cox, *A Swinger of Birches* [1957] (New York: Collier, 1961), p. 80.

12 Richard Poirier, in his recent *Robert Frost: The Work of Knowing* (New York: Oxford University Press, 1977), has called this statement 'the most misleading advice Frost ever gave for the reading of his or of most lyric poetry' (p. 19). But Poirier, as his title suggests, is more interested in Frost's intellectual milieu than in his place in poetic tradition. My own argument here supports Frost in this matter.

13 Lynen, p. 9.

14 Quoted in Nitchie, p. 140.

15 Quoted in Elizabeth Shepley Sergeant, *Robert Frost: The Trial by Existence* (New York: Holt, Rinehart & Winston, 1960), p. 229.

16 See Reuben A. Brower, *The Poetry of Robert Frost: Constellations of Intention* (New York: Oxford University Press, 1963), p. 30.

17 Lynen, p. 145.

18 Sergeant, p. 118.

19 David Jones, *The Anathemata* (New York: Viking, 1965), p. 65n.

20 See Brower, pp. 130–5, and Poirier, pp. 162–5.

21 Nitchie, p. 45.

22 Lynen, p. 158.

23 Brower, p. 156.

24 Sergeant, p. 118.

25 Lynen, p. 136.

26 Mertins, p. 107.

27 Lawrance Thompson, in *Robert Frost: The Years of Triumph* (New York: Holt, Rinehart & Winston, 1970), pp. 360–2, shows that the poem was written in response to traits which Frost detected in the young poet Wade Van Dore, but this information, though interesting, is extrinsic to the action of the poem.

28 See Lawrance Thompson, *Robert Frost: The Early Years* (New York: Holt, Rinehart & Winston, 1966), p. 284.

29 Compare also: 'I've got a man there; he's both ... a wall builder and a wall toppler. He makes boundaries and he breaks boundaries. That's man.' Frost, quoted in Reginald Cook, *Robert Frost: The Living Voice* (Amherst: University of Massachusetts Press, 1974), pp. 82–3.

30 See Sergeant, pp. 87–8. This incident is also discussed by R. George Thomas in 'Edward Thomas and Robert Frost,' *Poetry Wales*, 13 (Spring 1978), 29.

31 For a convenient gathering of these, see Thompson, *Robert Frost: The Years of Triumph*, pp. 546–8. For Thomas's remarks to Frost on 'The Road Not Taken,' see 'Letters to Robert Frost,' *Poetry Wales*, 13 (Spring 1978), 14–16.

32 William Cooke, in *Edward Thomas: A*

Critical Biography (London: Faber, 1970), p. 243, dates 'The Sign-Post' 7 December 1914. R. George Thomas, in *Edward Thomas* (Cardiff: University of Wales Press, 1972), p. 36, dates 'The Other' November or December 1914. Both poems are therefore among the earliest that Thomas wrote. Indeed, it is possible that 'The Other' was a direct result of Frost's encouraging Thomas to rewrite as verse certain passages from *In Pursuit of Spring* (1914), which used a double-figure as a continuing device throughout the narrative.

33 Quoted in Sergeant, p. 335.

34 Lionel Trilling, "A Speech on Robert Frost: A Cultural Episode,' *Partisan Review*, XXVI (Summer 1959), 445–52, reprinted in James M. Cox, ed., *Robert Frost: A Collection of Critical Essays* (Englewood Cliffs, NJ: Prentice-Hall, 1962), pp. 151–8.

35 Quoted in Nitchie, p. 34.

36 Quoted in Sidney Cox, *A Swinger of Birches*, p. 96.

37 Mertins, p. 288. To be fair, it should be recorded that Frost is also reported to have said: 'I think in all my work there's a consistency. It takes serious brainwork to see the consistency. You have to know how to take me' (*IRF*, 258). But the consistency claimed here would seem to be one of attitude and approach rather than formulated, applied belief – perhaps, indeed, a consistent refusal to be pinned down.

7 / EDWARD THOMAS

1 For Clare, see *Feminine Influence on the Poets* and *A Literary Pilgrim in England* (relevant extracts reprinted in *Clare: The Critical Heritage*, pp. 311–19); For Barnes, see 'Wessex in Poetry,' a review of Hardy's *Select Poems of William Barnes* (*Daily Chronicle*, 28 November 1908) and *In Pursuit of Spring* (London: Nelson, 1914), p. 186; for Hardy, see 'Thomas Hardy of Dorchester,' *Poetry and Drama*, I (June 1913), 180–4 (reproduced with some alteration in *In Pursuit of Spring*) and *A Literary Pilgrim in England*.

2 All quotations from Thomas's poems follow the text of R. George Thomas's recent edition of *The Collected Poems of Edward Thomas* (Oxford: Clarendon Press, 1978). Since a number of editions of the poetry are now available, page references are not given; line numbers are inserted for the longer poems. Special mention should be made of Edna Longley's edition of *Poems and Last Poems* (London: Collins, 1973), which is excellent but incomplete since six of Thomas's poems (notably 'Up in the Wind') did not appear in either of the volumes; but the notes to this edition are a major contribution to Thomas studies, and should be consulted.

3 R. George Thomas, ed., *Letters from Edward Thomas to Gordon Bottomley* (London: Oxford University Press, 1968), p. 107.

4 *The Heart of England* (London: Dent, 1906), p. 238.

5 See William Cooke, *Edward Thomas: A Critical Biography* (London: Faber, 1970), p. 185.

6 Ibid., p. 73. See also *Poems and Last Poems*, p. 396.

7 *The Country* (London: Batsford, 1913), p. 7.

8 I have discussed the prose, with a brief section on its relations to his poetry, in the chapter on Thomas in *The Rural Tradition* (Toronto: University of Toronto Press, 1974; Hassocks, Sussex: Harvester Press, 1975).

9 See R. George Thomas, *Edward Thomas* (Cardiff: University of Wales Press, 1972), p. 26.

10 Quoted in Cooke, p. 147.

11 Quoted in Louis Mertins, *Robert Frost: Life and Talks-Walking* (Norman: University of Oklahoma Press, 1965), pp. 136–7. For further discussion of their influence upon each other, see Frost's letter to Grace Walcott Conkling first published by William Cooke in *Poetry Wales*, 13 (Spring 1978), 22–3.

12 This was written before I had read the sensitive and persuasive discussion, 'Edward Thomas and the Georgians,' in Edna Longley's annotated edition of *Poems and Last Poems*, which established the close connection between Thomas and the Georgians with a wealth of literary-historical detail. For opposed views, however, see Jeremy Hooker, 'The Writings of Edward Thomas, II: The Sad Passion,' *Anglo-Welsh Review*, 19 (Autumn 1970), 65 and 75, and J.P. Ward, 'The Solitary Note: Edward Thomas and Modernism,' *Poetry Wales*, 13 (Spring 1978), 72.

13 Quoted in Eleanor Farjeon, *Edward Thomas: The Last Four Years* (London: Oxford University Press, 1958), p. 110.

14 See Cooke, p. 244.

15 Elizabeth Shepley Sergeant, *Robert Frost: The Trial by Existence* (New York: Holt, Rinehart & Winston, 1960), p. 202.

16 Robert Thornton, ed., *Recognition of Robert Frost* (New York: Holt, 1937), p. 29.

17 For an excellent detailed discussion of this poem, see Michael Kirkham, 'Edward Thomas's Other Self,' *Ariel*, 6 (July 1975), 65–77.

18 The poem is, however, topographically exact. The inn in question is the White Horse between Froxfield and Priors Dean, Hampshire, and the details recorded in the poem remain virtually unchanged, including the empty frame for the inn-sign. For further details of the local background to Thomas's poems, see W.M. Whiteman, *The Edward Thomas Country* (Southampton: Cave Publications, 1978).

19 See Cooke, pp. 163–6.

20 See Lawrance Thompson, ed., *Selected Letters of Robert Frost* (New York: Holt, Rinehart & Winston, 1964), p. 164, and John Moore, *Life and Letters of Edward Thomas* (London: Heinemann, 1939), p. 222.

21 Longley, ed., *Poems and Last Poems*, pp. 12, 231.

22 Raymond Williams, *The Country and the City* (London: Chatto & Windus, 1973), pp. 257–8.

23 *The Country*, p. 6.

24 R. George Thomas, *Edward Thomas*, p. 48.

25 *The Last Sheaf* (London: Cape, 1928), pp. 101–2.

26 John Burrow, 'Keats and Edward Thomas,' *Essays in Criticism*, 7 (October 1957), 413.

27 Michael Kirkham, 'Hardy and the Hardy Tradition,' *University of Toronto Quarterly*, 43 (Winter 1974), 184. Compare also J.P. Ward's discussion, *Poetry Wales*, 13 (Spring 1978), 73.

28 The setting for this poem has recently been identified as Priors Dean north of Steep. See Whiteman, p. 34, and a photograph in Jan Marsh, *Edward Thomas: A Poet for his Country* (London: Elek, 1978), facing p. 115.

29 Farjeon, p. 154.

30 'Letters to Frost,' *Poetry Wales*, 13 (Spring 1978), 16.

8 / THE GEORGIANS AND AFTER

1 Philip Larkin, 'Church Going,' in Robert Conquest, ed., *New Lines* (London: Macmillan, 1956), pp. 20, 21.

2 W.H. Auden, 'A Literary Transference,' *Southern Review*, VI (Summer 1940), 86; Philip Larkin, 'Wanted: Good Hardy Critic,' *Critical Quarterly*, 8 (Spring 1966), 179.

3 Auden, 85.

4 James Reeves, introduction to *Georgian Poetry* (Harmondsworth: Penguin Books, 1962), p. xv.

5 John Wain, 'Reason for Not Writing Orthodox Nature Poetry,' in *New Lines*, p. 83; later collected in Wain's *A Word Carved on a Sill* (London: Routledge & Kegan Paul, 1956).

6 C.K. Stead, *The New Poetic* (London: Hutchinson, 1964), p. 88.

7 Donald Davie, *Thomas Hardy and British Poetry* (New York: Oxford University Press, 1972), pp. 11–12.

8 D.H. Lawrence, *Phoenix* (London: Heinemann, 1936), pp. 304–7.

9 R.S. Thomas, *Poetry for Supper* (London: Hart-Davis, 1958), p. 14.

10 F.R. Leavis, *New Bearings in English Poetry* [1932] (Ann Arbor: University of Michigan Press, 1960), pp. 66, 68.

11 An exception might be made in the case of Hardy, but the display of a hardly won erudition which is an irritatingly conspicuous element in his prose-style is less evident and far less disconcerting in his poetry.

12 Edmund Blunden, *Poems 1914–1930* (London: Cobden-Sanderson, 1930), p. 227. All quotations from Blunden's poetry are from this volume, hereafter cited in text as *BP*.

13 Leavis, p. 68.

14 For a useful commentary on this procedure, see George Ewart Evans, *Where Beards Wag All* (London: Faber, 1970), pp. 169–70.

15 W.B. Yeats, 'Vacillation,' *Collected Poems* (London: Macmillan, 1955), p. 283.

16 Michael Thorpe, *The Poetry of Edmund Blunden* (n.p.: Bridge Books, Kent Editions, 1971), p. 11.

17 Andrew Young, *The New Poly-Olbion* (London: Hart-Davis, 1967), p. 30.

18 Andrew Young, *Complete Poems*, arranged and introduced by Leonard Clark (London: Secker & Warburg, 1974), p. 145. All quotations from Young's poetry are from this edition, hereafter cited in text as *YCP*.

19 Young employs the same image in prose in *A Prospect of Flowers* (London: Cape, 1945), p. 12.

20 Norman Nicholson, in Leonard Clark, ed., *Andrew Young: Prospect of a Poet* (London: Hart-Davis, 1957), pp. 61–2.

21 Ibid., p. 62.

22 Since this section was originally written, Roger D. Sell's full-length study, *Trespassing Ghost: A Critical Study of Andrew Young*, has appeared (Abo, Finland: Abo Akademi, 1978). It may be recommended as a thorough and detailed examination of the whole of Young's work.

23 Most of R.S. Thomas's rural poems appeared in his first three volumes to be published in London: *Song at the Year's Turning* (London: Hart-Davis, 1955); *Poetry for Supper* (London: Hart-Davis, 1958); *Tares* (London: Hart-Davis, 1961). References will be incorporated into the text as *SYT, PS* and *T* respectively.

24 R.S. Thomas, *Words and the Poet* (The W.D. Thomas Memorial Lecture. Cardiff: University of Wales Press, 1964), p. 22. Hereafter cited in text as *WP*.

25 *A Choice of Wordsworth's Verse* (London: Faber, 1971).

26 See Davie, p. 4n. Thomas included one poem by Hardy ('Afterwards') in his *Batsford Book of Country Verse* (London: Batsford, 1961), but this may represent no more than a dutiful gesture.

27 The fact that R.S. Thomas has edited *The Selected Poems of Edward Thomas* (London: Faber, 1964) strengthens the case for possible influence. In the introduction he stresses Edward Thomas's Welsh origins. 'Up in the Wind,' the poem containing the lines quoted in the text, is included in the selection.

28 *Batsford Book of Country Verse*, p. 7.

29 R. George Thomas, *R.S. Thomas* (Writers and Their Work series. London: Longmans, 1964), p. 31. Most of the poems in the two locally printed volumes were reproduced in *SYT*.

30 See my discussion of Sturt in *The Rural Tradition* (Toronto: University of Toronto Press, 1974; Hassocks, Sussex: Harvester Press, 1975), pp. 166–8.

31 See W. Moelwyn Merchant, 'R.S. Thomas,' *Critical Quarterly*, 2 (Winter 1960), 341–51; R. George Thomas, 'The Poetry of R.S. Thomas,' *Review of English Literature*, III (October 1962), 85–95; H.J. Savill, 'The Iago Prytherch Poems of R.S. Thomas,' *Anglo-Welsh Review*, 20 (Autumn 1971), 143–54.

32 *Frequencies* (London: Macmillan, 1978), p. 34.

33 Ibid., p. 12.

34 See Davie, pp. 4n, 13. The poem is collected in *Laboratories of the Spirit* (London: Macmillan, 1975), p. 35. In the same poem Thomas writes approvingly of Wordsworth 'looking into the lake / of his mind.'

35 Quoted in Byron Rogers, 'The Enigma of Aberdaron,' *Daily Telegraph Magazine* (7 November 1975), 29. Thomas rarely grants interviews, and the observations recorded in this article are of considerable interest.

36 R.S. Thomas, *Selected Poems 1946–68* (London: Hart-Davis, Mac-Gibbon, 1973), p. 100.

37 *New Lines*, p. xv.

38 Ibid., pp. 83–4.

39 Robert Langbaum, 'The New Nature Poetry,' in his *The Modern Spirit: Essays on the Continuity of Nineteenth- and Twentieth-Century Literature* (New York: Oxford University Press, 1970), pp. 101, 102.

40 William Blake, *The Marriage of Heaven and Hell*, plate 10.

41 *A Choice of Wordsworth's Verse*, p. 12.

42 Ibid., p. 18.

INDEX